Gandhi, Smuts and Race in the British Empire

Of Passive and Violent Resistance

Peter Baxter

PEN & SWORD
HISTORY

First published in Great Britain in 2017 by
PEN AND SWORD HISTORY
an imprint of
Pen and Sword Books Ltd
47 Church Street
Barnsley
South Yorkshire S70 2AS

ISBN 978 1 47389 621 5

Printed and bound in Malta by Gutenberg Press Ltd.

Typeset in Times New Roman by Chic Graphics

Pen & Sword Books Ltd incorporates the imprints of Pen & Sword
Archaeology, Atlas, Aviation, Battleground, Discovery,
Family History, History, Maritime, Military, Naval, Politics, Railways,
Select, Social History, Transport, True Crime, Claymore Press,
Frontline Books, Leo Cooper, Praetorian Press, Remember When,
Seaforth Publishing and Wharncliffe.

For a complete list of Pen and Sword titles please contact
Pen and Sword Books Limited
47 Church Street, Barnsley, South Yorkshire, S70 2AS, England
E-mail: enquiries@pen-and-sword.co.uk
Website: www.pen-and-sword.co.uk

Gandhi, Smuts and Race in the British Empire

To my darling Jude, for all the fun and inspiration

*   *   *

'The day will come, and perhaps is not far distant, when the European observer will look round to see the world girdled with a continuous zone of the black and yellow races, no longer too weak for aggression, or under tutelage, but independent, or practically so, in government, monopolizing the trade of their own regions and circumscribing the industry of the Europeans.'
—Charles Pearson, National Life and Character: A Forecast

Contents

Acknowledgements

Thanks to Bill Shannon for his interest and encouragement. Also to Claire Hopkins at Pen & Sword, and to Chris Cocks for placing the manuscript under Claire's nose.

List of Illustrations

1. Gandhi, the Transvaal lawyer.
2. Gandhi in about 1894.
3. Gandhi in 1908.
4. Gandhi during the Bambatha Rebellion, 1906.
5. Gandhi during the visit of Indian political leader Gopal Krishna Gokhale to South Africa, Durban, 1912. Below row, center, from left: Dr Hermann Kallenbach, Gandhi, Gokhale, Parsee Rustomjee.
6. Gandhi with Sonia Schlesin and Hermann Kallenbach, 1913.
7. The Great March.
8. Dadabahi Naoroji.
9. Jan Smuts, 1916. (Courtesy of Chris Cocks)
10. Jan Smuts, 1900. (Courtesy of Chris Cocks)
11. Lord Salisbury.
12. Cecil John Rhodes.
13. Elizabeth Maria Molteno.
14. Olive Schreiner. (Courtesy of Chris Cocks)
15. Paul Kruger.
16. Smuts in about 1914.
17. Joseph Chamberlain. (Courtesy of Chris Cocks)
18. General Lord Kitchener. (Courtesy of Chris Cocks)
19. Jan Hofmyer.
20. John Dube.
21. Leander Starr Jameson.
22. Henry Campbell-Bannerman.
23. Lionel Curtis.
24. Louis Botha.
25. William Phillip Schreiner.
26. John Merriman.
27. Punch Cartoon.
28. James 'Barry' Munnik Herzog.
29. Smuts at Cambridge.
30. Alfred Milner. (Courtesy of Chris Cocks)
31. Emily Hobhouse.

Introduction

'Destiny had laid her hand on him, at first gently, but gradually
with more force, till at last he became conscious of her mighty
presence.'

—Jan Christiaan Smuts

In the summer of 1894, a letter arrived at the home of the member for
Finsbury Central, Dadabhai Naoroji, dated 5 July of the same year, and with
a return address listed as Durban, Natal Colony, South Africa.

Seated at a rosewood Davenport, the elderly Naoroji, having disposed of
his more routine correspondence, turned his attention to the plain white
envelope that he had set to one side. The address had been scripted casually
in a style that seemed, in some respects, purposeful, and yet also, rather lazy.
Affixed to the top right-hand corner were two one-penny Natal colony
stamps. After slicing open the envelope with an ivory-handled paper knife,
Naoroji carefully extracted two crisp white sheets, which he then unfolded
and spread on the green leather desktop before him.

He read it through, and found, perhaps to his disappointment, that it was
no more than a formal salutation from a newcomer to the Indian nationalist
movement, a 25-year-old barrister by the name of Mohandas Karamchand
Gandhi. As he read on, Naoroji scratched the chin of a gaunt and aristocratic
face, bespectacled and bearded, his eyes deep set and coal black. It was a
curious letter indeed, quite unexpected, and although without specific detail,
it seemed to be nonetheless rich in implication.

The old man could recall Gandhi to mind without difficulty. Five or
perhaps six years earlier, the young fellow had made a courtesy call when
studying law in London, and after that the two had occasionally met and
exchanged a few words. That sort of thing was usual. Naoroji, a towering
figure in the Indian political and academic establishment, was headquartered
at the time in London, and it was his duty to act as host, patron and
intermediary to the steady stream of bright young Indians arriving in the
British capital to seek their fortunes.

He had at the time found Gandhi rather loose-tongued and jovial, with
neither firm ideas nor any particular commitments, and perhaps in

consequence a little shallow and pleasure-seeking. He took disapproving note of the young student's slightly showy appearance, urbane and composed, wearing a tight frock coat over a swept wing collar, and with a gold pin set in the centre of a red silk tie. His hair was Brilliantined and combed, his moustache clipped and his complexion dark. His manner was familiar, however, and friendly, and Naoroji, somewhat despite himself, was disarmed. The young man was clearly intelligent, and might, with some discipline and polish, own some modest potential.

With the passing of three or four years, however, Naoroji found himself mildly surprised, and then gratified as odd snippets of intelligence filtered through the grapevine revealing that M. K. Gandhi, now a qualified barrister, had surfaced in South Africa, and seemed at last to be taking life and career rather more seriously.

This was confirmed a few days later when a special messenger arrived at Naoroji's door, and handed him a dense manila envelope addressed in that familiar scrawl, and plastered with an unnecessary miscellany of postage stamps. This time he repaired directly to his desk and cut open the envelope immediately, spreading before him the pages of a carefully crafted legal petition. The document was accompanied by a brief explanatory note from Gandhi indicating that the document represented a plea directed to the British colonial secretary, Lord Ripon, on behalf of the Natal Indian community, urging that an exclusionary draft franchise bill, tabled by the Natal legislature, be disallowed by Her Majesty on the grounds of discrimination. The signatures of 10,000 Natal Indians had been attached to the original petition, which was quite unprecedented. Moreover, it was obvious that Gandhi was the architect of the document, and as such appeared to be leading some sort of constitutional revolt in South Africa.

This was exciting news, and Naoroji carefully read through the petition for a second and third time, acknowledging immediately the unspoken expectation that he advocate on behalf of the Natal Indians in London, and among an increasingly organized metropolitan British Indian community. The thrust of the new law proposed by the Natal government was to exclude by specific mention all Indians of the colony from any territorial franchise. This amounted to discriminatory legislation, and Her Majesty's government had long sworn to uphold no such articles of statutory racism in the overseas colonies. This was precisely the platform upon which Naoroji had built his political career, and he set to work with a great deal of vigour and enthusiasm.

At 69, Dadabhai Naoroji had established a reputation as the 'Grand Old

Man' of Indian politics, behind whom there now lay perhaps the most illustrious and successful Indian career of the age. He was the first Indian to be awarded a professorship – initially in Mathematics and Natural Philosophy at the prestigious Elphinstone College, Bombay, and later in Gujarati at the University College London – after which he distinguished himself as one of the earliest and most respected Indian nationalists. Despite this, and despite the tenor of the times, he remained throughout his career entirely uncontroversial. In many respects he was an establishment figure, venerable, moderate and cultured, and as an Indian of the old school, he was one that the British could do business with.

Balancing his spectacles on his nose, meanwhile, Naoroji returned his attention to the brief and rather plaintive note of a few days earlier that still lay on his desk. He read the few words once again, and found them now filled with an entirely different meaning.

'I am yet inexperienced and young,' Gandhi wrote with his usual disarming candour, 'and, therefore, quite liable to make mistakes. The responsibility undertaken is quite out of proportion to my ability. You will, therefore, oblige me very greatly if you will kindly direct and guide me and make necessary suggestions which shall be received as from a father to his child.'[1]

Reaching under his desk, Naoroji brought up a clean sheet of paper and, blotting his fountain pen, scratched out a few lines in reply. These Gandhi noted in his memoir as receiving a month or so later, although the letter that contained them was never archived. Nonetheless, one can imagine that Naoroji might have registered a brief note of congratulation on the drafting of an excellent petition, adding perhaps some words of encouragement and advice for a junior revolutionary set upon a path not of his choosing.

The older man, with the wisdom of a long and exemplary life to draw upon, was struck by an uncanny sense that this business in the Natal colony would prove in the end to be more than the sum of its parts. The 'Indian Question' was coming of age, and it seemed entirely rational that, if a confrontation between subject peoples and empire was in one way or another inevitable, the first blow to be struck for global emancipation should be struck in South Africa.

Nowhere on earth has there been a race landscape quite as tortured and complicated as South Africa. Across the divided ramparts of white history, Briton and Boer glared at one another in a mutual hatred so consuming that for generations it overwhelmed the parallel struggles of black, coloured (in the South African context, people of mixed blood), Indian and Chinese.

Similar tensions, of course, were felt and reflected across the European colonial spectrum, but in South Africa the race dichotomy of empire was consistently portrayed on a larger scale, always more delicately balanced, and ferociously contested to the extent that ultimately it proved formative of the entire character of the region.

Much of the inflammation of race and culture in South Africa came about because the European settler community could not, as had been achieved in the Americas and the Antipodes, numerically overwhelm the indigenous population. Both were thus forced to confront a fundamental incompatibility between two major races of the earth, on a battlefield upon which each held a valid and defendable claim. Peripheral battles, such as the Indian struggle, had about them more of a diasporic flavour, and were, in many respects, incidental to the great race war, the embryo of which was planted on the continent at the moment that the European races made landfall.

In one way or another, Europeans have been present in southern Africa for centuries, commencing in the fifteenth century with the first visitations of Portuguese maritime explorers, and concluding with the great migration that saw the colonies populated by Europeans fleeing the depression and destruction of post-1945 Europe. The mild, temperate climate of the Cape and the South African highveld rendered large-scale European settlement in the region practical, and the vast wealth incrementally unearthed from the soil of South Africa gave each and all the necessary incentive to stand and fight when claim upon claim began to be registered.

The first Indians to arrive in South Africa came as indentured labour, assigned to a period of contractual service in the emerging sugar industry of Natal, with only a handful later opting to return to India. A few re-indentured at the conclusion of their various contracts, but the majority chose to remain in the colony, forming, almost in anonymity, a separate class of cottage farmers, wage labourers and petty traders.

South Africa at that time existed in a state of unhappy matrimony between two British colonies and two independent Boer republics. In the British territories, as indeed throughout the British empire, Indians, at least in theory, enjoyed the same protection rights under law as any other race or people enjoying British protection. On the other hand, the Boer republics were entirely free of direct British control, and therefore, unambiguous racial discrimination existed on a primitive statute without the particulars of British legal ambiguity to smudge the clear lines of inequality.

Indians arrived in South Africa and, as with the various peripatetic

INTRODUCTION

European races that steadily populated the outer reaches of the globe, they filtered out into the countryside to make what could be made of the many opportunities. They were, however, almost immediately fettered by vexatious legislation that was unashamedly aimed at limiting their freedom of movement, and access to economic opportunities. One of many examples of this was Act No. 22, an 1890 legal instrument promulgated in the Boer republic of the Orange Free State that sought to outlaw all independent, non-white settlement and trade. This did not affect the black population directly, since black political and mercantile activity in the republic at that time was almost non-existent, but it resulted in the immediate dispossession of a small community of Indian traders, who were expelled from the territory forthwith and without compensation.

Blacks in the republics, and also, for that matter, in the colonies, at that point neither expressed nor were granted any particular political consideration. Most were content for the time being to remain subject to customary law, yielding only very few of their number to the cash economy, and even fewer to modern education.

Indians, on the other hand, were economically active. They conducted business on a large scale, and paid taxes, and were not as a consequence so easily dismissible on the Darwinian scale of civilization and savagery. Under the laws of the Natal colony, for example, where the vast majority of South African Indians resided, they were included alongside blacks as an uncivilized race. This separated them under law from the white, civilized races, and therefore subjected them to the various pass laws and social restrictions that governed the lives of blacks. It also served to merge Indians with blacks in the general race legislation of the colony, creating multiple unnecessary disabilities, and indeed, at the very core of the Indian grievance in South Africa was this far-too-close legal association between them and the black population.

In this regard, however, if such was what irked them, the Indians of Natal were not entirely blameless. They found themselves in an economically productive environment, and were content as a result, no matter what petty injustices were visited against them, to keep their doors open and their mouths shut in order to make the best of the available opportunities. The rewards of free enterprise in South Africa significantly outweighed any real and conventional social disabilities that they might confront, and it was widely acknowledged in consequence that the risks of opposition or protest were simply not matched by the rather ephemeral promise of reward. They simply kept themselves to themselves, expressed no opinions whatsoever and genuflected with equal opportunity to all and any who walked through their doors.

However, as the Indians of Natal began to outnumber the whites, and as Indian trade began to offer real competition to established white trade, the noose around the Indian neck began to tighten. Ever more confining legislative controls on Indian life began to appear. In 1895, for example, within the first year of Gandhi's South African experience, an immigration revision act was tabled in Natal that erected visible barriers against fresh Indian migration to the colony, and discouraged permanent settlement by the imposition of a penalty tax. Efforts were also made to legalize and enforce the repatriation of Indians back to India, but across that particular precipice, Her Majesty's government could not be induced to step.

Such laws and conventions, however, although present, of course, to some degree in all the settled colonies, nonetheless ran contrary to the social charter of the British empire. In the post-abolition age, a great weight of conscience appeared to settle on the shoulders of the English-speaking races, and the Victorian iteration of empire emerged as an institution conceived not only for the greater glory of Britannia, but also as an agency for the modernization and improvement of the world. This was reflected in many forums, but perhaps most notably in the Queen's Proclamation that underwrote and formalized the British imperial takeover of India. Here absolute equality and freedom were promised for Her Majesty's Indian subjects in exchange for their loyalty, and as something of an atonement for two centuries or more of plunder under British East India Company rule. This, of course, reflected the triumph of the age of enlightenment, a triumph that quite often did not manifest in the colonies and various overseas administrative districts of the empire.

In 1861, thirty years after abolition, and in the midst of the age of enlightenment, a Christian mission sponsored by the universities of Cambridge and Oxford attempted to establish itself in the region of the Shire Highlands, more or less at the southern tip of today's Lake Malawi. At the time, the East African slave trade was gathering pace, and the missionaries attracted enormous criticism from their metropolitan peers and governing organizations by engaging in armed conflict with the slave traders. By this they overreached the limitations of church and state in a territory as yet unclaimed by any European power, but at the same time in an environment riddled with endemic lawlessness. One member of the mission party was a certain Reverend Henry Rowley, who wrote in the defence of the mission that: 'No greater mistake can be made than to suppose that men who go out there can at all times act as though they possessed all the appliances of civilization and Christianity, or as though the antecedents of the natives were like our own.'

In other words, spare the man toiling in the tropics your effete observations. When in Rome we do as the Romans do. Until such time as one has attempted to administer a colony one cannot fully appreciate the difficulties involved. The high-minded proclamations of empire drafted in Whitehall, and delivered with hands resting comfortably on the dispatch box, hold no relevance to those on the frontier carving out a practical empire from the raw stuff of Africa.

Towards the end of the nineteenth century, in the meanwhile, and under these very expediencies of overseas government, India began to stir. The benign despotisms of the British Raj began to constrain a society capable of much that its occupiers were not. Through its imperial influence of some 250 years, the British united India into a single, unitary concept. Under the occupation, India became one kingdom, and with a common objection to occupation by the British, a national identity would relatively easily form.

From the British point of view, however, India *was* the British empire, for without it the edifice could hardly stand. The Indians, of course, were not long in reaching this same conclusion, and upon the essential truism that the British ruled India with Indian cooperation, the Indians were apt with increasing focus to warn the British to watch their step.

The British, however, were unwilling to award India the same degree of territorial autonomy that had been granted to the younger settled colonies of Canada, Australia and New Zealand. The reason for this was the same as their refusal to grant home rule to Ireland. Home rule was applicable only to those territories content to remain in the empire. To grant home rule to Ireland would have meant its immediate loss to the kingdom, and such was also true for India.

That is not to say that Indians were indifferent to the concept of full and equal partnership with the British under the rules of empire. There was no fanatical determination in India to shed British rule as there was in Ireland. No indeed. The Indians saw much of value in an equal partnership with the British, if only that equality could be achieved. The credentials of Indian civilization certainly gave the people of the subcontinent every ground to expect it; in an ideal balance of empire and subject, absorption is the reward of compliance, and first-class citizenship, by definition, ought to be absolute. The British, however, against all rational policy, maintained the invisible divisions of civilization and savagery, and were apt to be rather generous in their application of the latter to the Indians. Indians, however, saw the world in their own image, and were disinclined to acknowledge the social kinship that the British applied to them with the primitive, aboriginal races of the world, who naturally had no comparable claim to civilization.

Naoroji was of that very generation of Indians that admired the British, valued what had been gained under their rule, but were equally anxious that Britain be alerted to the saplings of Indian independence that were now growing strong under her imperial sunshine.

In 1855, Naoroji made the decision to travel to England, and there to mingle with the conquerors, to learn their ways and expose them to his. Indians, he intended to make clear, were not, in the words of contemporary British parliamentarian Thomas Babington Macaulay, the tattooed savage of the Pacific Ocean, the enslaved Negro, the Hottentot or the Mohawk, but an ancient and venerable people, and the product of a great many deep and creative civilizations. And no Indian could testify to this acme of culture and accomplishment better than Dadabhai Naoroji, and if it would profit the British to meet and understand a man such as he, he was more than willing to introduce himself.

Born in Bombay in 1825, Dadabhai Naoroji was a Parsee, which, in the kaleidoscope of religion, language and ethnicity of modern India, placed him among the broad Indo-Iranian, or Aryan, races. Typically a fair-skinned and aristocratic people, the Parsees own the exclusivity of Persian blood and manners. They are Indian, insofar as they reside in India, but they have remained culturally aloof, and have, or at least had in the time of Naoroji, retained strict consanguinity with their western Asian origins. Naoroji's accomplishments had been quiet, but notable, and his quest to present a picture of Indian achievement to the British proved wildly successful, although perhaps not in the way that he might have anticipated.

The failures of British rule in India, he maintained, occurred simply as a consequence of the mischief of distance, and the obscurity of cultural differences. What they could not see, the British could not remedy: 'I have not the least doubt in my mind about the conscience of England, and Englishmen, that if they once see the evil [of British administration in India], they will not shrink to apply the proper remedies.'

In a bold decision, therefore, Naoroji decided that he would contest a seat in the House of Commons, and thus introduce himself at the very heart of British democracy. This, of course, was easier said than done, but it was at least possible. Under the rules of British suffrage, any subject of Her Majesty enjoyed the right to contest any seat in any parliament.

INTRODUCTION

In India, of course, rule was more or less direct, and indigenous access to the higher echelons of the administration was therefore effectively blocked. Indians sat on the various governing committees, but never in an executive context. Universal or even qualified suffrage did not apply in India.

In England, however, no such barriers existed. Naoroji could seek the candidacy of any seat that he chose, assuming that he could win selection. It would be almost four decades before he judged the moment to be right to announce and contest his candidacy. In 1884, the landmark Third Reform Act passed in Britain on a very narrow majority, broadening the base of the electorate at a time when imperial hubris in Britain was arguably at its peak. The effect of this was to solidify the interest of the common man in the affairs of an empire that was daily becoming more central to the British self-image.

It was the Great Exhibition of 1851, held in the iconic Crystal Palace, that for the first time introduced the empire to the wider British public as an integral part of the whole, and central to that whole was India. In fact, if an average Englishman of the period thought about the empire at all, he would typically think first about India, acquiring then its status as the Jewel in the Crown. The sunburned colonial of Nyasaland, Kenya or Rhodesia was an afterthought, a concept of the early twentieth century, while Australia, Canada and New Zealand were more or less cultural extensions of Britain. The fascination during the late nineteenth century was always with India.

By the mid-1880s, therefore, thanks to this, to the development of the mass media and the post-abolition attitude of liberal paternalism, the voting public of London in particular had become far more international in outlook than ever before. The notion, therefore, of an Indian contesting an inner-city parliamentary seat, although improbable, was also novel and not altogether outlandish. Naoroji stood for and, somewhat to his surprise, won the Liberal Party candidacy for the Holborn constituency of Finsbury.

This naturally stirred up a frenzy of public discussion, and a press bonanza that swung from deprecating hilarity in the tabloids to mature scepticism in the broadsheets, tempered on both sides by a keen sense of sporting encouragement. Naoroji had an outside chance, to be sure, but the best of British luck to old Rammysammy if he thought he could pull it off.

The London *Times*, a liberal newspaper on occasion, remarked in an editorial of 26 June 1886, that 'by returning him [Naoroji] to the House of Commons, Holborn would prove itself one of the greatest constituencies in Great Britain'.

Naoroji contested Holborn in the British general election of 1886, but suffered a narrow defeat at the hands of the incumbent Tory candidate, a retired Royal Artillery officer by the name of Colonel Francis Duncan. What was of particular interest to the press, however, and no doubt what excited most commentary in the members' dining room, was not Naoroji's near victory, but old Colonel Duncan's narrow escape. The howling ignominy of a retired British cavalry officer knocked off the backbenches by an Indian would have been simply too dreadful to contemplate. Narrow it certainly was, however, and while Colonel Duncan might have kept up a brave face and laughed off the matter, he was surely mopping his brow in private.

What changed this preoccupation with Colonel Duncan's near defeat to Naoroji's near victory was a crass and poorly conceived comment, or series of comments attributed to Prime Minister Lord Salisbury. Upon addressing the Scottish parliament in the autumn of 1888, Lord Salisbury ruminated rather too freely on the matter. His comments run as follows:

> I regard the [1886] election at Holborn as a very valuable indication of public opinion at this moment. It is undoubtedly a smaller majority than Colonel Duncan won by last time, but then, Colonel Duncan was opposed by a black man; and, however great the progress of mankind has been, and however far we have advanced in overcoming prejudices, I doubt if we have yet got to the point where a British constituency will elect a black man to represent them.

At this point in his speech, and somewhat to his surprise, Lord Salisbury was interrupted by jeers and laughter from the gallery, which he allowed to subside before continuing in more measured language: 'Of course you will understand that I am speaking roughly, and using language in its ordinary colloquial sense, because I imagine the colour is not exactly black; but at all events he is a man of another race who is very unlikely to represent an English community.'

Lord Salisbury, prime minister of Britain on and off between 1885 and 1902, was a large and avuncular man, a respected academic and one of the great statesmen of his age. He was, however, rather known for this sort of thing. During the Irish home rule debate in 1886, for example, he remarked that the Irish were as incapable of governing themselves as Hottentots, adroitly debasing two races at once.

The reckless wit, however, of referring to an accomplished Indian scholar and intellectual as 'black' challenged not only the primary precepts of empire, but also the liberal self-image of Britain itself. It was all very well to exclude from the British social contract the Irishman, the Frenchman, the tattooed

INTRODUCTION

savage and the Hottentot, but to apply the same to an Indian was not only boorish in the extreme, but politically rather dangerous.

Over the weeks and months that followed, the British press, both liberal and conservative, reflected on the gravity and intelligence of the prime minister's remarks, producing in the process some of the most memorable copy of the age. One particular Lancashire daily, the *Accrington Times*, drew upon an astute analysis of history to observe:

> While Lord Salisbury's unknown savage ancestor was hunting wild beasts in the woad paint of Aboriginal Britain, the Indian plains were teeming with fertility and were ruled by principalities and powers. The finely woven fabrics of India adorned the ladies of Roman patricians and were esteemed more highly and were far more costly than the shawls of Cashmere known to our grandfathers.

In the great British press and parliamentary tradition, such pejorative flowed rich and virile, and usually just like water off a duck's back, but more carefully considered editorial comment drew attention to the fact that the Anglo-Indian relationship at that moment in history was one not to be trifled with. No more than 50,000 British troops controlled the combined homeland of some 300 million souls. The British did indeed rule India with the consent of the Indians, and if that were to remain true, a united and contented India was essential, and wantonly insulting her finest sons was not the way to achieve this.

To read these many outpourings, from those in whose higher conscience he had such absolute faith, must have been of quiet gratification to Naoroji. He certainly had suffered no aspiration to win a seat in the British parliament as a second-class Englishman, but as a first-class Indian. He wished to offer the loyalty of India in exchange for inclusion in empire, and moreover, a practical acknowledgement that India was deserving of a seat at the table of civilized nations.

From none of this, however, should it be inferred that the metropolitan English were entirely immune to race or class prejudice, for they were not. In this regard, the Indians were in good company, for the same was held true for the Irish, Scots and Welsh, and certainly the French. It was simply that in the subtle weights and measures of known race hierarchy, a higher-caste Indian could not, and should not in good conscience be compared to a black man.

However, the upshot of it all was that Lord Salisbury succeeded in projecting the humble name of Dadabhai Naoroji on the ballot ticket to the

19

very forefront of public attention. His name was known and traded where it otherwise would have been obscure. The press adored him, and soon enough, a spontaneous drum roll of popular support for his candidacy began to be heard.

In the general election of 1892, the Conservatives were returned to government, but for the opposition Liberal Party, the Right Honourable Dadabhai Naoroji won the seat for Finsbury Central. This he did by a very slim margin, earning him the nickname 'Narrow Majority' (from his principal name, pronounced *now-row-jai*); he held on to his seat for only three years, but the symbolism of what he had achieved was enormously powerful in the moment.

Thus, the thoughtful and heartfelt missive that Naoroji received from Mohandas K. Gandhi on that summer morning in 1895, united the moral extremes of the British empire. On the one hand, the British were prepared to embrace an Indian academic as an equal, and to defend vigorously his right to equality, while on the other, the same race was content to brush unabashed bigotry at the outer reaches of the empire under the carpet.

As the memory of that momentous general election faded, however, so would the name of Dadabhai Naoroji. Occasional street names, apartment buildings and school wings remain named after him in the liberal east of London, and a great many similar memorials throughout India, but few English-speaking people today could say with any confidence that they know who Dadabhai Naoroji was.

Mohandas K. Gandhi, on the other hand, would go on to achieve worldwide acclaim as a universalist, a philosopher of peace and the destroyer of empires. He began his political career, however, not in London, nor Bombay, but in South Africa. There he stood very much alone against the white Goliath of institutional racism, and from a sling of unimpeachable right, he hurled the pebble that would not only stagger the giant, but would in due course bring it to its knees.

Chapter 1

The Meeting

'It is infinitely more profitable to trade with civilized men than to govern savages.'

—Thomas Babington Macaulay

On the afternoon of Friday, 5 April 1907, six men cautiously entered the offices of the Transvaal colonial secretary, having lingered patiently in an adjacent wood-panelled waiting room for some forty-five minutes. After his umpteenth expression of apology and regret, the minister's private secretary, a tall and melancholy Englishman by the name of Ernest Lane ('Long Lane' as he was also known) finally bid the six to step through a heavy teak door. Standing to greet them on the other side was a man of medium height and build, dressed in a high-collared shirt and a dark woollen jacket. His hair was blond, somewhat thinning at the crown, and he wore a crisply clipped goatee beard that accentuated an already long face. Set deeply in that face, young, but burdened somehow, were eyes of ashen grey, open and clear, and although not friendly, neither were they hostile.

Introductions were cordial, and stiff, reflecting perhaps an adversarial predisposition. The minister apologized economically for the delay, explaining that labour unrest presaged a general strike in the colony, and that the situation was challenging his patience in many directions. Clearly, whatever was required of him at that particular moment, trivial by comparison to all that he had on his plate, was more than he was disposed to greet with amity.

Nonetheless, he was curious, and quick to identify the leader of the deputation. What he found was an Indian man of slight build but clean complexion, bright eyed and with a certain outward elongation of the face that emphasized a protrusion of the ears. When he smiled it was with every feature of his face, and the effect of it was unexpected and immediately disarming. Upon his upper lip he wore a neatly clipped moustache, and his hair, close cropped and thinning, was lightly salted with grey. Dressed in a simple woollen jacket, a waistcoat and white linen shirt, it was certainly not his couture that marked him out, for his companions were all more richly attired than he. With apparently sincere regret, however, and expressing earnest sympathy for the minister's tribulations, he was quick to assure his host that no time would be wasted, and that the matter would be abbreviated to the best of his ability.

With that, the minister dipped his head slightly, and ushered the small party towards a semi-circular arrangement of chairs laid out on an ancient Turkish carpet and facing an unlit stone fireplace. The curtains were drawn, and the room lit only by a tall iron lamp crowned by a gold-fringed, green chenille shade. A moment later, the door opened on oiled hinges and into the room came Ernest Lane, bearing a tray of tea that all but one of the Indians accepted.

The two principals at this meeting were General Jan Christiaan Smuts, a man of considerable authority and reputation, and a largely obscure Indian barrister by the name of Mohandas K. Gandhi. Gandhi's supporting deputation comprised men of Hindu, Muslim, Parsee, Pathan and Memon origin, quite obviously symbolic of a united community protesting the prejudicial conditions under which they lived, and for which they no less obviously held the minister responsible.

As the parties settled into their chairs, and as Lane poured the tea, Gandhi and Smuts began to spar lightly. Gandhi reported that he had journeyed up from Durban the day before, making a significant point of the fact that he had travelled first class, and that for this presumption had suffered no forced removal from the train. To this, no doubt, Smuts expressed his satisfaction, again with a simple dip of the head, revealing nothing of his mind at work. At a glance he calculated the weight of the five deputies, and ignored them thereafter. They were common men, community elders, businessmen and traders, with not one, he surmised, of an opinion worth hearing. The object of interest to him in that room was Gandhi, and no other.

The lives and careers of both of these men are well chronicled, although Gandhi, of course, enjoys far greater acknowledgement and recognition in the modern era. Smuts, however, built and enjoyed a career no less illustrious at the very pinnacle of British imperial power, overlapping Gandhi's in all of its key facets. Sadly, however, he left no memoir or autobiography, no formal chronicle of his own life, and, of course, the brilliance of his achievements has tended in recent years to be clouded by the deliberate discrediting of his ideological pillars, and the dissemination of a great deal of questionable and quack popular history.

THE MEETING

Thanks, however, to an archive of speeches, personal reminiscences and private letters, it is at least possible to determine that when Smuts bid farewell to Gandhi that afternoon it was with very mixed feelings. He had squandered more time than he could afford on what was, after all, a very minor matter, and at the end of it, he found himself conflicted. Gandhi was quite clearly a man of significant intelligence, and by his appearance obviously one of disciplined, perhaps even obsessive, commitment. His intellect might have lacked the discipline that Smuts could boast of his own, but Smuts had engaged sufficiently with the common man to understand the essence of Gandhi's philosophy, and he was of sufficient philosophical outlook to appreciate the obvious religiosity that underpinned the latter's appearance and manner.

Gandhi, on the other hand, who wrote numerous memoirs and autobiographies, appears to have declined the opportunity to honestly remark upon a man who obviously interested him. Perhaps he was intimidated, for Smuts applied absolute professional forbearance, and declined on the one hand to treat Gandhi with the same attitude of conceited hostility that many white civil servants and officials adopted towards Indians, but nor the fawning sycophancy of his followers and acolytes, that he also had by then come to accept, and even, perhaps, to expect.

Indeed, Gandhi makes absolutely no anecdotal mention of Smuts at all, other than, of course, that which would support his political position. He seemed to have no interest in Smuts other than as an opponent, and was alert as a consequence only to his inconsistencies and failures. He had been primed by long months of anticipation to expect a man of trenchant ideology and unyielding obstinacy, and he was reluctant now to absorb an impression that differed from this. Gandhi was disposed to draw very clear lines, and notwithstanding his belief in universal virtue, was often slow to identify that virtue in his enemies.

Smuts, on the other hand, despite the pressure of work, had found the time to select from an overabundance of bookshelves in his office a relevant volume or two in order to prepare himself for this encounter. Open upon his desk lay an illustrated copy of Charles Wilkins's translation of the *Bhagavad Gita*, alongside other publications on Hinduism, Zoroasterism, Buddhism and Islam. The Indian question in South Africa interested him, and gave him the opportunity to ponder and read, albeit superficially, on a subject that he had scant reason for the most part to consider.

Smuts was a man possessed of a rich and varied intellect, and the books that surrounded him reflected that fact. The walls of his office were clad in bookshelves, each crammed haphazardly with a diversity of subject matter. He was, for example, an admirer of German philosophy, and so there could be found the complete works of Goethe, Kant, Nietzsche, Hegel and many others. He also owned several hundred volumes of poetry, and had recently reread Rudolf Lotze's *Metaphysic*, Darwin's *On the Origin of Species* and Henri Bergson's *Creative Evolution*. He read widely, and avidly, devouring the usual subjects of philosophy and poetry, art and anthropology, but also languages, history, botany, political economy, finance, ethics, taxation, sociology, education, administration and of course law.

In addition, had Gandhi the interest or opportunity to look, he could hardly have missed a large copy of Wilhelm Bleek's 1862 study, *A Comparative Grammar of South African Languages*, and other various works on eugenics and race, papers and publications by Samuel Norton and Josiah Nott, by Voltaire and Karl Vogt. Smuts had recently furrowed his brow in moral perplexity over his umpteenth reading of the *The Descent of Man, and Selection in Relation to Sex*, wishing to understand what drove him, and his people, to such revulsion over the native in their masses, when at the same time he was so interested, and eager to explore the mind of the native before him.

No such conflict troubled Gandhi, for in his moral certitude he was unassailable. His preoccupations, moreover, were rarely technical, but spiritual. His interest was in diet, alternative medicine, theosophism, service, global community and, of course, religion. In general, he wrote more than he read; Smuts's office he would have found oppressive and confining, the clutter of books an offence to his simplicity and the lack of natural light a blasphemy.

Gandhi's power over Smuts was simply that he forgave him, despite his own identical prejudice. His objective in meeting Smuts, after all, had not been to seek relief for the subject races of the colony, no indeed, but simply to win a reprieve on behalf of the Indians. To him it was of vital importance that Smuts, and the legislative body of the combined territories, understand that the Indian and the black man were not the same. Under the evolving race legislation of South Africa, he wished that the classification of Indians under the law concur with white, in recognition of the fact that Indians enjoyed a comparable standard of civilization. Failing this they were to be classified at least as different from blacks, and not simply under the broad and indiscriminate taxonomy of *non-white*.

To all of this Smuts listened with his fingers held in a steeple before his lips, and his eyes never removed from Gandhi's. Eventually, however, he was forced to acknowledge the persistent eye-catching and mute appeals of Lane as he hovered about the door. Drawing the meeting to a close, Smuts shook Gandhi's hand with sincere warmth, surprised at its firmness, and assured him that he would look into the matter, and that the Indians might expect satisfaction in the very near future. Much of what he had heard, he admitted, was new to him, and he needed time to reflect, and to learn what he could about the matter before making known his decision.

This Gandhi received with obvious gratitude and pleasure, and with the credulity of an amateur, he remarked to his colleagues as they left the building that the colonial secretary was not quite the fiend that he had been reported to be. It was refreshing to find, in fact, that he was a reasonable and intelligent man, and despite the circumstances of the meeting, Gandhi found himself disposed to like him. His colleagues, however, were merchants in the main, wealthy men of substance and character, and they were less inclined to trust a man on his appearances, nor to celebrate a victory before its consummation.

As the door closed behind them, Smuts stood alone for a moment deep in thought. No doubt he reflected on the curious spectacle of this disreputable coolie barrister, of whose crimes against decency he had already heard so much. On the surface he seemed avuncular and harmless, charming indeed, all eccentricity and practical incompetence, but Smuts knew better than this. He was instinctively conscious of the threat behind Gandhi's friendly pragmatism, his dancing eyes and keen humour. Gandhi had been a presence in South Africa for more than a decade, and it would be a fool who took him lightly that had seen already the cut of his sabre upon others.

The man was an enigma, and he led an enigmatic people. His manners were not simply eccentric or harmless, but messianic, and extremely dangerous because of it. Smuts had never met a man quite like him. His gentle charisma was leavened by a fanatical determination to succeed, but yet his objectives were ethereal. He was impoverished by choice, and so incorruptible. It certainly was a conundrum, and Smuts was under no illusion that he had seen the last of Gandhi.

Soon enough, however, Lane was back, and with infinite regret, announced the arrival in the building of Mr Louis Reyersbach, president of the Transvaal Chamber of Mines, upon which Smuts took a moment or two to prepare. The matter of Gandhi and the 'Indian Problem' were put immediately out of his mind.

Chapter 2

Smuts's South Africa

'In 500 years of the College's history, of all its members, past and present, three had been truly outstanding: John Milton, Charles Darwin and Jan Smuts.'
—Lord Todd, Master of Christ's College, Cambridge

In the tranquil backwaters of the Cape Colony, a child was born, taking his first steps in a world that reflected the cherished memories of a faraway country. Here was a place still governed by the church and the seasons, where the highest standards of European culture remained rooted in the land, the soil and the ancient guilds. In 1870, the year of Jan Smuts's birth, Dutch-speaking settlers had been present on the southern tip of Africa for more than two centuries. Their culture, although somewhat hybridized, had nonetheless been thoroughly grafted, and as industry and capital scarred the face of Europe, the Cape lingered in the twilight of a bygone age.

The story begins in 1652, with the arrival on the southern tip of Africa of a small flotilla of Dutch trading vessels. A party of colonists was set down upon what came to be known as the *Kaap de Goede Hoop*, or the Cape of Good Hope, and there they set up camp. Soon, in the lee of a table-topped mountain, a settlement of the Dutch East India Company (Vereenigde Oost-Indische Compagnie, or VOC) was established to supply and service ships plying the lucrative East Indian trade. One of the first chores assigned to founder and company administrator, Jan van Riebeek, was to establish a boundary separating the new settlement from the surrounding aboriginal communities.[1] This he did by planting a hedge of bitter almond, within the confines of which the white man could reside, and beyond which he might not permanently venture.

The symbolism of this bitter almond hedge, the remnants of which can still be seen today, established a founding doctrine of separation – in the first instance to define the administrative responsibility of the Company, and thereafter to embrace the institutionalized separation of the races in South Africa as a definitive social policy. In part, this convention came into being as a device to protect the integrity of native land and culture against white expansion, but later it began to tilt more towards the preservation of white lifestyles and livelihoods against the danger of black domination.

As the history of the Cape would later prove, this early conservatism did nothing to inhibit European expansion, and nor ultimately to limit black domination. The hinterland of the Cape in due course came to resemble a gentle rendering of Vester, or van Goyen, with only the addition of rugged mountains and a setting of mystical drama to locate it not in northern Europe. The country was orthodox, but also substantially free of dogma. Around the Protestantism of Calvin was grouped the social organization of the various communities, and a burgher system of local government recalled very much its parent pattern.

Centuries of isolation from Europe, however, resulted in distinct peculiarities of language and culture emerging, but during the late eighteenth and early nineteenth centuries, distances contracted, and a strong undercurrent of modern intellectualism and political and social theory began to take root. By then the aboriginal races, or the Hottentots, had either been eradicated or assimilated, and the influence of the Bantu remained for the time being minimal.[2]

Almost as Smuts took his first steps, however, the doors to the outside world began to open. The *ancien régimes* of Europe, their hands bloodied by war and slavery, had at last begun to yield to the age of reason, of idealism, of faith in progress and optimism. The industrial revolution, the development of modern transport and communications, and advances in art, science and technology all increasingly linked the old world with the new.

Today, the district of Malmesbury, Smuts's childhood home, lies within the orbit of Cape Town, but then it remained a bucolic backwater cast very much in the common character. The elements and symbols of protestant reform were well evident, but overlaid also by a rustic serenity that insulated a safe and comfortable society. The tiny hamlet of Riebeek West, close to the Smuts's homestead, consisted of a whitewashed church, the stone and corrugated-iron parsonage and a handful of local merchants.

The village was set in a region known as the Swartland, or the Black Lands, named after the renosterbos (*Elytropappus rhinocerotis*), a heather-like shrub that darkens to black after a dousing of rain, an effect enhanced by the dense and bruised cloud cover of the wet season. A richly visual landscape, the Swartland is bordered to the north by the white-capped ramparts of the Grootwinterhoek, and in the south by the isolated whaleback of the Riebeek Kasteel. Today it is part of the Western Cape, but then it was a district of the British Cape Colony, and Smuts was born a British subject.

The British held substantive control of the Cape more or less from 1806 onwards, although formal annexation only took place under the terms of the Anglo-Dutch Treaty of 1814, which settled matters between the two kingdoms in the aftermath of the Napoleonic Wars. European history on the peninsula, however, began not with the Dutch, nor the British, but with the Portuguese, who waded ashore upon the *Cabo das Tormentas*, or the Cape of Storms, in May 1488, almost two centuries before van Riebeek. Their ship was the caravel *São Cristóvão*, and their captain the 37-year-old Bartolomeu Dias. Nine years later, a second Portuguese fleet followed, this time captained by Vasco da Gama, making landfall at St Helena Bay, some hundred miles north of present-day Cape Town, before continuing on to explore the east coast of Africa, arriving ultimately on the shores of India in May 1498.

This feat of navigation gave the Portuguese the first European foothold in India, and one of the earliest in Africa, after which they grew to dominate the lucrative trade routes between Europe and India. In support of this trade, and over three centuries or more, ports were established along the east coast of Africa, ranging from Lourenço Marques (present-day Maputo) to as far north as Somalia. And although the Portuguese remained interested in the Cape, they never established a permanent presence there.

Thus, the arrival of the Dutch on the peninsula was unimpeded, ultimately robbing the Portuguese of dominion over the entire southern subcontinent. This would have linked the two dominant Portuguese territories of West (Angola) and East (Mozambique) Africa in a federation that would certainly have given the Portuguese an enormous strategic advantage in trade with the East Indies. As it turned out, however, the Dutch ultimately wrested control of that trade from the Portuguese, establishing Cape Town first as a victualling station, and then as a distant port en route to India and South-East Asia.

Some 9,000 miles distant from its administrative home, this spore of European settlement quickly took root, and under a benign climate it flourished. A steady trickle of fresh arrivals broadened the base of the colony, which expanded steadily beyond the bitter almond hedge, although always retaining its essentially homogenous Dutch character. Towards the end of the seventeenth century, however, a wave of French Huguenots fleeing religious persecution in Europe took refuge in the farthest reaches of the known world.

In isolation, these two cultures mingled, and although remaining substantively European, here and there they absorbed the cultural and genetic influences of Asian and Micronesian slaves.

On the far and expanding frontier, however, a rugged variant of the breed evolved. These assumed the name of Boere (farmers), or Trekboere (migrating farmers), adopting many credos of the Old Testament, and choosing to reflect on the land that they encountered and occupied as a homeland upon which they, and they alone had the God-given right to settle. As semi-nomadic pastoralists, they drove outwards the boundaries of white settlement in South Africa, gradually coming to view themselves as the sons of Israel, and the tribes of the interior as the Canaanites.

By the 1770s, Boer frontiersmen had begun to encounter and clash with Xhosa tribesmen in the region of what would today be the Eastern Cape.[3] Thus, in 1779, began the first of the Kaffir Wars, or Frontier Wars, sparked over inevitable complaints of territorial encroachment and accusations of cattle theft. Thereafter, clashes ebbed and flowed over the course of the next century, eventually involving the British in an orchestrated and violent campaign of pacification.

The Eastern Cape was then, as it is to today, a substantively black region of South Africa, with a merger of mythologies and histories, and a turbulent and scarred political history. The Frontier Wars, however, were only the first of a number of campaigns to break the cohesion of black society, and to replace it with a second-class amalgam of European. Of these, the Anglo-Zulu War of 1879 was the last, and most dramatic. Indeed, the rise of Zulu militarism in South Africa forms arguably the main bedrock of 'native' history, and the icon of a Zulu warrior bearing an assegai and an elliptical shield remains embedded in both white and black popular consciousness.

In 1879, Jan Smuts was 9 years old, and for him the Anglo-Zulu War was the stuff of mythology, raging over the far horizon, its permutations remote. As the kingdoms of the east and north were smashed between the hammer and anvil of British and Boer expansion, his view of the 'native problem' was limited to trying to coax rational answers to life's many mysteries from his father's bucolic farm workers.

Throughout his life, in fact, Smuts made frequent and fond reference to being close to a particularly phlegmatic cattle herder of indeterminate age by the name of Adam, whom in very general terms he referred to as a Hottentot. The word Hottentot, however, might at that time have meant many things, for by then the true aboriginal people of the region had largely disappeared. The last confirmed sighting of a San (Bushman) in the Drakensberg

Mountains, for example, was recorded early in the 1880s, and certainly by the turn of the century, full-blood San and Khoisan people survived only in the inhospitable regions of the arid west.

The emergence of a mixed blood class in the Cape came about consequent to an intermingling of white and non-white at a time when Cape society was accepting of much that later generations would reject. The Khoisan – the Hottentots and Bushmen – were very quickly determined by the incoming colonists and expansionist Boer to be of little value as labour. They occupied land, and they had a proprietary attitude to all the beasts of the field, including domestic livestock. This precipitated endemic stock theft, which rendered their unaltered existence incompatible with the Europeans, and in many instances they were hunted down on a bounty.[4]

Those that were the product of miscegenation, however, survived and integrated better, and thus was laid the bedrock of the rural coloured community, which remains very much in evidence today. In the urban context, this merger of blood was enriched by the addition of Indian merchants and tradesmen, and slaves introduced from East Africa, Madagascar and parts of South-East Asia, generally referred to as Malays. This, again, is evidenced by the extraordinary diversity of appearance in the modern coloured communities of Cape Town.

What was not evident in the Cape at the time of Smuts's birth, however, was any significant presence of Bantu people. The advance of Bantu into the Cape had been largely halted on the eastern frontier, while the infamous *Mfecane*, or *Lifaqane*, had decimated those potentially entering the Cape from the north.[5]

Here, however, we journey into an historic record of divergent memory. It is generally acknowledged in academic circles that a vast demographic movement known as the Bantu Migration, or the Bantu Expansion, began at about the turn of the first millennium, proliferating the Bantu race from its origins in the Niger Delta, first into the fertile regions of the Congo, and then, incrementally into central Africa.

The term *bantu* is misleading, however, for it is an umbrella term used broadly to define the indigenous races of Africa that make up the bulk of its modern population. The word is a variant of *abaNtu*, meaning simply 'people' or 'the people', as an expression of humanness or simply *being* human. In this context, the name owes its origins to German linguist Wilhelm Bleek, who coined it in his 1862 study, *A Comparative Grammar of South African Languages*, from where it has since entered the established lexicon of African anthropology. The word Bantu, therefore, simply implies the black, Congoid, or Negroid races of Africa that dominate the sub-Saharan region, as distinct from the Capoid, or Khoisan, peoples who represent the earliest aboriginal inhabitants of most of the central and southern regions of the continent.

The Bantu Migration was driven primarily by advances in iron-working technology, and a shift from agricultural to pastoral practices. Over many hundreds of years, it expanded into central Africa and the Congo Basin before overflowing east into the Great Rift Valley. From there it moved substantively southward towards the Central Plateau of southern Africa, and thence to the great expanses of South Africa.

European mythology, however, will have it that the Bantu reached the Cape a century or more *after* the region had been settled by the Dutch, and in this there is some truth. Black memories, however, differ, but what is indisputable is that early Dutch colonists in the Cape did not encounter any Bantu until they began to clash with the southward pressure of Xhosa groups in the eastern Cape, or perhaps more appropriately, as Xhosa groups began to encounter the pressure of white expansion east- and northward.

The Bantu in general would prove to be infinitely more resourceful and adaptable than the Khoisan, resulting in the almost total absorption or expulsion of the latter along the entire line of Bantu advance. A small pocket of aboriginal hunter-gathers known as the Hadzabe currently survives in central Tanzania, while the vast majority continue to occupy the arid reaches of the southwest of the continent.[6] Throughout the remainder of the sub-Saharan region, the Bantu language groups predominate.

Those such as the redoubtable Adam in Jan Smuts's informal memoir represented at the time the only viable surviving thread of aboriginal society in the Cape, and their viability in the modern context was only shored up by their genetic merger with European, Asian and Bantu bloodlines. Where, however, the original Khoisan element is strongest, deep in the rural hinterland of the Western Cape, the maladies of alcoholism and social decay tend to reflect the struggles of similarly vulnerable aboriginal populations elsewhere in the world.

The preponderance during the early European settlement of the Cape of single males resulted in numerous unorthodox marriages and unions with indigenous women, the products of which was the first generation of coloureds, known as Basters, or Bastaards. This growing subculture enjoyed recognition and acceptance from neither their maternal nor paternal communities, and were therefore socially marginalized. Most adopted European manners and the Dutch (later Afrikaans) language, as well as a tendency towards independence and individualism. This saw them, like the semi-nomadic Boer, migrating steadily outward ahead of progressive European administration, until, by the early decades of the nineteenth century, independent Griqua communities under independent leadership were established both on the frontier of the infant Cape Colony, and in pockets of what would in the future be German South West Africa. The Griquas, however, did not survive far into the modern era. As the entirety of the Cape Colony came under British administration, their independence and militancy diluted, and in due course, they were absorbed into the wider Cape Coloured population.

The almost total disappearance of the pure Khoisan bloodline, however, was of limited social consequence at the time of Jan Smuts's birth. The region of the Cape that he called home was so deeply ensconced in the European heartland that any claim to the contrary would have been absurd. In the future, this would offer white South Africa an undisputed claim to ownership of the region, it having never been stolen, or claimed as a right of conquest from any Bantu group. Such would not be true north of the Orange River, and certainly not north of the Vaal River, and even less so east of the Drakensberg Mountains.

For the time being, therefore, Smuts and his generation existed in a state of grace removed from the great permutations of race and colour that would in future years define South Africa. For the moment, the fault lines of racial tension in the region existed not along the black–white axis, but along lines of white–white divergence that began almost at the moment that the British made landfall in the Cape.

The British arrived in 1795, consequent, as we have heard, to the dispensations of the period Anglo-French wars, and while the minutiae of this vast historical backdrop are not entirely relevant to this narrative, what is relevant is that the Netherlands entered the war on the French side. In 1795, republican France invaded the Netherlands, creating the short-lived Batavian Republic, and causing William V, Prince of Orange, to seek refuge in England. The Dutch East India Company was bankrupted, after which the Dutch were effectively marginalized from the first tier of international trading powers.

Soon afterwards, a small Royal Navy fleet dropped anchor in Simon's Bay and presented the Dutch Cape commissioner with a letter from William of Orange requesting that the colony be entrusted to British protection for the duration of the war. The local administration resisted, and an amphibious landing was launched. The British then held the colony until 1802, after which it was returned briefly to the Dutch upon the negotiation of a peace treaty with France. In 1806, however, as Anglo-French hostilities resumed, it was retaken, and held in effect as a British colony until the Union of South Africa was formed in 1910.

At the time, Cape Town represented the only notable British port straddling the strategic shipping routes between Europe and Asia, and the primary British interest in controlling it was to ensure that nobody else did. And having acquired the territory for those strategic purposes, the British were now constrained to take into account the fact that it consisted of a significant hinterland, and beyond that a wide frontier. The Dutch administration was purged, with only those prepared to swear loyalty to the British Crown allowed to remain in a private capacity. The rest were repatriated. In consequence, the mood within the orbit of Cape Town, although sullen, was at least cooperative. In the vast and ungoverned reaches of the interior, however, populated by a defiant breed of men accustomed to a freedom of thought and action impossible under British rule, the arrival of Pax Britannica upon the shores of their liberty was no less of an outrage than the rape of their daughters.

The British, of course, regarded these denizens of the wild frontier with a degree of disdain and distaste that only subjects of the greatest empire known to man could reasonably justify. An early history of the Cape Colony was written by Sir Colin Turing Campbell, an amateur historian and minor British official, and his view of the Boer spoke somewhat to the majority:

> The settlers that had been introduced by the Dutch were truculent, turbulent, and impatient of restraint of any kind. Many of their descendants were tainted with slave blood, and inherited the bad qualities of an inferior race. They were cunning, deceitful and unscrupulous. Having been accustomed to the use of slaves, and been constantly engaged in forays against the Hottentot races whom they exterminated when they could not capture them, they inherited an inborn hatred of the coloured population, and regarded them fit only to live on condition of lifelong servitude, and where it was impossible to acquire them by fair means or foul, their duty was to extirpate them.[7]

To contemplate bringing to heel such a wild and uninhibited people was a prospect indeed, and with the ebb and flow of the Frontier Wars, a report, dated 6 August 1809, was compiled and presented to the Earl of Caledon, Governor of the Cape Colony, suggesting as the only viable solution the forced removal 'of all Kaffirs' from the disputed frontier, and the orchestrated settlement of British subjects in such a manner as to alter the white demographics of the region in favour of the latter.[8] The result was a concentrated military campaign that culminated during 1811 and 1812, and which, in the words of Governor Sir John Craddock, shed no more black blood 'than would seem necessary to impress on the minds of these savages a proper degree of terror and respect'.

The conflict would continue, however, until in due course it overlapped into war with the Zulus, at the conclusion of which the various colonial authorities in South Africa were at last able to claim the end of substantive, independent native rule. However, as early as 1819, enough of the Eastern Cape had been pacified for the British to begin contemplating large-scale settlement, and thus the '1820 Settler' phenomenon came in to being. A public subscription was issued in Britain for assisted immigration to the Cape, and out of some 90,000 initial applicants, 4,000 were chosen. Modest land grants were demarcated in the recently secured districts of the Eastern Cape, and the settlement of Port Elizabeth established, after which the first wave of British immigrants began to arrive in the Eastern Cape.

With the British came all of the minutiae of administration, law and order, taxation and an influx of abolitionist British missionaries, none of which sat well with the Boers. As the British increasingly established administrative authority, so English began to proliferate as the language of justice and government. Land claims were investigated, demarcated and recorded in a manner that steeply proscribed the nomadic independence of the Boers. Various reports and investigations into the cause of tensions between black and white on the frontier pointed the finger at the Boers, which further disgruntled a people whose independence was prized above all else. The issue that set the match to the powder, however, was abolition. In 1833, abolition took effect throughout the British empire, and almost overnight this age-old institution disappeared throughout the territories of the world governed or controlled by the British.

Boer councils met, and a great deal of outrage and table thumping followed as dispersed communities coalesced over this latest British outrage. Slavery, in the context of a largely cashless society, was nothing if not a grey area, and certainly the British misunderstood and overstated its severity and application. As an institution, slavery in rural Boer society could hardly be identified alongside the industrialized plantation slavery of the New World, and nor with the cruel and brutal practice perpetrated in East Africa. The absorption of Hottentots, or typically a mixed-blood *indigenes* into the family as second-class members or dependents might be defined as slavery only in the biblical, or Abrahamic, sense of the word. The system was managed generally without coercion, and with no greater application of corporal punishment than might be applied under general law, which was broadly speaking applicable to all.

However, when filtered through the fine mesh of British legal statutes, the institution was duly identified as slavery, and was thus outlawed. This set in motion a painful reshuffling of social conventions in the rural areas of the Cape, which occasioned economic disadvantage, the full extent of which was probably never wholly appreciated by the British. Most Boer farmers did not believe that they owned any slaves, and so compensation in this context could not be calculated according to the same ledger, for example, as in the Caribbean. There a slave was a commodity akin to a horse or a steam engine, with a specific and codified market value.

Ultimately, however, frontier Boer dissatisfaction accrued less because of money and slaves than the constraint of time-hallowed institutions and lifestyles. A coloured man and his family passing their lives on a Boer farm may one day be slaves, and another not, without materially altering the facts of their existence. It is also true that irritation at British intrusion was less keenly felt in the urban areas and the immediate hinterland of Cape Town. Here the advantages of assimilation to a better educated and more sophisticated society somewhat outweighed the nuisance, but in the farther reaches of the Cape, and on the far frontier, anti-British feeling was nurtured, and as the years passed it grew increasingly acute and incendiary.

By the early 1830s, a combination of land shortages, weariness at the ongoing Kaffir Wars and chafing under British rule prompted a series of Boer explorations into the interior. These were undertaken with a view to locating viable new territories beyond the reach of British control. From this developed the momentum of the so-named Great Trek, one of the largest organized exoduses in modern history. Between 1835 and 1837, six individual treks left the Eastern Cape, crossing the Orange River and penetrating the central plateau north, northeast and northwest of the Cape.

By 1840, roughly 6,000 Boer souls had abandoned the Cape Colony, about a fifth of its population. Of the six original parties, one suffered annihilation at the hands of local tribesmen in the area of modern-day Gaza Province of Mozambique, having endured punishing conditions for several months. Others encountered and overcame resistance from Zulu and amaNdebele legions, fighting and surviving epic engagements that thereafter became the bedrock of Voortrekker (pioneer) mythology, and which underwrote the holy covenant that many believed existed between the *volk*, the people, and God in the matter of their claim to the land.

Three republics were duly founded: the South African Republic (Transvaal), the Orange Free State and the Natalia Republic (Natal). The latter did not survive, and in 1843 it was annexed and declared a British colony. The independence of Transvaal, however, was ratified in 1853 by treaty with the British, upon the key provisos that the rights of British subjects would be respected and that slavery would not be practised. The Orange Free State, although initially keen to remain under British administration as the Orange River Sovereignty, was handed over by the British in 1854, under similar terms of treaty.

Thus, upon the birth of Jan Christiaan Smuts, the Boer republics had been in existence for some fifteen years, and South Africa consisted of the uneasy proximity of four separate territories, two of which were British and two under independent Boer administration. The Zulus in northern Natal and the Basotho on the Drakensberg plateau still enjoyed a substantial degree of independence, although, as mentioned already, the Zulu monarchy would be broken by war in 1879, and Basutoland eventually declared a British protectorate in 1868, and later still absorbed into the Cape Colony.

Chapter 3

Gandhi's South Africa

'Even the heathen must acknowledge the hand of God in our history.'

—Paul Kruger

On the morning of 24 May 1893, the *Admiral*, a passenger steamer of the German East Africa Line, appeared off the coast of Port Natal, dropping anchor a half-mile or so offshore. A fortnight earlier, the *Admiral* had departed Brindisi, passing through the Suez Canal and calling in at Mombasa and Dar es Salaam before pausing briefly at the island of Zanzibar, where a large contingent of Indian passengers was taken on board. Among them was a 24-year-old Gujarati barrister from Porbandar by the name of Mohandas Karamchand Gandhi.

Gandhi travelled in second class, sharing a deck with a number of reasonably well-to-do Indian immigrants, while the upper decks were held for the most part by the handful of European passengers. Below deck, however, occupying the steerage cabins, were some 200 poor and illiterate Indians under transportation to Natal as contracted and indentured labour. Conditions in the lower decks, although relatively clean, were crowded, and inevitably there had been issues of smell and sanitation. Because of this particular passenger complement, the port authorities of Natal insisted on a comprehensive medical inspection of the ship before permission to disembark would be granted.

This was always a confused and rather pointless affair, and a distasteful chore for the official charged with its disposal. On this occasion, that official was a Scottish physician by the name of Dr Neville McLaughlin, more accustomed to diagnosing consumption in the slums of Glasgow than the diseases peculiar to a cargo of impoverished Indians. As usual, his inspection included a perfunctory examination of the steerage cabins, a cursory glance down the gullet of one or two wide-eyed passengers and a quick visit to the sick bay. There it was typically confirmed by the ship's doctor that dysentery and seasickness had been the only maladies recorded on board. Such was the result of this examination, and in the absence of bubonic plague, smallpox fever or any other pernicious and communicable disease, McLaughlin assigned his signature to a certificate of disembarkation and gratefully retired from the ship.

For the remainder of the day, passengers were ferried ashore on a convoy of lighters steered primarily by Indian coxswains, and powered by Indian oarsmen.[1] Gandhi was met on board by an agent of Dada Abdulla Sheth & Co., a prominent Durban merchant family, who respectfully accompanied the young lawyer to shore, and there left him for an hour or so as he dealt with the various shore-based formalities. Under a warm spring sunshine, Gandhi stood and observed with interest the busy commerce of Indian and Chinese coolies, of Europeans of many shades and languages, hundreds of black labourers and stevedores and the occasional oriental lascar. Passengers, Indian and white, milled about in confusion as a handful of uniformed officials attempted to separate the English-speaking Europeans from the others, and the Europeans from the Orientals and Indians.

Free Indian and Oriental arrivals in the colony – generally classified as Asiatics – were particularly thoroughly scrutinized, and subjected to rigorous inspection protocols that were not required of Europeans. Once separated out, they were herded into a roped-off section of the immigration hall to await the processing of various European passengers, only after which would their proficiency in a European language be tested. A table was set up in the middle of the floor and a line roughly formed. Then, one by one, those Indians and Orientals (and any East European Jews that could be identified) seeking a certificate of entry into the colony were required to dictate a passage in English, or alternatively in French, German or Dutch, and then write a few dictated sentences in the same language.[2] Of those that could not, a few were returned to the ship, although the majority were issued with a stamped permit and sent on their way.

The largest group, however, were not free immigrants, but the knot of imported Indian labour, both men and women, and these were expedited through the arrivals hall before being identified by name and region according to a tag or badge pinned to their clothing. A handful of white labour agents, assisted by Indian interpreters, then set to work dividing them up, and checking them against a register before marching them out of the gates of the harbour.

In Gandhi's case, however, the literacy test was waived for the obvious reason that his English was impeccable, and he thus passed out into the sunshine once more with a minimum of delay or inconvenience. With his bags identified and gathered up by an Indian porter, he dutifully followed the agent through the milling crowds towards ranks of waiting rickshaws.

Gandhi would no doubt have been startled, and perhaps even a little intimidated by the spectacle of a wildly accoutred Zulu rickshaw runner waiting sullenly in harness. Imported from Japan just two years earlier, rickshaws had been quickly adopted as an occupation by Zulu men, becoming thereafter ubiquitous on the streets of Durban. Initially, the municipal authorities required that rickshaw runners be uniformed according to the norms of domestic service, but before long various martial accoutrements began to appear among old soldiers separating into their traditional regiments and guilds. There is some anecdotal evidence that early Indian rickshaw runners attempted to form a guild of their own, but upon confronting Zulu competition, they wisely, and somewhat inevitably withdrew.[3]

In the meanwhile, the barefoot and sweating Zulu settled into a trot, and humming a methodical refrain, carried the pair of elegant Indians smoothly across the busy Victoria Embankment. From there the party travelled briskly up the bustling precincts of Broad Street, a wide and unpaved avenue laced with tramlines, and lively with rickshaws, bicycles and pedestrians. On either side, buildings and shop fronts of an imperial flavour were overhung by corrugated iron, fringed with lattice work and decorated with the livery of various British and European merchants.

Having passed alongside the impressive domed edifice of the Juma Masjid mosque, which at the time dominated the corner of Queen and Grey streets, Gandhi would have found himself suddenly in a more familiar and welcoming atmosphere. Scented with incense and spices, and enlivened by the vivacity, colour and noise of an Indian bazaar, he was now among his own people. Here the markets were not disciplined by shuttered doorways, but overflowed in an unruly jumble onto the street. Dark-skinned and barefoot Tamils blended with blacks and Chinese, and turbaned Muslims mingled with Hindu women in colourful saris, picking their way among the fruit and vegetable sellers, spice traders, fancy goods emporiums and street hawkers.

This was the Indian quarter of Durban, and although covering considerably less than a quarter of the metropolitan area, it was home to by far the largest non-white population of the city. The Juma Masjid dominated the district, because Muslims dominated trade, but the more humble Shree Thakurdwara Temple, larger, and located a short distance away on the seaboard side of the railway line, attracted a more vigorous and heterogeneous congregation.

The Muslims in the main were Gujarati, of lighter complexion and higher caste, while the Hindus tended overall to be darker-skinned Tamil, Madrassi and Telugu natives of southern India. These were of the lower and labouring castes, and most were ex-indentured workers, or the descendants of indentured immigrants, the founders of the Natal sugar industry and pioneers of Indian settlement in Natal.

It is here that the story of the Natal Indian community begins. As was true for much of the global Indian diaspora of the age, the local Indian community in South Africa owed its origins to the agency of sugar. Britain was the first major power to outlaw slavery throughout its empire, which resulted in the almost immediate manumission of some 100,000 slaves across the spectrum of British sugar islands. These were first transferred to labour contracts before a system apprenticeship came briefly into operation. Very quickly, however, it became evident that in the absence of cheap replacement labour, the British overseas sugar industry would soon be in crisis.

Plans for the importation of free African labour to make up the shortfall proved ultimately to have far too many unpleasant associations for it to be practical. Instead, international labour brokers began looking at the vast pools of dirt-cheap labour available in India and China. The first British territory to begin experimenting with Indian contract labour on a large scale was Mauritius, where the option was attractive because Indians had been imported in the past as slaves, so an established Indian community already existed. By the advent of the Natal sugar industry, some twenty years later, indentured Indian labour was well established on the island, and the results had generally been found to be positive.

Its negative aspect, however, not lost at all on the white community of Natal, was simply the fact that in association with free immigration, the Indian community grew at a marvellous pace, and quickly began to outnumber the white settler community on the island by a significant percentage. By the 1890s it was clear that Mauritius was overrun by Indians, and had become in effect a colony of India.

It was for this reason primarily that there was manifest in Natal a great reluctance to introduce low-caste Indians in significant numbers. A large potential workforce of indigenous blacks was already established in the territory, numbering upwards of 200,000, and for the time being idle and un-integrated into the cash economy. In the 1850s, however, neither the Xhosa nor the Zulus showed any early inclination to submit to white cultural domination, and certainly no interest in engaging in formal labour. Natives of the region clung with maddening tenacity to their traditional styles of life and economy, and so long as they did not want to work, nor had any need to work, it was hard to make them do so.

The latter half of the nineteenth century was a period of similar dislocation and adjustment all over the world, as indigenous societies were awakened by the arrival on their shores of mercantile Europeans, and then prodded and coerced into contributing labour and taxation to foreign economies. At the same time, sensitive to the dark moral residue of slavery, the British establishment was anxious that the colonization of the tropics be framed as a philanthropic and civilizing mission. As a result, the various charters and constitutions governing British overseas territories sought to entrench equality of treatment to all and any under British protection, which, quite obviously, ran contrary to the interests of British settlers who required, above all else, land and labour.

Local settler attitudes in Natal towards its black population were, therefore, ambivalent to say the least. There was, on the one hand, great interest shown in the potential utility of black societies, but on the other, their physical occupation of large tracts of agricultural land was inconvenient. Settlers therefore fought an unrelenting campaign of propaganda against unalienated blacks in order to provoke the imperial government either to look the other way, or to actively participate in the sequestration of native lands.

Blacks, who had, under the circumstances of white colonization, been forced to shift from free-ranging pastoral to static agricultural lifestyles, adopted in general a system of agriculture and animal husbandry that was seen by white colonists as harmful to the land. This led to stringent calls for ever more black-occupied land to be held in reserve for whites, who arguably were in a position to make better use of it, and for blacks to be forced in one way or another into formal labour to work that land on behalf of European agriculturalists.

None of this, however, would happen overnight, and in the short term an emerging agricultural and mining colony like Natal required labour. After a great deal of public debate, reams of anxious press reporting and much emotional hand-wringing, a parliamentary bill was finally tabled that in 1859 resulted in the passing of the Natal Coolie Law, cautiously opening the door for the controlled importation of contracted Indian labour.

The Natal Coolie Law, however, was drafted under the careful supervision of imperial authorities, and with due regard given at all points of its passage to a raft of rights and protections established for the purpose by the British and Indian governments. The British liberal establishment, extremely influential at that moment in history, had in 1839 shut down the pipeline of Indian labour to the Caribbean and Mauritius after a brief but effective abolition campaign. The revitalization of the practice was only permitted after both governments (British and Indian) applied exhaustive effort in ensuring humane conditions for indentured Indians, and ensuring moreover that the fact was widely appreciated.

Any individual recruited for labour overseas was required to present him- or herself to a British magistrate in order to attest verbally to the fact that recruitment had been both willing and free, and that the contractual terms were clearly understood. In addition, a free return passage was mandated for those desiring repatriation at the conclusion of their contract, and while under such contract, each individual was guaranteed various rights and protections as British subjects. Local agents, or *duffadars*, typically non-British, were to be contracted to undertake recruitment, after which, individual recruits would be housed in controlled depots in Calcutta, Madras and Bombay under the protection of a British Protector of Emigrants.

Before embarkation, various medical examinations were to be carried out, contracts vetted, ships inspected and further assurances sought that conditions of service were fully understood. To each ship would be appointed a European surgeon to examine every individual upon embarkation, and to monitor health and sanitation on board throughout the journey.

In the particular case of Natal, terms of contract stipulated five years of bonded labour, with free passage available for those wishing to return to India at the conclusion of their contract. Alternatively, those who had completed their contract could simply re-indenture, thereby earning full rights of free citizenship in the colony and a gift of crown land. In 1872, the official government Office of Indian Protector was established to adjudicate the rights and liberties of indentured labourers, outlawing, for example, flogging as a legal punishment.

Thus it was that on the morning of 16 November 1860, the citizens of Durban awoke to see a wooden sailing barque, the *Truro*, anchored offshore. On board were 342 men and women from the urban centres of Madras and Calcutta, crowding the decks and apprehensively contemplating the land of their adoption. This was a significant moment in the history of the colony, and as a lighter made its way out to sea, carrying the various agents and inspectors, a crowd gathered on the quayside to watch the business unfold. In due course a small flotilla of transport lighters was launched across the straits, pulling up alongside the *Truro* in order to begin ferrying her passengers to shore.

Both white and black greeted the newcomers with passive and not unfriendly curiosity. There were smiles and waves from both sides, and a festival atmosphere as if a small circus had arrived in town. Black stevedores paused in their work, and imitating among themselves the strange new words and enunciation that they heard, they created the onomatopoeic name *abakwaMnanyai*. This stuck, and remained in the Zulu lexicon for generations.

In general, however, while the spectacle was observed and enjoyed, it was not long before the citizenry of Durban dispersed. The business of sorting and allocation then saw parties of workers delivered to their employers, loaded onto wagons and transported in convoy up the North Coast road. The following morning, the *Natal Mercury* printed a colourful report of the event for the sake of those not present:

> They were a queer, comical, foreign-looking, very Oriental-like crowd. The men with their huge Muslin turbans, bare, scraggy shin bones, and coloured garments; the women with their flashing eyes, long, dishevelled, pitchy hair, with their half-covered, well-formed figures, and their keen inquisitive glances, the children with their meagre, intelligent, cute and humorous countenances mounted on bodies of unconscionable fragility, were all evidently beings of a different race and kind from any we have yet seen in Africa or England.[4]

Ten days later, following the *Truro* into Port Natal, the *Belvedere* dropped anchor. She had set sail from Calcutta, and from her recesses spilled a second contingent of Indians. Over the course of a year, nineteen ships would arrive offshore, bringing the total in that first wave of Indians to arrive in Natal to a little under six thousand. The cost of importation fell on the colonial administration, and through various tariffs, indirectly upon the local planter community.

Most, however, were generally pleased with the result, and the Indians soon blended into the rural landscape. Under their terms of service, each received a stipend of ten shillings a month for the first year, increasing yearly to a maximum of fourteen shillings. Thereafter, the options available were either reindenture, accept free repatriation or simply remain in Natal as free British subjects.

The first contractual term – from 1860 to 1865 – was obviously a challenge for both workers and employers, but most acutely for the former. Workers were typically housed in modest compounds, and for the first decade or so they lived and laboured very much in isolation. Without support or community, they undertook their tasks uncomplainingly, and although in general they received fair treatment, reports of abuses surfaced periodically. Very few, however, would ultimately avail themselves of their option to return to India.

Indeed, the Indian community of Natal established itself firmly and quickly, proliferating at such a rate that by 1904, the date of the second official census of the colony, Indians were found to outnumber whites.[5] Not all of these, of course, were descendants of the *Truro* and *Belvedere*, although that community certainly made up the majority. Many were 'Passenger' Indians, i.e. those who arrived in the colony as free immigrants in the aftermath of indenture. The sudden advent of such a large population of foreign and illiterate people, without community or cultural establishment, invited the rapid formation of a society, and before long the first Indian shops and trades in Durban were registered and licensed.

The Passenger Indians, however, were of a different demographic entirely. They were in the main Gujarati-speaking Hindus and Muslims from the west coast of India, and it was they, in service to the needs of the indentured community, who laid the foundation of an Indian trade and professional class in Natal. Before long, the names Abbobaker Amod, Abdoola Hajee Adam Jhaveri and Moosa Hajee Cassim began to appear above shop fronts in a number of 'locations', centred initially at the west end of West Street, close to the city centre of Durban, but later in concentrations around Grey and Field streets, and Commercial Road.

Thanks to the preponderance of Muslims, these enterprises and concerns became generally known as 'Arab' businesses. Many represented large, multinational Indian firms actively spreading into the new diaspora. More humble traders tended to penetrate deeper into the hinterland, serving the concentrations of indentured labour in the various magisterial districts of Inanda, Umlazi and Alexandra. Others established shops and stalls in Umkomanzi, Umgeni and Umvoti, and inland in the coal-mining districts of Dundee, Newcastle and Ladysmith.

Of the indentured workers that completed their contracts, and chose to remain in the colony, most entered formal employment either on the coalmines, the railways or in public works, or secured land and began to supply the urban centres with fresh produce. Others, who were unable to secure land or employment, entered such humble trades as laundry, shoe repair and hawking. None suffered any specific discrimination within colonial administration, inasmuch as they were all coolies without regard to caste or ethnicity. Within the community, however, the darker-skinned and illiterate contract workers tended to remain subject to the same disadvantageous stigma of caste they might have expected in India.

Early European accommodation began to wear thin as Indian numbers increased, and it was in the European mercantile community that initial disquiet found expression. This was mainly over Indian tendencies towards opaque financing and arcane record-keeping. A great deal of tax avoidance and devious accounting, for example, could be achieved simply by maintaining accounts in Gujarati or Urdu, and certainly the parallel banking, loan and financing systems that sustained Indian business proved intimidating to a majority of white traders.

Likewise, the exclusivity and clannishness of Indian business, and its heavy reliance on caste, regional and family associations seemed to create unfair advantage. Indian business, for example, could benefit from the importation of almost unlimited family reserves, profiting thereafter from low wages, or, indeed, no wages at all. Against this sort of thing, European employers simply could not compete.

It was thanks to all of this, and perhaps simply to a more finely tuned aptitude for trade, that by the end of the 1880s, Natal Indians found themselves in the happy position of dominating petty trade throughout the colony and, in particular, holding a monopoly over the African trade. The African trade, indeed, as more blacks entered the cash economy, had become an increasingly important pillar of rural business, and white traders watched their Indian competitors dominate this market with a growing sense of enmity.

Then, as the great mineral discoveries in the Cape and the Transvaal transformed the economy of the entire region into a spitting cauldron of capital, Indians rapidly moved into the Transvaal, and soon began dominating all levels of petty trade there too. With this came more Indians, and more still, until the complexion of the mercantile quarters of Durban and Johannesburg began to resemble an oriental bazaar.

All of this simply added fuel to an already incendiary anti-Indian atmosphere, the result of which was a growing clamour for restrictions to be applied, first against Indian immigration, but also against the unfair competition of Indian business. Stoking the flames was a steady chorus of hysterical and often spiteful press reportage, lampooning the Indians, and speculating on the future complexion of a colony dominated by Indians. The example of Mauritius became the template of a future Natal if an unleashed policy of Indian immigration was not somehow held in check.[6]

However, the unfortunate fact was that immigration controls to limit non-indentured Indian arrivals in Natal would be impossible for so long as the territory remained under substantive British metropolitan administration. Just as was the case with British whites, British Indians were regarded as equal subjects of Her Majesty, guaranteed all of the rights and liberties owed to any other imperial subject. If an Indian wished to emigrate from India to Natal, he enjoyed the same rights as a European wishing to do the same thing.

In 1858, upon the transfer of authority for the government of India from the East India Company to the Crown, a royal proclamation served upon the people of India, in the loftiest language of English legal penmanship, gave notice of full equality granted by Her Majesty on all of her Indian subjects: 'We hold Ourselves bound to the Natives of Our Indian Territories by the same obligations of Duty which bind Us to all Our other Subjects; and those Obligations, by the Blessing of Almighty God, We shall faithfully and conscientiously fulfil.'[7]

In order to ensure that all of Her Majesty's far-flung colonies respected this covenant, the Colonial Office required of each that it forward its pending legislation for approval before adoption into law. No immigration policy specifically identifying Indians as prohibited persons would pass such royal scrutiny, and certainly no civic ordinances that targeted Indian licences, businesses or properties would be allowed. This forced the white political establishment to consider alternative methods of proscription, and the local administration soon fell upon the matter of sanitation. In fairness, the Indian community in this regard represented a large and static target, and they were slow to recognize this fact and act.

Although standards of sanitation in lower-caste Indian communities were indeed deplorable, the homes and business premises of the larger Indian concerns were, of course, no more or less sanitized than their European counterparts, but thanks to a lack of official differentiation, coolies were coolies, the opportunity existed to spread the stigma of poor Indian hygiene standards to wherever it was most convenient.

In 1890, a general election was pending, and emerging as the key figure was John Robinson, co-founder of the hugely influential *Natal Mercury*, and a populist member of the local assembly. Robinson, who had hitherto been something of a moderate over the Indian question, recognized nonetheless its vote-winning potential, and quickly became a vocal and hard-hitting detractor. Among other choice epithets he was apt to trade, he referred to Indians as 'pernicious on social, political, commercial, financial and especially on sanitary grounds'.[8]

This sort of thing succeeded spectacularly in fuelling further public demands for the segregation of Indians on grounds of health and sanitation, which stirred up an almost hysterical reaction. In Pietermaritzburg, for example, the capital of the colony, the chief magistrate, who really ought to have known better, uttered the oft-quoted remark that the Indian 'still wallows in his native stench and filth'.[9]

Throughout it all, the Indians kept their mouths shut and their doors open. In 1891, however, as Natal was petitioning Her Majesty's government for a grant of responsible government, the Durban Indian Committee was formed, and counter-petitioned the Colonial Office and the government of India to disallow responsible government in Natal, pleading that it would undermine Indian rights and liberties, and jeopardize their ability to live and trade. This, of course, was ignored by both, and achieved nothing more than to further infuriate the settler community.

In 1893, Crown approval for responsible government was indeed granted, as was inevitable, and the first prime minister of Natal, none other than John Robinson, wasted no time in attending to the Indian question. Early the following year, the Powers of the Municipal Corporations Bill was introduced, intended to authorize town councils and municipalities to regulate sanitary conditions, and to abate such nuisances as overcrowding, excessive noise and smell, the keeping of livestock in living apartments and the depositing of refuse in the streets. Despite ambiguous wording, the principal thrust of the statute was to provide an official pretext for the refusal of business and trading licences to Indians based on real or imagined transgressions of the law.

The issue closest to the heart of the average white townsman in Natal, however, was not business licences, but immigration and repatriation. A majority argued for a complete ban on the unregulated entry of Indians into the colony, and a means to rid the colony of those already there. This, however, was beyond the competence of a local legislature. The next best thing was deemed to be discouraging permanent settlement by the imposition of a heavy tax on any immigrant determined to remain in Natal after the expiry of his or her contract.

This, however, was but a finger in the dyke, and was corollary to another and potentially much more serious issue. Indians, as British subjects, enjoyed the same access to the franchise in Natal as any other taxpayer. The ballot was protected by modest education and property qualifications, which increasing numbers of Indians were satisfying. If left unchecked, Indians would in due course dominate the electorate, and eventually take over government. This struck to the very core of European fears. It had happened before, and it could happen again.

These, and other similar issues, came increasingly under discussion in the territorial parliament, in the members' lounge and, of course, in the various clubs and parlours around the colony. At the time the white political establishment was somewhat complacent, having experienced or observed no organized Indian efforts to coordinate, lobby or make representation. Therefore, as a bill to deny Indians access to the franchise entered parliament, the parties to the debate felt no particular urgency, and the draft enjoyed a leisurely passage through the house.

Changes, however, were afoot in the Indian community. Among Indian merchant dynasties in Natal, there was none more prominent than Dada Abdulla Sheth & Co. Dealing in European and Indian imports, and engaged in transport and shipping, Dada Abdulla represented the local interests of a wealthy and influential Indian family. By the early 1890s, the firm had established its local headquarters in Durban, and from there it began to spread its activities throughout Natal and Portuguese East Africa, with perhaps its most lucrative branch associated with the goldfields of the Transvaal.

That particular branch was managed by a cousin of the family, a certain Tayob Haji Khan Mahomed, who later negotiated, and reached an agreement, with Dada Abdulla to purchase the Transvaal operations on the strength of a promissory note. A dispute erupted, however, and Tayob defaulted. The amount in question was significant, some £42,500, and the matter appeared to pivot on how and when items in stock would be valued. Each party claimed a different date, with the difference in value ranging from between £4,000 to £6,000.

Dada Abdulla & Co. initiated a suit in the High Court of the Transvaal, and representing the firm was a prominent and liberal English lawyer by the name of Albert Weir Baker. Although something of a scholar of Indian history, and unusually knowledgeable in this field, Baker's expertise did not extend to the intricacies of Indian accounting, and certainly not to the wiles of Indian accountants. Indeed, a mystery of Tayob's bookkeeping defeated even local Gujarati interpreters, whose duties typically ran to nothing more complex than counting pennies in the pay packets of disgruntled indentured workers. Baker desperately needed a Gujarati-speaking research assistant, but no such Indian professional was to be found anywhere in South Africa.

GANDHI'S SOUTH AFRICA

So it was, that on 24 May 1893, Mohandas K. Gandhi found himself leaning on the railings of the steamship *Admiral*, gazing across a mile or so of breakwater to the low urban horizon of Durban. The aging vessel, less than optimum in its appointments, and carrying a cargo of ragged immigrants, rolled on the swell as a convoy of lighters plied the straits. An hour or so later, Gandhi was in the midst of the city, and soon after that in the scented and cool interior of Dada Abdullah's home.

Gandhi accepted a contractual term of one year in the service of Dada Abdulla, for no reason other than to gain the preliminary experience necessary to establish a legal career at home. He had trained in London, and later joined the English bar, but at no time had he excelled. The best that could be said of it was that he had enjoyed a lengthy junket in educated society, which had polished his manners and overlaid a veneer of sophistication, but which had left him nonetheless disadvantaged in the matter of law. As a rule, in order to function as a barrister under any British system, an informal apprenticeship was obligatory, something that typically came about through connections and not aptitude.

Gandhi, therefore, arrived in South Africa with no particular interest in the territory other than to dispose of his contract and leave with the money and the experience. The advice that he had been given prior to his arrival was simply to do his work and keep his mouth shut, which to him must have seemed curious counsel. In London he had encountered a great many Englishmen and -women of every class, and had met nothing but accommodating attitudes and friendly curiosity. He had formulated his early acquaintances among like-minded people, taken dance lessons, debated in the local theosophical society and cultivated numerous alliances on the fringes of liberal politics. None of this, however, could have prepared him for the blatant snobbishness, the frosty disregard and petty pinpricks of racism that greeted him in Durban.

He was, it is true, not quite the orthodox Indian that the white townsmen of Durban were accustomed to, and he was granted in consequence a little more respect and courtesy than most. He eschewed the loin cloth or pyjama of the lower or merchant classes, as he did the robes and turbans of his Muslim hosts, preferring a frock coat and club collar, stove-pipe trousers and a pair of black, patent-leather shoes. Upon his head, however, he was inclined to wear a turban, which was his only accommodation to tradition.

This, in combination with his abiding courtesy, his disarming amiability and his faultless English did indeed effect a dulling of the sharpest edges of his encounters with whites, although nothing could this do to rescue him from the derisive and overarching classification of coolie. For an educated man accustomed to the intricate caste and class consciousness of India, this lack of distinction proved odious, but at the same time, it was an unassailable fact of life in the African colonies, and about it nothing could be done.

Abdulla Sheth also did not initially appear to care a great deal for his new appointment, and for the same broad reasons. He found himself uncomfortable in the company of such an urbane Indian, sophisticated and lettered, untraditional, and a Hindu besides.[10] Gandhi, however, quickly disarmed his host, and then impressed him with his general competence, and his detailed and specific knowledge of Islam. Gandhi, of course, was at all times willing to discourse on faith and religion, and always without trace of prejudice. World religion, as history would prove, was to remain of abiding interest to him, perhaps even an obsession.

Although always accommodating, and unfailingly pleasant, Gandhi was nonetheless also capable at times of a forceful and unyielding obstinacy. He was invited one morning to accompany Dada Abdulla to the High Court of Durban, to be introduced to the firm's lawyer, and to observe the form and protocol of the local judiciary. The case was a trivial one, and as Gandhi took his seat in the gallery he became aware that the magistrate was regarding him coolly. This continued for some time, before in due course Gandhi was addressed by the court and ordered to remove his turban. Dada Abdulla also happened to wear a turban, but in combination with his traditional robes, this was not, in the eyes of the law, incongruous. Gandhi, on the other hand, was dressed in western style, and his turban therefore seemed to sit ill with the court. He courteously declined to remove it, however, explaining that such was not required in India, where, indeed, it would be disrespectful to present an unadorned head. The magistrate nodded, accepting this argument, but nonetheless Gandhi was ordered to remove himself from the court if he refused to comply with its traditions, which he willingly agreed to do.

This impressed Dada Abdulla considerably, who forbade him thereafter ever to remove his turban in a court of law. It also introduced him to the wider Natal public, for the incident was reported in detail the following morning on the front page of the *Mercury*. Very rare it was in those days that an Indian stood his ground, and the matter prompted some admiring conversation in the various clubs and chambers of the city. Gandhi was of a sudden greeted by Indians with esteem, and by Europeans with polite interest. Within a few weeks of arrival, he had established his presence in both communities, a gratifying fact, for Mohandas K. Gandhi was not without vanity.

In due course, Dada Abdulla felt the moment opportune to introduce

Gandhi to the matter at hand, and arrangements were made for him to travel by rail to Pretoria. On the evening of 31 May 1893, at the onset of winter, he set off from Durban, travelling in a first-class compartment, which he felt befitted his status and objective. This raised no particular concern in Durban, where wealthy Indians regularly travelled first class, but as the train slowly mounted the escarpment, and began to ply the high and chilly reaches of the Drakensberg foothills, the sight of a brown man in a first-class compartment began to excite comment. Soon enough, as the train halted at Pietermaritzburg station, a white man entered the doorway of Gandhi's compartment, where he paused for a moment before spinning on his heels. Soon, however, he was back, but this time in the company of a railway official who in some evident discomfort informed Gandhi that he would be required now to move to a third-class compartment.

At this Gandhi protested, and held his ground. He had, after all, paid for and been issued a first-class ticket, and he intended to complete his journey in first class, or not at all. He would, he declared, yield to nothing but force, which proved acceptable to both Europeans. Soon afterwards Gandhi found himself standing on the cold concourse of Pietermaritzburg station, luggage at his feet, watching glumly as the train, the last of the day, disappeared into the gathering dusk.

There he sat all night, shivering without an overcoat, consumed by the simple injustice of what had taken place, and determining with a mounting sense of moral outrage that he would simply not accept it. The following morning, he dispatched two telegrams, the first a bitter complaint to the railway authorities and the second to Dada Abdulla. The first achieved nothing, but the second mobilized the local Indian community that immediately rushed to his rescue.

The next day he resumed his journey, once again in a reserved first-class compartment, arriving this time at the end of the line without incident. From there he was booked on a stagecoach to Standerton, but the driver prevented him from entering the coach, pointing instead to the luggage box at the rear. Gandhi remonstrated, quite naturally, and argued persistently as the white passengers looked the other way. Then, quite unexpectedly, a sharp slap caught him across the back of his head, persuading him at last that if he wanted to reach Pretoria at all he had no alternative but to bite his tongue and climb up on the rear of the coach.

For six hours he brooded, breathing dust and cultivating a rich spleen. Arriving in Pretoria that evening, filthy, angry and exhausted, he was met by Albert Baker, who listened to this tale of mistreatment unhappily. Such, Baker explained, was all too common in the Transvaal. A deeply religious man in his mid-thirties, tall, balding, blue eyed and kindly, Baker took Gandhi in hand as gently as he could. Not every European in the republic, he explained, was so unfriendly, although it would be wise to expect such things from time to time. An unpleasant fact, to be sure, but butting heads with the establishment was no remedy.

Gandhi, however, had taken the matter very much to heart. He was wounded and aggrieved, his dignity, which then he held very dear, had been injured, and he was disinclined to simply sit back and accept it. He determined that somehow he would make a stand on the matter. Precisely how and when was not clear to him, but at that moment the modern world shifted upon its axis, and the end of the British empire was set in motion.

Chapter 4

Equal Rights for all Civilized Men

'By liberalism I don't mean the creed of any party or any century. I mean a generosity of spirit, a tolerance of others, an attempt to comprehend otherness, a commitment to the rule of law, a high ideal of the worth and dignity of man, a repugnance for authoritarianism and a love of freedom.'
—Alan Paton, South African novelist

In 1691, the Dutch East India Company, the Vereenigde Oost-Indische Compagnie, superseded the Office of Commander in the Cape with that of Governor, creating from an overseas out-station, administered by a private company, a constituted colony superintended by the Dutch state. The first governor of this new colony was a gifted Dutch administrator by the name of Simon van der Stel. Arguably van der Stel was the father of the modern Cape, and it is to him that many of the finer aspects of this gifted region can be traced.

Simon van der Stel was very much a product of his age, with all of the transitional social and political contradictions that this might imply. As the son of a senior Dutch colonial administrator, he spent his childhood in the Far East, and through the prism of liberal parentage, emerged into adulthood with a sense of social awareness that presaged in many respects the first philosophical works of the Age of Enlightenment. He first set foot in the Cape more or less at the age of 40, with his wide-ranging, initial experience tempered and fashioned by a thorough-going and sophisticated metropolitan education.

The Cape at the time had been under the utilitarian rule of a series of company commanders who had done little to advance the culture of the region beyond the strict requirements of its mandate. The city of Cape Town consisted of a fort, various battlements, the administrative quarter, a port and a rusticated sprawl of smallholdings and ramshackle estates founded for the purpose of producing essential supplies. Simon van der Stel, however, looked around him, and in this temperate region, set against a backdrop of singularly rare drama and beauty, pictured an outpost of Dutch metropolitan society and manners. Little at that point was known about the interior of the subcontinent, and although the outer fringe of pioneer society had begun already to develop its bucolic and individualistic mood, the hinterland of Cape Town was accessible, beautiful and not without the raw material of culture.

The colony was run along lines of strict economy, and there was little that van der Stel could do to circumvent this. Nonetheless, and although he undertook much in the way of civic improvement in Cape Town, his most notable achievements were the founding of the settlement of Stellenbosch, the acme of Cape Dutch architecture and civic planning, and the creation of his own private estate, Groot Constantia, today regarded as the signature stately home of the Cape.

In the shadow of the Tafelberg, Table Mountain, the main homestead of Groot Constantia displays the stolid surety of its north European influences, but is embellished by the fine gables that have since come to define the particular architectural standard of the Cape. Set at the end of a tree-lined avenue, and planted with a higher grade of vines, it established the tone for the development of life and industry in the Cape that would mark the beginning of its great cultural advance.

In 1685, the Edict of Fontainebleau was enacted by Louis XIV of France, stripping the protestant Huguenots of France of their immunity from persecution by the Catholic Church. This set in motion an exodus of Huguenots from France to various Dutch overseas territories, where a culture of liberalism and tolerance promised sanctuary. In 1688, a contingent of some 180 Huguenots arrived in the Cape, following a piecemeal immigration that had been ongoing for some time, and which would continue well into the eighteenth century. Many of these were allocated farms and holdings in the beautiful valley of Franschhoek, and here another district of high culture was established, embellished also by sprawling vineyards and the emergence of an amalgam of these two distinct European artistic styles.

Simon van der Stel, in the meanwhile, wearing the pale skin of his Dutch father, but also the raven hair and coal-black eyes of his Indian mother, might under later regimes have been classified as 'coloured', in consequence of this mixed-race parentage, and would have been conceivably restricted from all that he had created in an earlier age. One can only speculate, however, how he might have regarded the native Khoisan who were still present in viable numbers in the hinterland of Cape Town, and who occasionally ventured onto the flatlands between Table Mountain and the Hex River range to graze their herds. Only the anecdotal record of a conversation between him and his son hints at a continuation into this matter of his evident social liberalism. He, and one can imagine a majority of those enlightened among the settler population, saw the Hottentot as innocent and wild, and deserving therefore of the gentle usage and the protection of the colonists.

One of the great discourses of the Age of Enlightenment was that composed by French philosopher Jean-Jacques Rousseau, contained in his 1755 *Discourse on Inequality.* As the title suggests, Rousseau sought in this discussion to identify the causes of inequality in man, and the facets of primitive, or Natural Man in defence of his theory of the unchanging nature of humankind. The minutiae of this theory, and Rousseau's conclusions upon it, probably stray beyond the scope of this narrative, and it might perhaps be sufficient to conclude that this, along with other associated works of the period, marks the moment that the European races began to question, and ponder, the place and order of mankind against a growing appreciation of its complexity and diversity.

The frontispiece of the Dutch edition of the *Discourse on Inequality* features an engraving of Simon van der Stel, portrayed in classical elegance, surrounded by a committee of sorts, and seated equidistant between the ramparts of a European castle and a collection of crude native shelters. Here he reflects upon a half-naked Hottentot youth, who stands before him over a nondescript bundle, the entire composition captioned, '*Il retourne chez ses Egaux*'.[1] The engraving illustrates a story that Rousseau included in his discourse as evidence of the immutability of mankind. Simon van der Stel is purported to have adopted this Hottentot youth as an infant, brought him into his home, clothed and educated him, instructed him in several European languages, and upon adolescence, apprenticed him to a Dutch commissary-general of the Indies.

Some years later, however, upon the death of his master, the child, now a grown man, returned to the Cape, and without visiting his adoptive father, crossed the bitter almond hedge, never to return. It was claimed that he was seen on occasions in the mountains of the Hex River, adorned in a sheepskin cape, attending to his herd and engaged in simple, pastoral pursuits.[2] Soon afterwards, a bundle of clothing was delivered to the home of Simon van der Stel, those very clothes that the young Hottentot had left Cape Town wearing, accompanied by a note that read: 'Be so kind, Sir, as to take notice, that I forever renounce this apparel. I likewise forever renounce the Christian religion. It is my firm resolution to live and die in the religion, manners and customs of my ancestors. All the favour I ask from you is to leave me the collar and the hanger I wear. I shall keep them for your sake.'[3]

With its fairy-tale reference to the prodigal return, this parable alludes to a quality of equal intellect that could not of itself save its owner from savagery. The conclusion, therefore, presented by Rousseau, was simply that, despite the very best efforts applied to the civilization of the savage, and although its veneer he might display, he cannot be removed from his fundamental condition, no matter what his training. The savage, the moral implied, although not to be despised or abused, was neither to be tamed nor lived among.

Simon van der Stel died in 1712, and his office was inherited by his son, whose legacy was poorer. The age of Dutch ascendency, however, soon gave way to the age of British, and the higher values of culture and living established by the father and son van der Stel were duly inherited. The British were also bequeathed of a liberal political tradition, born under Protestant midwifery, before the advent of the Frontier Wars, and before the needs of assimilation.

The retreat of the Dutch and the advance of the British in the Far East saw the gradual consolidation of British India, and the more concentrated settlement and administration of Australia and New Zealand, both with vulnerable aboriginal populations. In each case, as in the Americas, those populations fell victim primarily to the introduction of strange diseases, although in the Cape, the controlled extermination of the Khoisan presaged genocide, and the advent of the Frontier Wars, the exodus of the Voortrekkers and the settlement of Natal all hinted at more and greater catastrophes in the future.

In general, however, it was accepted and understood in the age of abolition that the impact of colonization on indigenous societies was proving calamitous. This prompted the rise of the European humanitarian movement that evolved in parallel with the expanding exploitation of the populated tropics. In 1837, the British Aboriginal Protection Society was founded by a corps of interested parties, included among them liberal politicians, artists, writers, explorers and missionaries.

One such was parliamentarian Sir Thomas Foxwell Buxton, an early abolitionist who also sat on the chair of a parliamentary select committee authorized to investigate the condition of aboriginal peoples in the colonies. This was an important moment in the development of an imperial contract, and the preamble to the report details the mandate of the inquiry:

[to] consider what measures ought to be adopted with regards to the native inhabitants of the countries where British settlements are made, and to the neighbouring tribes, in order to secure to them the due observance of justice, and the protection of their rights; to promote the spread of civilization among them, and to lead them to the peaceful and voluntary reception of the Christian religion.[4]

The report spoke to all of the major settled colonies of the empire: Canada, New Zealand, Australia and of course South Africa. It spoke also from the vantage of British global predominance, but at the same time it underlined the responsibility of the British people to balance their global ambitions with the humane usage of its aboriginal peoples. Of South Africa, the report opens with a lengthy recapitulation of the race history of the Cape, from Portuguese observations of the wealth in livestock of the Hottentot to their almost complete dispossession and enslavement to the 'Boor'. According to the results of a survey of South African missions:

From the gradual manner in which the Cape Colony has been extended; from the peaceable manner in which the Hottentots had submitted to the Colonial Government; from the extermination of the Bushmen between Graaff-Reinet and the Orange River; and from the manner in which the Kafirs [sic] had retreated before us from the Sunday River to the Fish, and from the Fish River to Keiskamma, I had formed an opinion that in this way the aborigines of Africa would ultimately be exterminated, and that future ages would have nothing but tradition to tell them where the tribes and nations now inhabiting this continent.

Such was the British state of mind in the early nineteenth century. The guilt of that monumental crime against humanity – slavery – sat heavy on the conscience of every salient man and woman in Britain, and the quest for absolution created an almost frenzied regard for the wellbeing of those earthly cousins of a ruder state. This might not necessarily have facilitated or prompted a more liberal and humane view of indigenous societies in the wider empire, but it certainly contributed to the emergence of the Cape liberal tradition.

In 1853, the British Cape Colony was granted representative government, which, although largely symbolic, did grant the colony the right to form its own parliament, and to draft and adopt a constitution. That constitution enshrined as a facet of its humanitarian code a multiracial franchise, in some respects forced on it by the imperial charter, but also reflective of a leadership determined to make real that fabled egalitarian and colourless society.

The franchise, however, in and of itself, was irrelevant to the indigenous population of the Cape without the associated facilities of education and property. It was the first governor under the representative government, Sir George Grey, who sensed that the key to mature and popular political involvement in the colony lay, in the first instance, in education.

Grey arrived at the Cape in 1854, close upon his appointment as governor of New Zealand, and prior to that of Australia. He was a military man, firm in his ideas, resolute, physically prepossessing and unwilling to suffer fools. He had seen the empire first hand, and with an acquired sympathy for the aboriginal based on lengthy explorations of the Australian interior, he approached his tenure in South Africa intending to solve the frontier crisis through means other than force.

At that point in history, Britain was confronting war in the Crimea, and later the Indian Mutiny, and Grey's mandate in the Cape was simply to keep the peace on the frontier and in Natal, and to project tactful but firm diplomatic relations with the Boer republics. He also, however, taking advantage of British abstraction, implemented many unauthorized policies of engagement with the Xhosa, encouraging and supporting integration, education and social improvement. He further encouraged evangelism and missionary education, supporting the establishment of industrial schools as a first phase of practical education. These offered instruction in carpentry, wagon-making, blacksmithing and other useful trades, offering also a reasonable standard of academic education to those so disposed to accept it.

The results, however, were mixed. Some in indigenous society embraced the opportunities with enthusiasm, adopting western dress and manners, and seeing in these innovations a doorway to 'civilization'. Others, however, mainly among the traditionalist Xhosa, were less enamoured, seeing the effort as an attack on their cultural traditions and political autonomy. With the annexation to the Cape of the Transkei, under the short-lived British Kaffraria, a large population of unalienated Xhosa were abruptly absorbed into the Cape, placing them under direct British administration. In desperation, the remaining independent Xhosa began to look to the supernatural.

In April 1856, after almost 80 years of sporadic frontier war, a young Xhosa girl by the name of Nongqawuse was visited by spirits as she tended the family crops. The spirits informed her that only the slaughter of all Xhosa cattle and the destruction of all stored foodstuffs would herald the emergence of a new and glorious nation, at the advent of which the white man would be driven into the sea.

This preceded what has variously been described as the Xhosa Cattle Killing Movement, or the Xhosa Suicide, both of which are reasonably apt. The prophesy was taken seriously by the community and adopted, and between 1856 and 1858, some 400,000 head of cattle, virtually the entire national herd, was slaughtered, along with the burning and fouling of stored grain and crops in the field. The promised revelation, however, failed. Nongqawuse was arrested and detained by British authorities on Robben Island while some 75,000 Xhosa perished from hunger.

This episode finally broke the back of Xhosa resistance, and almost destroyed the nation. In it, however, Sir George Grey recognized an opportunity, and he instructed frontier colonists to provide assistance to starving tribesmen only if they accepted labour contracts. The depopulated lands of the Eastern Cape were soon afterwards settled by Europeans under generous land grants, largely to members of a German legion that had served alongside the British in the Crimean War.

Fingers were pointed at Sir George Grey, however, whose efforts at cultural and religious conversion had exceeded his mandate, and were decried for sparking the tinder of what was seen as a millennialist mass suicide. The episode, nevertheless, solved a great many problems for the colonial government, and although in due course the bulk of surviving Xhosa returned in one form or another to the land, after which frontier tensions resumed, a great many submitted to labour, and many more to education and assimilation. From this the bedrock of an educated black elite began to form.

On to the stage then stepped another remarkable man, and the head of a no less remarkable family. John Charles Molteno arrive in the Cape in 1831, at the age of seventeen. He was of an Anglo-Italian family, and founded a business empire in the Cape based on wine exports and the production and export of wool. Molteno was of the first generation of Cape parliamentarians, and what makes him interesting in this context was his willingness to marry the coloured daughter of a local business partner, and the lack of obvious stigma attached to this. That marriage, however, proved to be short-lived, for Maria Molteno died during the birth of their first child. Molteno remarried soon afterwards, and this time fathered nineteen children, including his eldest daughter, the much-storied Elizabeth Maria Molteno.

Elizabeth, or Betty Molteno as she was known, achieved prominence in a family of high-performing siblings thanks largely to an effervescent personality, great physical beauty and an uncompromising political liberalism. As a teacher, she revolutionized the Victorian codes of learning in the colony, but was hounded out of the profession for a determined anti-war position during the Anglo-Boer War, plunging thereafter into energetic political activism.

She was allied to Gandhi during the climax of his *satyagraha* protests, and remained a friend, and supporter of his political and spiritual activities until her death in 1927. Friends also with Gandhi was writer Olive Schreiner, arguably one the loudest and clearest voices in the Cape liberal movement, and all were friends with Emily Hobhouse, the Irish feminist and nationalist Alice Stopforth Green and a great many other female activists of the period.

In frustration at the lack of real political development in the Cape, in the meanwhile, John Molteno joined fellow parliamentarians and liberals Saul Solomon, John Fairbairn and William Porter (the latter a long-time attorney-general) to lobby Whitehall for a grant of responsible government.[5] When in 1872, this was finally approved, John Molteno became the first prime minister of the Cape Colony. A revision of the constitution saw the principles of the Cape qualified franchise coming under some pressure, but Molteno and his ministry mounted a stout defence, and the tradition continued, and was, indeed, fortified. William Porter, who had turned down an invitation to serve as prime minister himself, argued in fact for a reduction in the terms of qualification, potentially opening up access to the franchise to a wider population of natives. To bitter criticism of this he responded with a prophetic question:

> Why should you fear the exercise of franchise? This is a delicate question, but it must be touched upon. I do not hesitate to say that I would rather meet the Hottentot at the hustings, voting for his representative, than in the wilds with his gun upon his shoulder. Is it not better to disarm them by granting them the privileges of the constitution? If you now blast all their hopes and tell them they shall not fight their battles constitutionally, do not you yourselves apply to them the stimulus to fight their battles unconstitutionally.[6]

John Molteno would serve the Office of Prime Minister of the Cape Colony for six years, establishing a political philosophy that would endure into the next century. Supporting him was a strong movement of English- and Dutch-speaking liberals who would form the bedrock of a society generally welcoming of black participation, and cautiously willing to move forward in tandem.

One particular member of the Cape parliament at that time was a certain Jacobus Abraham Smuts, Jan Smuts's father. Smuts senior was a centrist member of the assembly, a local burgher and a church elder, and in common with his fellow parishioners, just and fair under the broad umbrella of paternalism.

It is unlikely that Jacobus Smuts was among those that advocated the free and uninhibited inclusion of civilized blacks, or indeed any non-white on the common voters' roll, but he would certainly have been a humanist in regards to what he felt was the just usage of those that fell beneath him in the social hierarchy. However, within the narrow parameters of Malmesbury, the delineations of race were narrow indeed, and no member of that community, besides those engaged in the far-off clamour of the frontier wars, was ever constrained to deal directly with a black man of Bantu origin.

The family lived in the modest circumstances of a stone-built farmhouse in the shadow of the Riebeek Kasteel, a large sandstone whaleback that separated the Swartland from the Peninsula, and the conservative wheat farmers of the valley from the vineyards of the coast. In common with the wider region, the Smuts farm existed almost as a community within itself, with the hierarchy set along the predictable lines of an almost feudal distribution of resources. The land was owned by the Smuts family, but upon it there also lived various Hottentot, or Coloured families. These shared in the common elements of faith and language, and existed as a kind of non-landowning service class, with certain predefined rights of cultivation, and an obligation, either for wage or kind, to contribute labour. The relationship was paternalistic inasmuch as the Coloured families tended to regard Smuts senior as a patriarch, falling not only under his authority, but also under his responsibility and protection.

In later years, Smuts would reminisce frequently about the relationship that he enjoyed with Adam, a junior member of the workforce, under whose care he would often find himself. He probably made political use of these stories in order to soften his public position on the colour question in South Africa, but it is also true that Adam exerted a strong influence on his formative thinking, and was the source of much of his early naturalistic philosophy.

It was from Adam, for example, that Smuts acquired his appreciation of allegory, and through the folk tales and parables of the countryside that Adam told him that he developed a lifelong interest in the supernatural. Adam, of course, was a Christian, but at the same time he remained linked to his animistic roots, and from him Smuts adopted into his own evolving belief structure elements of rural superstition and shamanism.

At other times, however, Smuts found himself alone on the veld, and exposed to the wondrous diversity of the Cape biome without the filter of Adam's bucolic simple interpretations. At such times his mind foraged, wandering freely, unearthing the complexity of his surroundings with a more scientific perception. On the surface, the patterns and sequences of nature seemed to be without rationale or order, and yet the clear interdependence of the whole implied a totality that he was as yet unable to identify. His mind was, of course, influenced by the orthodoxy of his society, and so he pictured nature in the context of creation, which obliged him then to brood over this diversity until he began to see it less in the complexity of its divergence than the simplicity of its concord. His sense of belonging within a wider spectrum of nature, and his appreciation of the greater whole within it, set an intellectual string vibrating that would hum steadily for the remainder of his life.

In all of this, undoubtedly, there lay the genesis of a great mind, but the gathering force of his intellect would also be a source of much confusion and frustration in his life. Throughout his life he alluded to the beautiful simplicity of his upbringing, the uncomplicated world view of men like Adam, and the enchantment that he would thereafter ever nurture for the simple and fundamental. And yet, more or less from the moment that he learned to read, that comfort of simplicity would elude him.

'All great truths,' he once remarked, 'are simple; and the absence of simplicity of statement only shows that the ultimate form has not yet been reached.'

In his early fascination for the complexities of nature, Smuts began to establish the seedbed of a unique philosophical theory. Nature, although infinite in its variety, was singular in its purpose, and comprised of a unity to which all elements belonged. This unity, or the 'Whole', held within it the intangible element of life – 'something more' as he eventually settled upon defining it – that could not be appreciated or understood simply by an analysis of its components. This Smuts would later term 'holism', which at its simplest can be defined as a predisposition for the elements of nature and society to amalgamate to the general advantage of the whole; or, in other words, the tendency in nature to form wholes that are greater than the sum total of their parts.

EQUAL RIGHTS FOR ALL CIVILIZED MEN

On this simple foundation, Smuts would construct a philosophical edifice so profoundly complicated and inaccessible that in the end it would have even his closest friends and admirers throwing up their arms in despair. His obsession with this concept would peak in the almost-completed manuscript of his book, *Holism and Evolution*, which saw publication in 1926 only as a curiosity to illustrate an otherwise brilliant life.

In the overcomplicated pages of this book, Smuts attempted to reconcile being with personality, individuality within the whole, the study of mankind in a holistic manner and the persuasion of himself, and the political community of his age, that mankind was mandated by forces of creative evolution to bond in some form of common destiny. This journey would carry him far, but it would be a journey that he would never complete, for somewhere along its passage there appeared an obstruction over which he was never able to climb.

His principal biographer, Australian academic William Hancock, asked the question on his behalf, in a chapter dedicated to Smuts's philosophy, if the study of man, like that of mechanics, could be understood merely by a deconstruction of its parts? A study of cellular biology, he remarked, had relevance in medicine, zoology and biology itself, but it appeared to offer nothing to explain the differences between a plant, an animal and a man.

This segued almost automatically into another question, one that transitioned from the pure theory of philosophy into the practical application of politics, and it concerned the developmental graduations of man. The question of 'personality' began to preoccupy Smuts's thinking as he commenced to ask himself precisely what that 'something more' was. The concept of 'personality', in his mind at least, defined the varying abilities of individuals and races to leverage their biological endowments, cultural memories and lived experience to achieve a higher state of moral equilibrium, self-awareness, spiritual integrity and social integration.

In due course he began to explore the idea that the development of the personality was integral to the evolutionary process, and that, by definition, there were higher and lower orders of personal and communal development. What, he asked himself, differentiated between a tribesman of the hinterland, without wheel or written language, and the creator and curator of the Industrial Revolution? What was this difference between him and Adam? He could, of course, in his early life, call upon no direct knowledge of a black man, but the dichotomy was to him as clear as day, almost from the moment he was born. It was what was said around him, it was how society was configured, and it was what he understood.

Herein lies Smuts's great failure, and this precisely the unscalable obstacle of his entire philosophical trajectory. 'The many are held and contained in the one, not mechanically, not added together in their separateness, but as it were in solution, all of their separateness swallowed up in one indivisible Whole.'

In this, a rare moment of brevity, Smuts offered up a succinct definition of holism. However, if applied to sociology and politics, which he tried to do, how can this be interpreted as anything other than an endorsement of universal human integration, and the common destiny of all inhabiting one earth? But not so. Smuts would never dare to cross that threshold. Instead he would accept the imposition of a hierarchy over the question of black and white in South Africa, which he would support through the doctrines of cultural relativism, palaeoanthropology and evolutionary divergence. This, in turn, would allow him to rationalize a social policy of segregation, and separate development. He never took the step of attempting to codify apartheid, but at the same time he never stood apart from it.

In fairness, however, and under the circumstances of his age, it was impossible for him to do otherwise. He was a product of that age, and that society. The state of the world in the 1890s was such that there were those displaying technical and intellectual capabilities almost celestial in their scope, his own people for example, and others so far distant from this, who appeared, at least to the untutored mind, to grope in a miasma of ignorance and superstition. How was it possible, at that moment in history, to view the wider social landscape otherwise than as a divided whole? How were the two irreconcilable elements of the same tribe to be accommodated upon a single estate? The ideal of absolute inclusion might have served the purpose of a class and generation at no risk of experiencing it, and it might have dwelt well in the text of a liberal constitution, but the moment was not far off when the practicalities of the Cape liberal tradition would begin to challenge the commitment of its architects.

Chapter 5

Influence

'I contend that we are the finest race in the world and that the more of the world we inhabit the better it is for the human race.'
—Cecil John Rhodes

On 1 September 1870, the roadway of Port Natal was visited by the steamship *Eudora*, en route from Portsmouth to Sydney, calling in briefly at Las Palmas and Madeira before the long haul south to the Cape. A small complement of passengers disembarked in Durban, among them a tall and strikingly fair youth, shabbily dressed, his eyes almost translucent blue, his complexion sallow and his breath escaping his lungs with a ragged whisper.

Cecil John Rhodes, then just 17 years old, had been dispatched to the colonies by his despairing father in the hope that an early death could be delayed. The fifth son of an English country parson, Rhodes was sparsely educated, for there had seemed little point in investing much in a life predicted to be short. When he bid farewell to his son on the station platform of Bishop Stortford, the Reverend Francis Rhodes had no expectation that the two would ever meet again.

In his pocket, however, Rhodes carried the respectable sum of £3,000, lent to him by his Aunt Sophia, and intended to be invested in the Natal cotton farm that his brother Herbert had acquired a year or so earlier. On board ship, however, Rhodes found himself mingling with a strong corps of prospectors travelling to the Cape upon news of diamond discoveries.

Arriving in Durban, he was met by his brother, a charming and charismatic man in his early twenties, robust and energetic, who threw up his arms in derision when his younger brother queried progress on the farm, offering up the entire holding if Rhodes so wished it, for he intended to travel inland to test his fortune on the diamond diggings.

As Rhodes applied himself to cotton, his brother applied himself to diamonds. Around a small promontory in the mid-Karoo, there formed the rough and tumble mining settlement of Kimberley, and as 1870 yielded to 1871, diggers and prospectors from across the empire flooded into the Cape, migrating in droves to the diamond fields. Herbert Rhodes acquired a handful of claims, but when an immediate fortune eluded him, he was quick to offer them up to his younger brother in order that he might follow the scent of gold in the Transvaal.

Rhodes arrived in Kimberley in October 1871, having travelled overland from Natal with a mule cart, a handful of tools and the company of a single native boy with whom he shared no common language. In his pocket he carried a companion edition of the *Meditations of Marcus Aurelius*, which throughout his life he would rarely be found without.

In the beginning he worked his claims, and he made some money, but diamond yields were spread over several thousand specific claims, and so individual returns tended to be limited. In due course, therefore, Rhodes began to experiment with business and capital manipulation, after which he began to make real money. He purchased, for example, pumping equipment and ice-making equipment, both of which proved lucrative, but ultimately he would use his enormous gumption and obvious financial genius to win the support of the influential Rothschild banking family, and thus begin the acquisition of failed and abandoned claims that he would eventually combine under the monolithic De Beers Consolidated Mines.

In 1873, however, at the age of 19, Rhodes did a curious thing. He left the management of his growing business in Kimberley in the hands of a partner, and returned to England with the intention of enrolling at Oxford University. With a mediocre academic history, however, his overtures were not particularly well received, but through persuasion and considerable persistence he gained a place at Oriel College. This, incidentally, set in motion the signature love affair that Rhodes would enjoy with Oxford University, which he would consummate many times, and with multiple endowments, not least the Rhodes Scholarship Trust.

Why he felt it necessary to enter Oxford at all remains one of the mysteries surrounding the life of this enigmatic man, but in all likelihood his objective was simply to add to his growing wealth the prestige of an education, as a means, perhaps, of securing access to British ruling classes.

While at Oxford, however, he fell deeply under the influence of a prominent Victorian philosopher and social thinker by the name of John Ruskin. In 1870, Ruskin took up a professorship in fine art at Oxford University, and spoke at his inaugural lecture to the rights and obligations of English youth to fulfil a destiny of World Empire.[1] Identifying the students of Oxford as the worthiest and most energetic sons of England, he entreated them to go forth and claim on behalf of the Crown as much of the globe as remained unconquered, and to create of England a 'Sceptred Isle', founded by God 'to guide the human arts, and gather the divine knowledge, of distant nations, transformed from savageness to manhood, and redeemed from despairing into peace'.

By these words, and upon these sentiments, Rhodes was immediately captivated. He had grown up on the banks of the River Stort, leaning over the garden gate of the vicarage as laden barges plied between the new industries of the Midlands and the trade networks of the globe. As with all of the children of his generation, he took for granted the emerging power of England, and was taught to embrace the superiority of his race without question. His journey to South Africa had revealed to him the size and scope of the world, and the fine language of Ruskin, who sculpted in verb every sentiment that Rhodes struggled to express, simply completed the incubation of a vision. 'I contend,' he suggested, more or less at this time, and indeed, more than once,

> that we are the finest race in the world and that the more of the world we inhabit the better it is for the human race. Just fancy those parts that are at present inhabited by the most despicable specimens of human beings what an alteration there would be if they were brought under Anglo-Saxon influence, look again at the extra employment a new country added to our dominions gives.

At the end of 1873, Rhodes returned to South Africa. His degree was only partially complete, but now he was consumed by a new idea that superseded any other. He could picture a world united under the dominion of the English-speaking races, the return of the United States to the British empire, and the addition thereafter of every other habitable corner of world. His acquisition of wealth ceased now to be its own objective, but became the means by which he would fulfil this great destiny. He returned to the diamond fields and, with a renewed sense of purpose, set to work to accumulate.

Then, in 1877, at the age of 24, Cecil Rhodes suffered the first of a number of increasingly severe heart attacks that would intermittently blight the remaining years of his life. This episode served immediately to introduce him to his own unstable mortality, setting in motion a desperate haste to achieve what he could as the hours of his life slipped through his fingers.

As he began his convalescence, Herbert suggested that the two take a lengthy sabbatical away from the diamond diggings, and in a scotch cart drawn by two mules, the brothers traversed the highveld, pondering the vast expanses of undeveloped land, and dreaming of a nation forged under the British hammer. As they travelled, Rhodes put pen to paper, commencing what would prove a lengthy manifesto with the following introduction:

> It often strikes a man to inquire what is the chief good in life. To one the thought comes that it is a happy marriage, to another great wealth, and as each seizes on his idea, for that he more or less works for the rest of his existence. To myself thinking over the same question the wish came to render myself useful to my country.

From this beginning, in some 2,000 words, he ruminated on a destiny that he believed, with absolute conviction, had been granted by God to the English-speaking races. In his mind he saw this as something almost supernatural, transcending the common rules of earth and man, a divine agenda, no less than that, and that those such as he who were touched by its mystery were powerless to resist.

> 'Why should we not form a secret society,' he wrote, 'with but one object the furtherance of the British empire and the bringing of the whole uncivilized world under British rule, for the recovery of the United States, and for making the Anglo-Saxon race but one empire.'

To this end, he resolved to bequeath a fortune, as yet unmade to, among others, the secretary of state for the colonies, at that time the 4th Earl of Carnarvon, whom he instructed, on his behalf, to and for

> the establishment, promotion and development of a Secret Society, the true aim and object whereof shall be for the extension of British rule throughout the world, the perfecting of a system of emigration from the United Kingdom, and of colonization by British subjects of all lands where the means of livelihood are attainable by energy, labour and enterprise, and especially the occupation by British settlers of the entire Continent of Africa, the Holy Land, the Valley of the Euphrates, the Islands of Cyprus and Candia [Crete], the whole of South America, the Islands of the Pacific not heretofore possessed by Great Britain, the whole of the Malay Archipelago, the seaboard of China and Japan, the ultimate recovery of the United States of

America as an integral part of the British empire, the inauguration of a system of Colonial representation in the Imperial Parliament which may tend to weld together the disjointed members of the empire and, finally, the foundation of so great a Power as to render wars impossible and promote the best interests of humanity.

One can only imagine what the colonial secretary would have thought had he ever had occasion to read such a preposterous document. Rhodes, however, superseded it with seven revised versions before the final draft was ratified by his death. By then he had reduced his vision of global British sovereignty to the more practical, if still monumental objective of a unified African colony stretching from the Cape to Cairo.

A decade later, in the summer of 1888, at the age of 35, Cecil John Rhodes was invited to address the student body of Victoria College secondary school, located in the picturesque hamlet of Stellenbosch. There he spoke on what had by then become an obsession: the unification of the four separate territories of South Africa into a single, amalgamated colony, superintended by Britain, but independent in the matters of internal politics and economy. The almost unimaginable potential of a great nation was hobbled by the squabbling of four unhappy partners, and only with unity, with the forging of a whole, could the united nation of South Africa be born.

Rhodes was by then a parliamentarian in the Cape assembly, and one of the richest men of the empire. He engineered the acquisition of British Bechuanaland to the Crown, and was poised to expand his interests deep into the interior. His achievements had been astronomical. In South Africa, the weakling had grown into a man, but on the diamond fields of Kimberley, and the gold fields of the Witwatersrand, that man had emerged as a titan.

Rhodes would ultimately bring under British rule all of the unclaimed territories south of the Congo, but yet he remained unable to find a cure for the determined and unwavering disunity of South Africa itself. To an audience of British and Dutch youth, therefore, the cream of the Cape Colony, and the leadership of a nation of the future, he appealed for a healing of the rift between Briton and Boer, and the creation of one South Africa, a single, vital and functioning political entity.

At the conclusion of his speech, he stood panting, the sweat beading his brow, surveying his audience with disappointment. Applause was polite, but perfunctory, and he blushed as he retook his seat at the back of the stage. However, to his pleasant surprise, a tall and rather spare youth, with striking blue eyes and the sharp, chiselled features of a blond El Greco, cautiously approached the podium and, resting his papers upon it, cleared his throat. Then, with a tremor in his voice, his English heavily accented, he began to speak.

This was an 18-year-old Jan Christiaan Smuts, head of the Victoria College Debating Society, who had been selected as an obvious choice to deliver the formal response on behalf of the school to the Right Honourable Cecil John Rhodes. Smuts had prepared a speech, which lay on the podium before him, but which he abandoned, launching instead into a richly passionate confirmation of everything that Rhodes had said before him.

He had listened carefully to the words of the master and, in that hour or so, had experienced a transformation. Not only had he been captivated by the spectacle of this prematurely ageing man ranting with such unruly passion, but he found also that the loose threads of his own small vision were tethered in a concept that he understood immediately. Now, standing at the podium himself, he addressed the same audience, and repeated in clear and educated terms, with brevity and precision, the same essential message.

Rhodes was astonished. He listened to the steady drumbeat of applause achieved after just ten minutes of oratory, and he was impressed. While making no effort to be introduced to Smuts at that encounter, he leaned across to his companion, a man by the name of Jan Hofmeyr, to whom he remarked:

'You keep an eye on that young man Smuts, he is destined to go far.'

Chapter 6

A Changing World

'You are the descendants of Ishmael and therefore from your very birth bound to slave for the descendants of Esau. As the descendants of Esau, we cannot give you rights placing you on an equality with ourselves. You must rest content with the rights that we grant you.'

—Transvaal President Paul Kruger

In the summer of 1891, two students crossed paths briefly in London en route to their individual destinies. The first was the 21-year-old Mohandas K. Gandhi, who had already been called to the bar, and was making ready to return to India, and the second was Jan Christiaan Smuts. The two never met, of course, but their experiences and impressions of London, and the British people, would likely have been very different.

Smuts had no exotic heritage to leverage in a search for companionship, and indeed, he made no such search at all. He was tightly budgeted, and although granted a partial scholarship, could barely afford the passage, let alone books and tuition. He would no doubt have clung to the cold interior of his guest house, resisting entirely any temptation to learn the foxtrot, or to debate *Das Kapital* in a coal-heated tea room off Chancery Lane.

If, however, he had chanced to meet the great Indian academic, Dadabhai Naoroji, as Gandhi had a year or two earlier, it is probable that the elderly Parsee would have been more immediately impressed. Smuts habitually wore a dark frock coat over a swept-wing collar, a neck-tie, loose woollen trousers and a pair of brown leather shoes. He was seldom disposed to smile, but this ought not to imply that he was unattractive. To a person searching for evidence of character, Smuts would have been of immediate interest, for it was his intelligence, evident at the moment that he opened his mouth, which was his most striking feature.

A few weeks later, both men left London, Gandhi in the direction of

Portsmouth, where he boarded a steamer for Bombay, and Smuts to Cambridge, where he entered Christ's College. Here, the halls of academia welcomed him like an old friend, and he excelled immediately, achieving in just three years of study a law tripos. Thanks to the difficulties of underfunding, however, he was compelled often to his own company, and to the long walks in nature that had always been his comfort, and much of his education. Nonetheless, his academic achievements, within and without his courses of study, were nothing less than exceptional.

When questioned by a mentor on his choice of law as a field of study, Smuts responded by producing his first book-sized manuscript, entitled *The Nature and Function of Law in the History of Human Society*. In some hundred pages, he traced the evolution of legal codification through its phases of natural law, the philosophy of law and its binding agents in systems, natures, states and empires. He pondered the independence and interdependence of mankind, proposed a single law for all of humanity and argued for the rights and protection of individual freedom regardless of race, class or distinction.

He then returned his mind to natural philosophy, a canvas upon which his intellect had, and always would range free. In his second year at Cambridge he completed an exhaustive and densely packed essay of some thirty-six pages, entitled *On the Application of Some Physical Concepts to Biological Phenomena*. Within the text of this treatise, he once again plunged into a deep pool of obscure philosophical thinking, in which he sought, almost, to define the meaning of life.

'Life' he wrote, 'is not energy; it is not development; it is not motion; it is not an equilibrium of motions or a harmony; it is a force.' (A life force, one might suppose, and how Gandhiesque that would appear to later scholars of soul force, and the *satyagraha* theory.) He went on:

> Life is a regulative principle, latent in the material substratum, which rises into activity whenever, and continues to act as long as, certain parts of matter have certain relations to one another or form certain collocations. Life is not the totality or the aggregate of the constitutive particles, nor the aggregate of the relations of those material particles. It is something more, something over and above all that.

What was Smuts stating here, or perhaps asking? Nothing less than a discussion on what lies in the darkness beyond the evolutionary theory, beyond the universe of time and space: life, creative evolution, soul force.

He seemed to be grasping for a reconciliation of God and Science, perhaps even a search for some principle that would marry together the simple and obvious mechanics of evolution with higher values of meaning and purpose – the *something more*. It might perhaps even be said that he emerged from his education less as a scientist vexed by spiritual intangibles than a spiritualist vexed by science.

As his mind toured these regions, often alone, but quite often in conversation or correspondence with mentors and tutors, he returned to that curious avenue of intellectual exploration, the study of personality, choosing as a rather random subject of study the American transcendental-realist poet and philosopher Walt Whitman.[1]

In 1894, Walt Whitman had been dead for just over a year, and apart from his own works, there was little in the way of biographical material and academic analysis from which Smuts could draw. Nonetheless, the result of this exercise would be Smuts's first serious book, entitled *Walt Whitman: A Study in the Evolution of a Personality*. But in fact, the seminal element in this title was not so much 'Walt Whitman' as a subject, but 'The Evolution of a Personality' as a concept, and as such the book would be written.

Smuts admitted later that he might just as willingly have written about Goethe, for it was not so much the man that mattered, but *man* in general, and not any specific personality, but *personality* in general.[2] He sought to define a method of examining and explaining what eluded orthodox scientific analysis, the complex and indefinable elements at the higher levels of existence, of intellect and of being. Morality, perception and progress, reacting also against the psychological preference for the examination of the personality as separate from the process of evolution, or from the person, when in truth, as Smuts saw it, they were but one and the same.

Sadly, the complexities of Smuts's relationship with Whitman, and the many other aspects of his private study, fall outside the strict scope of this narrative, other than perhaps to illustrate a personality itself under the metamorphosis of discovery, and self-discovery, in preparation for a future of almost inconceivable challenge.

Smuts from time to time shared the footpaths of the Shire with two high-born Indian Muslim brothers, Ahmád Khán Sultan and Ahmád Khán Aftáb, both of whom would go on to achieve high positions in Indian/Pakistani education and law. For the time being, however, they were, like Smuts, reading law at Christ's College and, constrained of funds, they tended, like him, to take their pleasures on long strolls in the countryside. During these sojourns, the two no doubt suffered at various times the relentless interrogation of facts and ideas, philosophies and doctrines that Smuts, even then, had established as his social hallmark.

The Khan brothers were not the only Indians at Cambridge during Smuts's period of study. Attending Trinity College was H. H. Jam Saheb Shri Sri Ranjitsinhji Vibhaji, sometime county cricketer and future ruler of the Indian princely state of Nawanagar. Another was Sarojini Naidu, poet and activist, first woman leader of Congress and a peace marcher alongside Gandhi in 1930, who studied literature and languages, first at King's College London, and later at Girton College, Cambridge. And another was Aurobindo Ghosh, or Sri Aurobindo, Bengalese nationalist, philosopher, yogi, guru and poet. And yet another, briefly overlapping Smuts's career, was Kaka Joseph Baptista, who likewise read law at Fitzwilliam College, earning the rather exaggerated sobriquet of Father of the Home Rule Movement in India.

Smuts could therefore hardly have shared the anxieties and concerns of his fellow countrymen regarding the unholy proliferation of Indians, and their lamentable standards of cleanliness and civilization. When in later years he met and grappled with Gandhi, it can be taken for granted that he knew and appreciated the minutiae of Indian cultural brilliance more acutely perhaps than Gandhi himself.

There were, however, no blacks at Cambridge, but had there been, Smuts would certainly have considered the fact with interest. His obsession with the unity of systems in nature and society did not appear to strike him as incompatible with a distaste for racial merger in a world where cultures were mingling ahead of their ability to assimilate. Clearly he was unable, or unwilling, to judge either India or his own native majority by the standard of their elite, as he was content to judge the nations of Europe. He did not, for example, question his appreciation of the charm and beauty of German philosophy, art and music simply because of the blunt and bellicose German militancy that he could see and hear.

It is also evident from his various correspondence that he had begun to recognize the gravity of the colour issue in South Africa. He was, for example, quoted as remarking on the eve of the Anglo-Boer War:

The war between the white races will run its course, and pass away and may, if followed by a statesman-like settlement, one day only be remembered as a great thunderstorm, which purified the atmosphere of the sub-continent. But the native question will never pass away. It will get more difficult as time goes on, and the day may come when the evils and horrors of this war will appear as nothing in comparison with its after-effects produced on the native mind.[3]

However, the first war in South Africa would indeed be between the white races, and not until a settlement of that debt would the more divisive struggle between the colours begin. Upon emerging from Cambridge with a double first in law, he entered the Middle Temple, having unsurprisingly passed the bar exam with distinction. Then, offered a Cambridge fellowship in Law, he refused, preferring after a brief period of practice as a barrister in London to return to the Cape, there to join that great work of nation-building that had begun for him when for the first time his ears heard the siren call of Cecil John Rhodes.

Chapter 7

The Asiatic Problem

'Your beliefs become your thoughts, your thoughts become your words, your words become your actions, your actions become your habits, your habits become your values, your values become your destiny.'

—Mohandas K. Gandhi

In 1881, Sheth Abubakar, a wealthy Muslim trader from Natal, established a branch of his business in Pretoria, acquiring through a local agent freehold on a substantial lot in a prime location. Pretoria in the 1880s was a dusty, ramshackle settlement of wide and unpaved avenues, its buildings of red brick and corrugated iron, and its frontier aspects hardly diminished by four decades of settlement.

The South African Republic, or the Transvaal as it was also known, was at that point almost entirely rural in complexion, landlocked and underdeveloped, boasting neither industry nor organized commerce on any meaningful scale. Its attraction to the Indian mercantile community of Natal, therefore, was obvious, and Sheth Abubakar was the first Indian trader to venture into its precincts.

Soon a gabled façade was erected, proudly proclaiming its date and proprietorship, and Sheth Abubakar & Co. was open for business. In general, the new arrival was well received, and business was good. Before long, however, a second Indian shop opened its doors, and then a third, until, within a year or two, Pretorius Street began to resemble West Street in Durban. It was then that the townsmen of Pretoria began to take notice, and both Dutchman and Englishman pointed to Natal as an example of what might be expected if the republic did not begin to control its borders. Press commentary grew steadily more antagonistic, as it had in Natal, and before long, parliamentary debates on limiting citizenship and burgher rights for Indians began to be heard.

THE ASIATIC PROBLEM

As things stood, Indians, or Asiatics as they were known, occupied a grey legal area in the republic, and some head-scratching went into the ultimate decision of how to classify them. The constitution of the republic recognized as citizens only those of European heritage who were born in the republic. Alternatively, to qualify for an oath of naturalization, a foreigner was required to have resided in the republic for two years, to be of good character and to have been accepted as a member of the Reformed Church.

Blacks could become citizens under no circumstance at all, and were granted no access to the franchise. This was a simple article of faith that came about thanks to a long-held Boer belief that a covenant with God had been forged in the wake of victories over the Kaffir, granting primary overlordship of the land to the *volk*. The Boer view of blacks, although rarely hostile on an individual level, was of a sub-race not included in the general human charter, and considered in matters of state and law as chattel, or livestock. Above all laws was the word of the Bible, and the Bible, under select interpretation, generally supported this position.

Standing immigration laws restricted access to the republic to all but those of provable European heritage, no matter what other considerations might be taken into account, which offered some legal protection against Indian immigration. This, however, was complicated by the fact that Indians were technically British, and therefore protected by treaty with the British imperial government. Although technically classified as black, or non-white, Indians thrived in the cash economy, owned property, paid taxes and conducted business. Although burgher rights could obviously not be granted to them, for they were not Christian, they were free under current regulations to enter the Transvaal and trade without restriction.

The matter was finally addressed in 1885, by which time the Indian community of the republic had grown to several thousand heads of households, upon the promulgation of what was known as 'Law 3'. The target of this law was persons belonging to any of the native races of Asia, including Indians, Arabs, Malays and subjects of the Turkish empire, none of whom could henceforth enjoy, or be granted rights of citizenship or access to the franchise. Moreover, no Asiatic could own fixed property except in such streets, wards and locations as the government, for purposes of sanitation, assigned, and each was obliged to inscribe in a register at the cost of £25 if he intended to settle with the object of trade.

In spite of this, the Indian community grew and flourished, for although stripped of all citizenship rights, Indians remained in a position to trade, which was their fundamental objective. Besides this, all laws and bylaws in

77

the Transvaal could be relied upon to be haphazardly applied, if at all, and so long as the community traded in its quarter, and minded its business, it tended to be left to its own devices.

Then, in 1886, the greatest gold rush in human history began. The Witwatersrand region of the Transvaal was transformed overnight into one of the most significant theatres of capital adventure in the world. Word spread quickly, and before long the republic was flooded with immigrants, primarily British of all classes, but also Lithuanian Jews, German mining engineers, Australian, Canadian and American diggers, Dutch civil engineers, railway workers from all over Europe, Portuguese builders and artisans, Italian and Swiss restaurateurs and hoteliers and indigenous migrant labour from across the region.

In this free-rolling atmosphere, Indian businessmen and traders simply entered and left with the same impunity as everybody else. The Transvaal authorities were completely overwhelmed, and in such a chaotic eruption of industrial and urban development, foodstuffs, equipment and materials were required at a rate that only the Indians through their established trade networks could supply. Conditions in the cash-heavy settlement of Johannesburg were so disordered, and so unregulated, and prices so inflated that the opportunity to make an easy fortune was available to anyone with wit and capital.

It was into this energetic and frenetic environment that Mohandas K. Gandhi arrived one evening in the spring of 1894, riding on the luggage box of a Zeederberg coach, coated with dust and his ear swollen from the blow he had received from the coachman. From Johannesburg he continued on to Pretoria, and there he remained in the company of Albert Baker until the autumn, completing his work before returning to Durban in preparation for his return to India. In the interim, he maintained a low profile, as he had been advised to do, but nonetheless he observed, and took every opportunity to engage with the local community to better understand the conditions under which they lived.

What he identified was statutory and conventional discrimination not dissimilar to that in Natal, and while he acknowledged that trade under these conditions was no less profitable, he was offended by the transgression of a stated contract between the British empire and its overseas subjects. The Transvaal was not a British colony, of course, but an independent republic over which the British government had little if any direct control. A treaty, however, existed that guaranteed British rights and protections in the republic, and Gandhi could hardly fail to notice that the enthusiasm applied to the defence of white subjects of the empire was not similarly applied to Indians. In theory, Indians were protected in the Transvaal under the same terms as any British subject, according to Article XIV of the London Convention of 1884, which restored Boer autonomy in the Transvaal after a period of British annexation. This guaranteed the rights of British subjects in the republic, in particular in relation to the large numbers of British engaged in mining and industry. The London Convention, however, was generally powerless in a predominantly antagonistic atmosphere, and, of course, allowed for no avenue of direct intervention in the internal affairs of the Transvaal.

It would be wrong, however, to imply that the discrimination authorized by the law was universally applied, for Gandhi was easily able to escape many of its more particular articles. A man of his appearance and social habits was quite able to spend the best part of a year in Pretoria, residing nowhere near the Indian locations and, as would continue to be the case throughout his life, acquiring colleagues, associates and followers among Indians, but friendships primarily among whites.

The first of these was, of course, Albert Baker, with whom he boarded, and who tried diligently to convert him to Christianity. Gandhi took this in good humour, and it was through Baker that he was introduced to a good many other Europeans. One was a certain Michael Coates, an English-born Quaker missionary whom Gandhi befriended soon after his arrival, and with whom he would remain in contact for the rest of his life. Coates and he spent a great deal of time together, and through this association, Gandhi was introduced to many other sympathetic whites, mainly British and Jewish, who comprised an alternative fringe of liberals and non-conformists in the Transvaal displaying no race consciousness at all.

Despite this, he was touched by the day-to-day injury and inconvenience imposed upon him by the prejudices of the establishment. He was disdainfully attended to in the various libraries and archives that he visited, and directed to the tradesman's entrance when entering court. He was unable to take tea with any of his white friends in a public facility, disallowed on any city tram, forced to travel third class on a train and prohibited from appearing in public after nine o'clock in the evening without the permission of his European employer.

By the latter restriction he was often inconvenienced, for he was not employed by a white man, so could obtain no written permission, and his frequent evening strolls through the suburbs of Pretoria were interrupted often by questions and harassment. He was eventually able to make the acquaintance of the Transvaal state attorney, Albert Ernest Krause, who happened by coincidence to be a barrister of the same inn as he, and by dint of this professional association, Krause granted Gandhi special dispensation to visit any part of the city of his choosing, and at any time.

On one particular evening, Gandhi happened to be walking past the residence of the president, and was roughly manhandled off the pavement and pushed onto the street by the white policeman guarding the gates. Gandhi was black, or at least in the darkness he appeared so, and all blacks were compelled by law to walk on the roadway. None could step on a pavement.

This incident happened by chance to be witnessed by Michael Coates, who climbed out of his horse carriage and attended to his friend, offering to act as a witness should Gandhi choose to pursue a case. Gandhi, however, dismissed the incident, forgiving the officer on the basis of his probably being unable to distinguish in the darkness between an Indian and an African, and he accepted the man's apology once the latter had been thoroughly dressed down by Coates.

The paradox of all of this, however, was not lost on Gandhi, and while his time in Pretoria was fulfilling and successful, and rich with new friends and acquaintances, it was also depressing and frustrating. He resented the fact that he, an educated member of one of the greatest of all human civilizations, should be so roughly handled, and so arbitrarily discriminated against by such an unaccomplished and undeserving people.

There was, however, nothing that could be done about it, and he simply bent to his task, enjoyed his friendships and thought ahead to India. The work that he did was routine, involving chiefly the role of research assistant and interpreter to Albert Baker, and when the matter was heard in the Pretoria High Court, it came as no particular surprise that judgement was handed down in favour of Dada Abdulla.

Dada Abdulla, of course, was delighted, but the judgement left his cousin facing bankruptcy, and the family in disarray. Gandhi then took it upon himself to arbitrate, eventually brokering an agreement between the two parties for the debt to be paid off in instalments, thus rescuing the business and saving face on both sides.

Once again, Dada Abdulla was impressed, and this time he urged Gandhi to consider remaining in the colony, for he would be hard to replace, and there was money to be made in South Africa by a competent Indian lawyer.

Gandhi, however, was disappointed. His years in London had predisposed him towards a fondness for the British, and imbued in him a sense of pride in belonging to the same empire. But the year past had been bruising, and he felt betrayed. Had it simply been Boer discrimination, he might have understood it better, but the English of South Africa were not the same people that he had known in London. India at that moment seemed very attractive to him, and he found himself counting the days.

Fate, however, was poised to intervene. As the story goes, Dada Abdulla hosted a farewell reception for Gandhi at the Juma Masjid mosque a few days before he was scheduled to sail. Coincidentally, on that very day, the *Natal Mercury* printed for the first time the full contents of the draft bill under debate in the Natal legislature that proposed to strip all Indians in the colony of their right of access to the franchise. The reception was attended by a full complement of Durban's wealthiest and most influential Indians, and discussion was naturally dominated by the proposed terms of this act.

Since 1865, blacks had been effectively blocked from accessing the franchise in Natal by a provision in the law that prohibited those subject to customary law from access to the institutions of state. Black residents of Natal were automatically assumed to be subject to customary, or tribal law, and for an individual to apply for inclusion on the electoral roll, it was necessary for him first to prove twelve years of consistent residence in the colony, after which a letter of exception from customary law was issued by the government, required to be in effect for a further seven years. Only then would an application for inclusion on the electoral roll be considered, assuming, of course, that the individual qualified in terms of education and property, which, of course, almost none did.

Indians, on the other hand, enjoyed theoretical access to the electoral roll as British subjects and taxpayers, and the objective of this proposed law was simply to close that loophole. The background to this, of course, was the steady increase of Indian immigration into the colony. The importation of indentured labour was still ongoing and, naturally, as the wealth of the territory developed, a vast majority did not reindenture, and chose to remain. This precipitated the continued importation of fresh reserves of labour, which was now made somewhat easier by the fact that Indians were clamouring to access the colony. Although serving the interest of the industry, this continuum stoked a steadily rising paranoia in the general population that by the 1890s had reached a fever pitch.

Early in 1894, a delegation of parliamentarians from Natal travelled to Calcutta to petition the Viceroy of India to accept the forced repatriation of Indians from Natal. Their continued importation would be more charitably viewed if those completing their contracts could simply be sent home.

The Viceroy of India at the time was Lord Elgin, a Scottish peer, and a man precisely of that liberal/intellectual class that drove the late-nineteenth-century imperial agenda. He received the Natal delegation and dutifully heard their petition, which he immediately and curtly rejected. Under no circumstances, he said, would he advise Her Majesty to deny access to any British subject to any British territory, no matter what the circumstances. It was not only beyond the scope of the law, but it was repugnant to him personally. His actual words, in part, were: 'I have little sympathy with the views that would prevent any subject of the Crown from settling in any Colony under the British flag.'

The delegation then returned to Natal and, somewhat chastened, pursued the repatriation effort no further. The next best thing was to limit the powers and capabilities of Indians in the colony to access and shape public policy. It is hard to understate the seriousness with which this matter was regarded at the time. Indians almost outnumbered whites and, in view of this, a steady paranoia was building. Although a vast majority of Indians in the colony remained poor and illiterate, and unlikely in their lifetimes ever to qualify for the vote, the steady growth of an educated and propertied class of Indians in the colony served clear notice of a pending catastrophe.

Gandhi asked why nothing was being done to protest the passage of this bill, for quite obviously it was discriminatory, and as such it was at variance with the rights of British subjects abroad. In reply, he was asked who he thought could lead such a movement. The only person qualified in the colony to undertake such a task was he himself, and he was about to leave. If the passage of the bill was to be opposed, then he would need to delay his departure for a few weeks at least in order to draft the necessary papers.

For Gandhi this presented an unexpected opportunity, not only to satisfy some of his intellectual vanity, but also to answer to the irritation and sense of injustice that had been building in his mind for the few months past. It would gratify him enormously to break the cycle of passive compliance that the white community had come to expect of the Indians, such that they imagined they could pass a law such as this without a breath of Indian protest.

The final reading of the bill was scheduled for a few days hence, and clearly there was no time to lose, but agreement among the assembled guests was not by any means absolute. What, some asked, did the vote matter to the Indians anyway? Was it really worth the risk of antagonizing the white community over such a minor and rather academic point? The community was affluent and well founded, and if the white political establishment could satisfy itself that the Indians posed no risk, the community would be left alone to prosper. A protest against the passage of this bill, on the other hand, would simply alert the white community to the fact that the Indians were developing political ambitions, as had been long predicted, which would in turn justify the passage of the law and, moreover, invite renewed hostility and perhaps more orchestrated oppression.

These were all valid points, but in reply, a younger corps of educated Indians, led by Gandhi himself, argued that the time had come to assert the political maturity of the Indian community in Natal, and that doing so would set a precedent both for India itself and the diaspora. Indians were taxpayers, after all, and British subjects to boot.

In the end, the latter argument carried, and it was agreed that some sort of an expression of Indian concern must be made upon the reading of the bill and, moreover, that Gandhi would delay his departure long enough to undertake the necessary preparations.

That evening, however, as he rode a rickshaw from the Juma Masjid mosque to the Dada Abdulla compound on Grey Street, he felt a mingled sense of excitement and apprehension. It was probably that very night that he sat at his desk and composed the letter to Dadabhai Naoroji, laying bare his sense of inadequacy to the task. Several months had passed since that cold night seated on his trunk on the concourse of Pietermaritzburg station, when he had determined that such would not stand, and this, perhaps, was the moment to make his voice heard.

Chapter 8

Protest

'Thus God laid the foundations of my life in South Africa, and sowed the seeds for the fight for national self-respect.'
—Mohandas K. Gandhi

The very next morning Gandhi drafted and dispatched a telegram to the speaker of the Natal parliament requesting a delay in the final hearing of the franchise bill, which, despite the novelty of such a request, was agreed to. Then, at the head of a small committee of advisers, he set about drafting an abbreviated petition, which was received by parliament and given due consideration. It did not, however, alter or divert the passage of the bill, which was debated and passed by a respectable majority of members before being dispatched to London for the consideration of the colonial secretary.

This raised the stakes somewhat. The matter now resided in Whitehall, and to challenge it there would not only internationalize the South Africa Indian question, but would serve notice on the Natal establishment, and indeed white South Africa as a whole, that the Indians of the colony had drawn a line in the sand.

A number of high profile and influential Natal Indians stepped back at this point, fearing an escalation, but the majority held firm, again mainly the younger and educated members, who advocated the drafting of a more formal petition to the British imperial government, and the commencement of wider and more comprehensive action.

At this point Gandhi searched his soul deeply. It began to occur to him that he had fetched up a heavy load indeed, and he wondered if he really had the commitment to carry it to the end. Who, after all, was Mohandas K. Gandhi, but an obscure, 26-year-old Gujarati attorney with less than a year of professional experience? His constituency amounted to something less than 100,000 Indians, fewer than might be expected to reside in an anaemic slum of Calcutta, and what possible interest could this minor episode inspire at the metropolitan heart of the empire?

And yet, when, within a fortnight, the draft of the Natal franchise bill arrived on the desk of the then colonial secretary, George Frederick Samuel Robinson, 1st Marquis of Ripon, he could not help a nagging intuition that he was dealing here with something much more than a simple review of colonial legislation. His suspicions were confirmed a week or so later when the draft bill was followed by a significant petition of protest submitted by a committee of concerned South African Indians. The document was long and detailed, conspicuously well-crafted and accompanied by the signatures of 10,000 prominent Natal Indians. The thrust of the petition was a plea to the Office of the Colonial Secretary to disallow the new law on grounds that it unfairly discriminated against Indian subjects of Her Majesty.

Lord Ripon happened to be another such moderate peer as Lord Elgin, then Viceroy of India, and as he thoughtfully pondered the two dispatches on his desk – the draft franchise bill and the Indian petition of protest – he was struck with an uncomfortable sense of déjà vu. At about the same time, Dadabhai Naoroji received his courtesy copy of the same petition, sans the signatures, as did also his parliamentary colleague, Sir Mancherjee Bhownagree. Grasping immediately the significance of this, both men set to work advocating in London on behalf of their South African comrades, and suddenly the name Mohandas K. Gandhi began to feature in telegraph traffic and various newspaper editorials traded back and forward between the two hemispheres. By the end of that year, the Natal Indian question was under discussion in a variety of formal and informal offices and assemblies, from London to Calcutta, and Lord Ripon, quite unexpectedly, found himself juggling an extremely hot potato.

Between 1880 and 1884, Lord Ripon had served the Office of Viceroy of India, and during that time had burned his fingers rather painfully in an attempt to relax many of the institutionalized rigours of British rule in the colony. He had stimulated Indian education, facilitated Indian advancement in the civil service and encouraged free political expression, which, although it won him some affection among Indians, achieved also significant disapprobation at the hands of the British ruling establishment, securing him, among other disabilities, an early recall.

Lord Ripon was at the time a protégé of Prime Minister William Gladstone, arguably the original British liberal, and his administration in India had been intended to reflect that very liberalism. The appointment of viceroy of India was the prerogative of the British prime minister, in consultation with parliament, but the Indian government itself was separate from, and often antagonistic towards the imperial government in Whitehall. Both Ripon and Gladstone shared a moderate and progressive view of India, and a rather forward-thinking perspective on the function of the Indian civil service. Gladstone's most quoted, and instructive utterance over the question was perhaps this:

> The question of who shall have supreme rule in India is, by the laws of right, an Indian question; and those laws of right are from day to day growing into laws of fact. Our title to be there depends on a first condition, that our being there is profitable to the Indian nations; and on a second condition, that we make them see and understand it to be profitable.

It had been Ripon's brief but unenviable responsibility to ensure that, by one means or another, the Indian public did indeed understand British rule in India to be profitable, an effort that in the end proved entirely detrimental to himself. As colonial secretary, therefore, and despite his natural sympathies, his first priority was to ensure no repetition of past mistakes.

In the end, however, Lord Ripon simply sat on his hands, a venerable strategy, until an opportunity to pass on the responsibility came with the 1895 general election. This would almost certainly usher in a Tory cabinet, at which point Natal would be in the happy position of dealing with a conservative colonial secretary, under whose jurisdiction a bill such as this would almost certainly receive kinder consideration.

Privately, however, Ripon advised the government of Natal that, while his department was sympathetic to the desire of the colony to protect its franchise, he thought it inadvisable to antagonize the local Indian community in the light of growing Indian militancy. Calls in India for home rule, although still faint, were insistent, and growing louder, and nothing that was likely to further inflame Indian grievances could be considered prudent at present.

To say that the political establishment of Natal was taken aback by all of this would be an understatement, and when it was discovered that Mohandas K. Gandhi, that little coolie barrister, was behind it all, a noticeable tone of defamation began to brew in the local press.

Gandhi responded with a handful of defensive replies, the thrust of which were to refute accusation of personal ambition, but also to argue the case of the Indians, denying institutionalized squalor and forswearing on behalf of the community any overt political ambition. He also attempted to illustrate the advantages the Indians offered to the economy of the colony and, of course, to argue their qualification for equal and fair treatment.

The effect of all of this was to pitch Gandhi firmly into the fray. The petition would clearly not be the end of the matter. The franchise bill had not been abandoned and, if anything, its delay, and the reason for its delay simply underlined the fact that the Indians truly had begun to emerge as a real political threat. This had been predicted for decades, and now, with their numbers comparable to blacks, and creeping ahead of whites, the arrival in their midst of a scallywag like Gandhi was all that was needed to ignite a revolution.

Gandhi, in the meanwhile, agreed to remain in the colony indefinitely, and having made this commitment, applied his furious energy to organizing and publicizing the new movement. Prior to this, he had been a member of no political organization, and certainly he had no affiliation with the Indian Congress, so it was with considerable caution that he proposed the establishment of a Natal chapter of Congress. The motion, however, was well received, and in May 1894, the Natal Indian Congress was inaugurated. Gandhi was appointed secretary and, although not listed among the executive leadership, it was manifestly his energy and expertise alone that drove the agenda.

His first priority was funding and organization, and in an initial rush of enthusiasm, the organization was floated by the wealthy merchants and traders who formed its founding membership. The movement, however, was no less welcomed in the rural community where a lack of representation was most acutely felt, and at the head of a corps of young volunteers, Gandhi set about spreading the news through pamphleteering and outreach. Small subscriptions were collected from those in the countryside that could afford it, and in a very short time the Natal Congress had accrued a sizeable rural and urban membership.

These opening moves established a pattern that would characterize Gandhi's political style into the future. He fired off a fusillade of communication, from open letters to the Natal and British governments to various petitions and communications as well, of course, as numerous letters to the press. Initially, the establishment response was muted and observant, for nothing like this had ever happened before. This, however, would not remain the case for long.

In the meanwhile, Gandhi submitted an application for membership to the Natal bar, which simply added to the confusion, and which was in the first instance greeted by the Natal Bar Association with scorn. This response, of course, was perfectly reactionary, and reflective of the wider play, for there was no reason why one British-trained lawyer should be different to another. Gandhi was Indian, that much was true, but he was a British subject no less, a member of a British Bar Association and a graduate of a British university. There were no rational grounds to reject his application but for the visceral and unreasonable reaction of an establishment simply unwilling to do so.

His case was taken up, however, by the Natal attorney-general, a prominent local barrister by the name of Harry Escombe who, swimming somewhat against the tide, took it upon himself to argue on Gandhi's behalf in the Natal high court. The case was unanswerable, of course, and judgement was duly handed down in Gandhi's favour, after which his application was allowed.

Escombe, however, did not do this for any love of Gandhi, whom he did confess to finding charming on a personal level, or any sympathy for the Indian cause, but simply because it was necessary. The law required it and, moreover, if the Indian question was to be dealt with constitutionally, then the rules of constitutionality and fair play must at all times be seen to be upheld.

The case, however, attracted considerable interest, some of it respectful, insofar as Gandhi was at the very least acknowledged to be competent, articulate and intelligent, but in most cases the attention was circumspect and hostile, breaking entirely a brief but pleasant season of speechlessness in the press.

The basis of Gandhi's platform, which he repeated often, and in a variety of forums, was simply that the Indians of Natal represented a race and a society rich with accomplishment, and deserving of full inclusion in the social and political processes of the colony. He sought to differentiate between Indians and blacks, arguing that the blanket legislation applicable to non-whites in the colony should not comingle blacks and Indians as a single caste.

In this regard he tended to create a monochromatic picture, painting the entire Indian community as virtuous and long suffering, and the entire white community as discriminatory and racist, which in neither case was accurate. The actions of Harry Escombe, as just one example, illustrated a higher standard of response, and the fact that so many Indian immigrants were of a low caste, despised even by their own countrymen, lent some credibility to European claims that Indian settlements were an unsanitary eyesore requiring careful regulation.

In general, however, although argumentative and persistent, and certainly apt to raise the hackles of his opponents, Gandhi set about building a unique political philosophy based on non-violence and the metaphysical aspects of activism. In some part he drew his inspiration from the tenets of *ahimsa* (non-violence) in Hinduism, his interpretation of which tended to be quite liberal, but also from the many threads of spirituality that his natural liberalism and curiosity allowed him to ponder. Surprisingly, the Natal colony at that time, perhaps as a microcosm of the homeland, was home to a great many experimental branches of spiritualism, religion and lifestyle, all of which Gandhi appeared to be open to, and selective of.

His particular focus of interest, however, remained the more abstruse works of Tolstoy, in whose uncompromising meditations on the meaning of life, on the significance of achievement and the impermanence of fame and eminence Gandhi found a curious brilliance. He had commenced his reading of Tolstoy in London, beginning with the great, esoteric work *The Kingdom of God is Within You*. Although framed upon Christian ideals, the central tenet of this book, of turning the other cheek as a device to eliminate violence, even violence of a defensive nature, inspired Gandhi deeply.

'You may not know the best individual, external aims, there may be obstacles in the way of achieving them, but the approach to inner perfection and the increase of love within yourself and others cannot be stopped by anyone or anything.'

This was written, and spoken by Tolstoy in a language that could hardly but appeal to a Hindu activist determined to remain true to his faith. However, in regard to his fundamental theory of non-violence, Tolstoy remained always somewhat vague and impractical, and there was much in his model of passive non-cooperation that required improvement in practice.

In theory, non-involvement in the power politics of society, as Tolstoy defined it, or in the principles of war, law, crime and punishment might satisfy an individual's desire to detach from the world, but it would serve no purpose in the practical achievement of revolution. The motivation and channelling of a popular movement using non-violence as its basis was in itself revolutionary, and would require something far greater than simple individual non-engagement. One can, however, debate into eternity how, and under what influences Gandhi founded his own particular raft of ideals.

His preparation, however, doubtless commenced in London, where he began for the first time to assert control over his own appetites, choosing abstinence and morality as the guiding principle of his life. As the years passed, a gradually deepening internal examination followed, and considerable dissociation from the temporal experience of life resulted, laying, inadvertently perhaps, the groundwork for the challenges that were written into his destiny.

In the meanwhile, once the political establishment had gathered its senses, Gandhi found himself the subject of much public rancour, and he was dutifully reviled and demonized by a slavish European press. He was portrayed as a self-serving, publicity-hungry barrister plundering for profit the susceptibilities of his illiterate compatriots. However, as was proven by Harry Escombe, he was not universally despised by whites and, indeed, those that met him were often attracted to him despite themselves. He wielded charisma, in part because of his courtesy, his amiability and natural familiarity and charm, but also because he was quite obviously a man for whom principle was paramount, and for whom truth was a guiding tenet.

In Durban, he established himself in practice, determining to use his qualification only as a means to support himself and his family as he supplicated himself to service as an expression of humility, love and truth. The political work that he undertook at this time was routine and organizational, and although he had begun to view it as a corruption, it was through his legal work, in particular among the poor, that he began to develop his reputation. Many of the poorest Indians were those serving labour contracts, and without language fluency, literacy or protective institutions, they fell victim frequently to an uncaring system.

Indian interpreters were often themselves simple people, and at times corrupt, and thus for an indentured worker to seek legal relief against exploitation by employer or state was near impossible. Gandhi bridged this gap, in part through his legal work, but also in part because he gave a dispossessed community of Indians a sense of leadership, and an inkling of the power of a political presence. He served the needs of the elite as an attorney as might be expected, but his common touch, and his unique fraternity with the masses of low-caste, labouring Indians was what established the bedrock of his following.

Chapter 9

The Green Pamphlet

'This, then, is the naked truth. In obedience to the popular outcry, justly or unjustly, the Asiatic must be put down.'
—The Green Pamphlet

Early in June 1896, Gandhi set sail for India on a six-month sabbatical from his work in South Africa. Ostensibly his objective was to collect his wife and sons, but perhaps more practically he hoped to introduce himself to the emerging Indian nationalist establishment, and to introduce to it to the work underway in South Africa.

He chose not to travel to Porbandar directly, but instead he disembarked at Calcutta, from where he commenced a journey inland by train. No mention is made in his memoir, or anywhere else for that matter, of any interest in the wellbeing of his wife and sons, and even as he describes his eventual return to Porbandar, his preoccupation appears to remain with his political work. This might cause a casual biographer to suspect that dissociation from his family, alongside other temporal interests, had already begun.

Be that as it may, as he travelled, his networking, correspondence and public speaking was feverish. It does not appear, however, that initially he was taken very seriously, which, at least according to his own accounts, was humbling but constructive, for it allowed him to offer himself in service to the movement in the lowest of capacities. This anonymity, and the general disinterest of the Indian political establishment towards the emerging struggle in South Africa, changed somewhat when he wrote and published a pamphlet, known as the 'The Green Pamphlet', which, somewhat to his surprise, ran to two editions, registering a distribution total of 10,000 copies.

The Green Pamphlet, or 'The Grievances of the British Indians of South Africa: An Appeal to the Indian Public', was widely circulated and avidly read throughout India, with copies quickly finding their way back to London for the perusal of the metropolitan establishment. Inevitably, second- and third-hand press reports filtering through to Natal dramatized the more sensational aspects of the publication, which had the effect of utterly scandalizing the European community. Gandhi had unleashed a finely crafted article of propaganda that listed a daunting litany of horrors inflicted on the Indian community, ranging from simple and petty instances of spite to actual and real injury.

In every respect the contents of The Green Pamphlet reflected the reality of day-to-day life for Indians in South Africa, although not without considerable production and a full measure of the sort of pathos that Gandhi was by then rather expert at blending. It would be wrong to say that he lied, not at all wrong to say that, outside of a shooting war with the French, that such nakedly inflammatory language in criticism of British conduct overseas had never been deployed.

Needless to say, the white population of Natal erupted into a ferment, stoking the flames of anti-Indian sentiment in the colony to a fever pitch, and setting the pot of Gandhiphobia to such a furious boil that the little coolie barrister, that quaint curiosity of yore, transmogrified almost overnight into an ogre of unimaginably diabolical intent.

In the meanwhile, somewhat unawares, the subject of this wrath finally rendezvoused with his family and made ready to return to South Africa. He had been warned by friendly correspondence that his activities in India had stirred up a hornets' nest, but it is unlikely that he appreciated the true depth of feeling that had built against him in Natal. However, as the SS *Courland* drew up alongside the mouth of Durban harbour, with the Gandhi family and several hundred other Indians on board, friends were quick to warn him.

Unfortunately, in the wake of the *Courland* came the *Naderi*, also arriving from the sub-continent with a large passenger list of Indians. This was seen as no less than an invasion, and soon enough a hostile phalanx of local whites had gathered at the gates of the harbour, supported by a smaller but no less threatening corps of blacks. Disembarkation was delayed for several weeks by a temporary quarantine imposed on both vessels because of an outbreak of plague in Bombay, and imperial officials hoped that the interim would see a damping down of white anger, but such was not to be.

The legacy of Mohandas Karamchand Gandhi enjoys as many devotees as it does detractors, but what can never be denied is that Gandhi was a man who possessed the courage of his convictions. He continued to be warned by a number of well-wishers that harm was intended against him onshore, and many suggested that he not disembark at all. He gave a press interview on board the *Courland* in which he made the simple point that exclusion was obsolete. Equal rights for all civilized men had been the words of the great Cecil John Rhodes, and could it be doubted that the Indians existed among the most civilized of the races of earth?

If the British empire was gnawing its fingernails at the prospect of losing India, let not India be offended by the actions of a minority of British expatriates building ramparts against the inevitable in southern Africa. If Victoria had not wished to include civilized Indians in her imperial charter, then why, in 1858, had she touched the shores of India with her majesty?

On 12 January 1897, authority was at last granted for the two ships to disembark. An angry mob gathered at the gates of the harbour to deal with Gandhi if he could be identified among the Indians stepping onshore and hurriedly dispersing into their own quarters of the city. Harry Escombe appealed to the mob for calm, reminding all those assembled that it was the diamond jubilee of their esteemed monarch, and as such it behoved the men of Natal to ensure that nothing grieve her in the twilight of her reign.

This appeal to patriotism did indeed have a sobering effect, and a gradual dispersal began. Gandhi stepped off the gangplank of the *Courland* later that afternoon, almost the last to do so, his wife and sons already ashore. He was rowed to the quay by southern Indians, Tamils probably, dark-skinned men, lean and muscular, seldom meeting the gaze of a superior, but talking softly among themselves as their sinews stretched.

Gandhi, it can be imagined, was anxious. Driven by nervous energy, he was not a physical man. At five foot five inches and weighing no more than 140lb, he could hardly stand his ground against an average meat-eating Englishman of the day. Nonetheless, he stepped ashore and, in the company of an English lawyer by the name of Frederick Laughton, hurried across open ground towards a rickshaw that was ready to spirit him away.

However, a knot of white youths lingering on the boards recognized him, and raised the alarm. Under severe threat, the native rickshaw runner left the scene, abandoning Laughton and Gandhi in plain view to then cross the Victoria embankment on foot and make their way northward on Stanger Street.

Soon enough, the mob began to coalesce around them, hissing and jeering, and occasionally lobbing anything that came to hand. The lash of a horsewhip fell across Gandhi's back, and he was slapped and kicked from various vantages.

It is not difficult to imagine how frightening this must have been, and in many respects it is a credit to Frederick Laughton, who was himself not a substantial man, that he remained steadfastly close to Gandhi throughout, tight lipped, himself afraid but unwavering.

Gandhi, bleeding and beset with tremors, kept a grip on his suitcase, stood straight and held his tread steady. He was, however, relieved beyond words when a doughty woman of some age, armed with a parasol, cleared a space around him, declaring herself to be the wife of the chief constable. And indeed, the chief constable himself appeared soon afterwards, warning those assaulting Gandhi that the consequences for such actions in a jubilee year would be severe.

The four then removed themselves ahead of a pack of venomous troublemakers to the home of Parsee Rustomjee, where Gandhi took refuge, and from where he was secreted a short while later disguised as a policeman. Thereafter, the chief constable addressed the mob and informed them that their quarry had flown, and that if they disbelieved him they could search the house if they chose.

A certain abashed silence prevailed in the press in the immediate aftermath of this incident, until the *Natal Mercury* was moved to remark that it had been Gandhi who invited violence upon himself by painting the whites of the colony 'as filthy and black as his own face'.

To this Frederick Laughton responded in a lengthy and considered letter to the newspaper which defended Gandhi, and in many respects introduced him to the colony less as the little coolie barrister, but for the first time as a political leader. This was reinforced in the United States by an essay published in the radical New York weekly, *The Nation*, which brutally took to task the British for betraying the very principles that had once made the empire great. Gandhi was extolled as an authentic champion of the people, a true David wielding a sling of truth that would one day topple the Goliath of empire.

Thus Gandhi was internationalized; but the matter itself – the assault and harassment of an imperial subject, and indeed the question of even deeper institutionalized restrictions against Indian immigration, and their ability to trade in the colony – remained. While the Natal Franchise Bill sat on the desk of the colonial secretary, a general election was fought that returned an alliance of Conservatives and Liberal Unionists to power. The mood of the new British administration, headed by the brilliant, but aggressively imperialist Lord Salisbury, marked the end of the age of indifference, and the beginning of a period of forceful imperial consolidation.

Chapter 10

The Imperial Factor in South Africa

'The day of small nations has long passed away. The day of Empires has come.'

—Joseph Chamberlain

On 29 June 1895, a key government appointment was announced by the office of the new British prime minister, Lord Salisbury. Fifty-nine-year-old Joseph Chamberlain, a retired businessman and past president of the Board of Trade, was admitted into the cabinet as secretary of state for the colonies, one of the most important and influential administrative positions of the day. Upon entering his office, Chamberlain assumed responsibility for the administration of the territories of India (shared with the India Office), British North America, the British Antipodes, various sundry possessions in Southeast Asia, the Caribbean, South America and the South Pacific, as well as, of course, the various colonies of Africa.

By then the British empire was nearing its greatest extent, encompassing over a third of the world and, thanks to India, considerably more than a third of its population. Upon the empire, the sun never set, and once consolidated, the day-to-day administration of this gargantuan entity fell to a handful of technocrats of limited creativity, but monumental competence.

Joseph Chamberlain was one such as this. Unaffiliated to the aristocracy, he was, instead, a middle-class businessman and industrialist who sat upon a self-made fortune. His world view was coloured less by an hereditary right to rule, founded in the clubs of Eton and Oxford, and more with the boiler-room credo of the working man. He had advanced by steady increments from the shop floor to the boardroom, and thereafter to the apex of imperial power by the application of what he had learned. His perception of empire dwelt less upon highbrow notions of diplomacy and manifest destiny, and more on the ideology of mergers and acquisitions.

95

Such was his view of South Africa. A consolidation of the four territories was no new idea; in fact it was widely regarded as an inevitability. Chamberlain's predecessor, the Earl of Carnarvon, had gone so far as to try and force an amalgamation by annexing the Transvaal, but this floundered, most historians tend to agree, upon a misappreciation of the full depth of Boer aversion to the British.[1] Chamberlain, however, looked at the same map and realized that if the Boer could not be persuaded to voluntarily acknowledge British seniority, then at some point a war was inevitable.

Chamberlain was also influenced by geopolitical factors absent a generation earlier. In 1871, for example, the Franco-Prussian War had given birth to the German empire, girding a third power to enter the contest of European global expansion. A complicated series of events then followed that saw Britain, France and Germany jostling over a number of strategic and prestigious territorial acquisitions, in Africa and elsewhere, which added to internal European tensions, and precipitating what came to be known as the Scramble for Africa.

In 1884, the German empire laid claim to the territory of German South West Africa, the future Namibia, followed by the annexation in 1891 of German East Africa, the future Tanganyika. This placed the German empire, an emerging naval power, in a commanding strategic position with regards to the security of British and allied shipping in both the Atlantic and Indian oceans. Bearing in mind the deep and unresolved regional antipathies between Boer and Briton in South Africa, and the natural ideological allegiance between Boer and German, a very real potential existed for the two Boer republics to ally with Germany, threatening British strategic interests in the Cape and potentially handing Africa south of the equator to the German empire.[2]

At the very heart of this situation lay Anglo-Boer relations, a festering sore on the body of South Africa that had remained unhealed for long enough for there now to be a real sense that healing was impossible. War in Europe, although a possibility, was not quite yet a probability, but the prospect was strong enough for Chamberlain to regard South Africa less in terms of its embellishment of British values than as a key element in a global structure that would at some point need to be mobilized in imperial defence. Other elements included the colonies of Canada, Australia and New Zealand, within each of which strong political elements existed that were opposed to any alliance with Britain in a world war. There was the question of Japan, and the security of the western Pacific and Indian oceans, and of course India.[3]

India was without doubt a key constituent of Chamberlain's thinking, and one can imagine that this was brought into sharper focus still when he found upon his desk, a desk recently vacated by the browbeaten Lord Ripon, the draft bill of the Natal Franchise Act, not yet suitably amended and, after more than a year, still unresolved.

This apparently simple dispute had kept Lord Ripon up at night. He realized that to judge in favour of the Indian would outrage white sentiment in Natal, with all of its values of kith and kin, but to judge in favour of them would unleash upon himself a fresh wave of polite but unrelenting protest from the Natal Congress. He fudged the issue, delaying a definitive judgement until he could leave office and assume the much safer agency of a seat in the House of Lords.

Perusing the original draft of the bill, meanwhile, Chamberlain took a pragmatic view. While acknowledging that the unsanitary masses of the Indian population ought to be prevented from overwhelming the colony, or any colony for that matter, he confirmed that the current wording and spirit of the draft made it impossible for his office to recommend a grant of royal assent.[4] It did not, for example, take into account the higher Indian castes, two members of which had won sufficient approval of the British electorate to sit in the House of Commons, and whose social attributes fully qualified them for all the duties and privileges of imperial citizenship.[5]

He did, however, also accept the pragmatic view that, if the destiny of Natal was to continue to be shaped by the white races, then some muscular limitation against Indian immigration and franchise in the colony would be necessary. He therefore posed the Natal government an interesting conundrum. If all overtly racist verbiage could be removed from the draft, even if it retained its essential elements, it would be granted his approval.

Receiving this news, the drafting committee of the Natal legislative assembly, mindful of the need to carefully select its battles, returned thoughtfully to the drawing board to review the text of the law, settling in due course on a rather brilliant solution. All specific racial reference was expunged from the document, with just a subtle and innocuous clause added that prohibited admission to the franchise of any resident of Natal who did not enjoy the same privilege in his home colony. India at that time remained a British colony governed by an appointed committee headed by a viceroy, and was without a popularly elected government or legislature. Indians, therefore, under the terms of the new draft, did not qualify for the vote in Natal.

When the amended draft arrived on Chamberlain's desk a month or two later, he no doubt shook his head and chuckled at the ingenuity of it. It was indicated that if the draft was approved by the Natal legislature, then he would offer his recommendation to Her Majesty. Thus, in 1896, the Natal Franchise Act passed into law, after which the Indians of the colony were encouraged to vote where the franchise was available to them, and with the best of British luck.

Needless to say, Chamberlain was briefly rocked by an outpouring of written and verbal protest unleashed by the Natal Congress, but as a lawyer, Gandhi soon acknowledged that he had been outmanoeuvred, and that he too would be wise to apply his energies to selected battles. Thus, the act came into law and was filed away, and he set off for India on his mission to collect his family, leaving Chamberlain to apply his mind to the wider issues of South African unification, and the powder keg of latent white-on-white racial dichotomy that would sooner rather than later blow up in his face.

Chapter 11

The Colossus

'With the eye of understanding he reads his age; with the eye
of faith he surveys its future. In the doubts of his age he sees
only the beginning of a vaster faith, the outlines of which he
does not hesitate to draw with a bold hand.'

—Jan Smuts, *Walt Whitman: A Study in the Evolution
of a Personality.*

In 1894, the 24-year-old Jan Christiaan Smuts passed the bar examination,
and thus entered the British legal fraternity. Soon afterward, he returned to
the Cape with the limited ambition of repaying the debts that he had accrued,
establishing himself in practice and marrying his high-school sweetheart. He
took chambers in Cape Town, but briefs proved sporadic, and money, as
would often be the case in his life, worryingly scarce.

With time on his hands, he took to writing, composing lengthy political
polemics in support of the unionist position, and in general on contemporary
political themes. These were published in various newspapers and journals,
and for a while he contemplated a career as a journalist and writer. The
unpublished manuscript of Walt Whitman remained on his desk, returned
from a number of publishers with notes expressing admiration for his
treatment of a unique and difficult subject, but admitting too little public
interest in the subject to justify publication. He attempted to have it serialized
in the British literary periodical, *The Nineteenth Century*, but this too was
turned down.

In the meanwhile, he took to spending long hours in the public gallery
above the floor of the Cape parliament, tapping a pencil on the empty page
of a journalist's notepad and slowly developing an interest in practical
politics. He observed the technique of debate, the power of oratory and the
vitality of personality. At home he practised and developed his own style,
and was more than once observed walking the cobbled streets of Cape Town

99

addressing an imaginary audience. It was, however, the parliamentary performances of Cecil John Rhodes that he most admired.

At 42, Rhodes stood at the pinnacle of his career. He was head of a number of major corporations, and one of the wealthiest and the most influential figures in South Africa and, since 1890, prime minister of the Cape Colony. In response to the German annexation of Damaraland in the South West Africa territory, he had engineered the advance of British protection over the territory of Bechuanaland, and under the aegis of his British South Africa Company, founded the two British territories of Northern and Southern Rhodesia. In achieving this, he had successfully checked German ambitions to link their two colonies of German East and West Africa, and at the same time advanced by several thousand miles his own vision of a through route from Cape to Cairo.

By all of this Smuts was enthralled, and how could he not be? What Rhodes had achieved in ten years of hampered life exceeded the accomplishments of many lesser lifetimes. He was a genius, and Smuts could hardly help himself from juxtaposing his own humble objectives against those of this great man. His own emerging concepts of holism in nature and society conformed with uncanny precision to Rhodes's often expressed ideals of union.

Rhodes spoke frequently in parliament, and no less frequently, hidden somewhat in the unlit seating above the main chamber, Smuts could be found listening. Rather tall, loose limbed and shabbily dressed, Rhodes had by then turned heavy, bloated and purple in complexion. His eyes were bruised and rheumy, and had lately begun to water. In the silence of the chamber, as he paused for breath, the rasping in his lungs could clearly be heard. Standing thus, with his hands on either side of the dispatch box, his voice at a quivering falsetto, economical of gesture, but verbose and inelegant of prose, he was nonetheless a powerful and persuasive speaker.

And thus, from the saturated lungs of this dying man continued to rise the soaring vision of a unified South Africa; but more even than this, for Rhodes had not lost sight of his united states of Africa; and nor the global government that would obviate future war, drawing the human race into a unified whole; an organic, cosmically aligned body of one thought, one action and one religion.

Underwriting this, of course, would be British moral and economic capital, the highest human standards expressed in a charter of empire that might have been, and perhaps had been decreed by God. Indeed, on the right-hand of God sat the Son, but on His left sat the Daughter, Regina Victoria, upon whom the promise of the world had been gifted, and under whose light the children of God would bask and proliferate.

But for all of his achievements, the fact remained that Rhodes had so far failed to unite the four territories of South Africa. He had outmanoeuvred the Germans, browbeaten the Portuguese and coerced his own government to act where they would have preferred not to, but so far he had been defeated by the obstinacy of a bucolic and uneducated population of Boer.

While his acquisition of Bechuanaland and the Rhodesias had been achieved by the blunt instruments of wealth and power, the amalgamation of South Africa would require a degree of diplomatic virtuosity that few believed him capable. When he addressed the student body of Victoria College he had been a relatively junior parliamentarian, but quite as he had implored the cream of Cape Dutch youth to acknowledge the inevitability of union, so now he laboured to cultivate their parents. By minute increments he had gained their trust, ultimately to broker an alliance between his Progressive Party and the Afrikaner Bond, the base upon which he had formed a government, and inherited the instruments of power in the Cape.

And, of course, Smuts was precisely of that Cape Dutch lineage, and he for one was utterly convinced of the same inevitability. It was his generation, indeed, and his social strata that Rhodes was appealing to most directly. If the men of Smuts's generation could be influenced by this message then they in turn would influence the republics, helping to throw across the slender lines of amalgamation.

From Smuts's articles and correspondence during that period, it is easy to measure the growth of his enthrallment with Rhodes. He heaped praise on his mentor, citing him as the prophet of the new age, the Colossus, and answering every critic with the clear and icy intellect that would be his political signature.[1] He was also quite unafraid to point out the obstruction standing in the path of this shared dream. It was that gnarled old tree, none other than the ageing Transvaal president, Paul Kruger, with the roots of his nation sunk into an ancient past, but its leaves basking in the sunshine of the century.

It was the monumental taxation levied against foreign mining activities that fed the moribund treasury of the Transvaal, but the entrenched rural element, stuck fast to their feudal ideals, who owned the country. How would it be possible to move this obstruction, Smuts mused, without upsetting the delicate house of cards of existing Anglo-Boer relations?

But we can sympathize with the ideal of the old cattle-farmer President. He fought for the freedom of his country because England threatened to interfere in the natural development of his pastoral people. Now he fights against industrial society in his country, because he sees that this is a still greater threat to its natural development. As true Afrikaners [Cape Dutch] we also would wish to see the burghers a strong and influential part of the future Transvaal: that is why we feel for the old President.[2]

What was required, Smuts cautiously advised, was a closing of the drifts, meaning, in Dutch idiom, a bridging of the gap, and an understanding of the terror felt by the old *volk* in the face of a changing world, and perhaps even a friendly hand to guide them. Rhodes, Smuts surmised, based on evidence that had convinced more experienced minds than he, was the only man currently breathing with the wit and sincerity to achieve this. In his youthful enthusiasm, Smuts even went so far as to proclaim a new era, challenging those critics to point to a single instance where Rhodes had abused his position for any reason of personal gain.

In his first significant political speech, delivered in 1895 to the De Beers debating society, Smuts addressed the strategic partnership of Rhodes and the Afrikaner Bond. It was, he said, 'an organic and natural advance of that at first somewhat narrow national movement which – when it has extended to all South Africa and infused its spirit into all white men living here – will be the basis of a politically united South Africa.'

What was the Afrikaner Bond? Referred to more often as simply the Bond, the Afrikaner Bond was a guild of sorts, rather more than a fraternity, but initially at least, somewhat less than a political party. Founded originally in the Orange Free State, the Bond could perhaps best be described as the emerging manifesto of a race – the Afrikaner race – that in an age of British political domination sought to retain its cultural autonomy. It was the precursor, indeed, to the later rise of Afrikaner nationalism, and its mission statement, like that of Rhodes himself, was the political unification of the separate territories of South Africa. The two positions, however, differed on the question of governance. Rhodes, on the one hand, pictured a unified British self-governing colony, while the Bond saw something entirely different. It pictured the future somewhat more in an independent federal, or confederal context, without the additional burden of British imperial overlordship. A republic of South Africa, independent of any European power and allied to the British only as a diplomatic consideration, perhaps within the British sphere of influence, but neither governed from Whitehall nor superintended by a British governor.

The question of engagement with the British was, of course, inescapable. The two Boer republics were, after all, landlocked, and in sharp contrast to the British colonies, they were socially and politically torpid. That besides, the Transvaal was host to a large and growing community of British workers, and a powerful clique of wealthy British capitalists and industrialists, all of whom were agitating for equal representation, and relief from taxation.

For the leaders of the Transvaal Republic, this was a conundrum indeed, for taxation levied against foreign mining activities in the Transvaal was extremely lucrative, as were the national monopolies placed on such commodities as dynamite, but to extend the franchise to the Uitlanders – foreigners, or outsiders – in exchange for this, as they were demanding, would be political suicide.[3] In terms both of numbers and capital influence, British and British-allied voters in the Transvaal would simply overwhelm the Boer, and gone in an instant would be that defining ideal of self-determination, sovereignty and freedom from British domination.

This, in a nutshell, was the white–white contradiction in South Africa, and it represented the first tier of the great South African race conundrum. During the formative years of South Africa, 'race' was a word that dominated the collective political language of the territories, but it did not involve people of colour in any consequential way, but was strictly a question of relations between Briton and Boer.

Rhodes, of course, spoke for British interests, but on behalf of the Boer spoke a man of no lesser reputation than he, a man whose name was Jan Hofmeyr. Hofmeyr was leader of the Afrikaner Bond, and it was he who had sat alongside Rhodes on the stage of the Victoria College assembly hall when Smuts had so impressed them both. Although he and Rhodes were close personal friends, more important was the fact that they were political allies, acting in roles both practical and symbolic of the new age of Anglo-Boer cooperation.

Onze Jan (Our Jan), as Hofmeyr was affectionately known, was the scion of a modestly wealthy and liberal Cape Dutch family, and a deceptively friendly and avuncular man. He was tall, bearded and bespectacled, round of belly and upright of posture, a well-respected political strategist and capable consensus builder. When Cecil Rhodes first entered the Cape parliament as an abrasive and opinionated novice, he was quick to identify Hofmeyr, among all of the back-benchers, as the man he most needed to get to know.

Rhodes had a mantra that he had adopted during his Kimberley years, which very well defined his approached to matters of business and politics. He preferred in the first instance to 'square' his opponents, and would only crush them once he had exhausted all efforts to achieve this. To this end he was gifted with powers of persistence and persuasion that amazed associates and opponents alike. Many powerful men, some much older and wealthier than he, were inclined to shake their heads and marvel at how it was that Rhodes was able to persuade them to act against their judgement. For all of his lack of physical attraction, and perhaps even because of it, Rhodes wielded extraordinary charisma.

Thus, he was able to 'square' Jan Hofmeyr with relative ease, and his argument ran more or less along these lines: Yes, indeed, the full potential of South Africa would never be realized before union, but the moment was premature for a full republic. At that point in history, the great empires of Europe controlled the globe, and the rapid growth of industry and communication worldwide was ongoing under imperial impetus. An enlarged British dependency would serve the interests of any new nation far better than a shackled republic existing solely by the leave of British capital, and dominated by English-speaking interests. Ride on the coattails of Victoria Regina, Rhodes advised Hofmeyr, and slip off some time in the future when the world would surely be more accommodating of the republican concept.

And like a gadfly, if one approach happened to fail, Rhodes would try another, until, in July of 1890, a full ten years after his first entry into politics, he finally succeeded in forging that alliance.[4]

Then, one day, Rhodes, who happened to own a significant stake in the Argus group of newspapers, noticed an editorial in the *Cape Argus* written by a young barrister by the name of Jan Christiaan Smuts, and his mind returned to that afternoon in 1888. He researched the matter, and unearthed the impressive academic record that Smuts had established in Cambridge, and he realized that here was precisely the type of young man that he needed. Rhodes briefed his friend Jan Hofmeyr, and a message was sent to the chambers of Jan Smuts by Hofmeyr, a voice that Smuts could not ignore, advising him that Prime Minister Rhodes wished to meet him.

Chapter 12

God's People

'I do not say of monarchy, or of aristocracy, but of all law, of all order, of all property, of all civilization, of all that makes us to differ from Mohawks or Hottentots.'
—Thomas Babington Macaulay

The issue that dominated the 1895 Cape parliamentary session was not the Anglo-Boer question, but Rhodes's spirited defence of the Glen Grey Act. The Glen Grey Act was an article of legislation that Rhodes piloted through parliament in 1894, and which has since come to be regarded as the first segregationist law passed in South Africa. This, in fact, is not true, for there had been one or two others, but the Glen Grey Act triggered an emotive response at the core of the Cape liberal movement, ageing now, but still with a handful of spry voices. It has also been cited, and most historians agree, that the Glen Grey Act brought an end to the age of Christianity and Commerce, and introduced the age of the Sacred Trust.

Christianity and Commerce was the clarion call of a generation of Englishmen responding to the death of Dr David Livingstone. Livingstone, arguably the greatest explorer of his age, began his career as a humble missionary, but gave himself over to exploration very soon afterwards, and in the modern context could perhaps best be described as a human rights activist.

Livingstone's career spanned the period between the early 1850s and the early 1870s, a time of abolition, but also of epidemic slave trading throughout the East African interior. This branch of the slave trade, older and far more established than the Atlantic, had at its root the ancient trade relationship between the Arabian Peninsula and the east coast of Africa.

The main agents of this trade were dominant African tribes, funded and supported from Zanzibar, and factored by Islamic, Swahili-speaking middlemen at the coast. The main market for slaves sourced in East Africa was Arabia and the Persian Gulf, and to a lesser extent India and the various French Indian Ocean islands. To this was added rogue Portuguese slave traders, shut out of West Africa, who rounded the Cape to source fresh supplies from their East African territories.

In general, however, the East African slave trade was a home-grown endeavour which lay under the control of the Zanzibari sultanate. The reason that it survived for so much longer than any other was due primarily to British diplomatic engagement with the powerful Omani sultanate, a familial branch of the Sultanate of Zanzibar.

At that time, it was the British Indian government that administered to all British interests between the Gulf of Aden and Burma, including the Arabian Peninsula and India, and there could be no profit in compromising such vital strategic relationships merely to satisfy the howling of a brace of metropolitan liberals. Slavery in black Africa was seen as an expression of culture and tradition, and so for much of the period up to the 1870s, the British were content to look the other way.

It was David Livingstone, however, who stumbled on the effects of this trade, hitherto hidden somewhat by the obscurity of Africa. Private armies raised and funded by Swahili traders ranged the interior, inflicting a reign of terror justified by the exclusivity of Islam, in what might accurately be described as the first humanitarian disaster in modern African history.

It was the forlorn voice of Dr Livingstone, travelling alone and unsupported through the south–central region, that sought to expose and publicize this unfolding horror. His plea was for a distracted Victorian public to fund the deeper exploration of Africa, in particular the navigable rivers, in order to introduce Christian values and legitimate commerce to supplant paganism and supersede the illegal slave trade. To appeal to the human instincts of the perpetrators would, of course, be futile. Nothing but the implementation of international law, and its practical enforcement could hope to bring an end to the suffering.

Livingstone died in 1873, expiring in excruciating loneliness somewhere in the dark heart of Africa. His body was transported to the coast by loyal servants, and received in Britain with a mixture of reverence and shame. That this great son of the empire had been allowed to die alone and in poverty, single-handedly carrying the torch of civilization in the pagan reaches of the world, touched the conscience of the Victorian public, spurring it to finish the work that Livingstone had begun.

By then, in any case, a treaty had been negotiated by the British, outlawing slavery throughout the territories of the Zanzibari sultanate. Thereafter, thanks in part to the development of malaria prophylactics, the interior of the continent became increasingly accessible, allowing missionaries to enter, followed by hunters and explorers.

Once the European capital element was able to take stock, it became evident that Africa was home to vast reserves of cheap raw materials, and almost unlimited markets for cheap European-manufactured goods. This was the age of industry, and soon European, and in particular British, capitalists forged their own passage into Africa, founding chartered companies and mapping out vast private concessions, until, in due course, the continent fell under direct imperial control.

The concept of Christianity and Commerce, therefore, came to define that period whereby it fell to the Europeans to repair the societies of Africa that they had contributed so much to breaking. European moral values, deemed to be universal, supported by economy and labour, would lift the pagan savage out of the concussive daze dealt him by centuries of horror and depredation.

And true enough, comprehensive European administration in Africa did indeed evict the adventurer elements. Tribal war largely fell away, slavery was banished and the worst tropical diseases were brought under control. Perhaps the most far-reaching effect of European rule, however, was to loosen the pressures of Bantu orthodoxy, releasing the potential of the individual through conversion, and equipping him for modern life through education. Traditional leadership suffered an erosion of relevance, but new doors began to open, and there were many who found the opportunities attractive.

The question then became one of conditioning black Africans to most profitably embrace the opportunities of Christianity and commerce now on offer. The first agents of this change were, of course, the missionaries. In exchange for conversion, it was they who provided medicine and education. And, in general, colonial governments were supportive of this, for it was in their interest to have available literate and educated blacks for the menial ranks of the administration, the military and various local constabularies.

Complications, however, arose towards the end of the century as settled and liberated native communities began to grow and repopulate traditional areas, areas that incoming white settlers also sought to claim. This was particularly the case in Kenya, where centuries of war, disease (human and livestock) and slavery had reduced the indigenous population of the desirable Central Highlands to a remnant.[1] However, as both populations grew, and land pressures began to manifest, the overlap of cultures became rancorous, prompting more creative and adaptive strategies to systematize separation.

It was at this point that discussion began to be heard in Africa of the Sacred Trust. The Sacred Trust, notwithstanding its lofty implications, was simply an admission that the long-term interest of European colonists were proving incompatible with the long-term interests of natives. The latter, however, remained vulnerable to exploitation, and unable to resist the forceful appropriation of land and the coercion of labour.

The Sacred Trust implied an imperial obligation to protect the interests of the natives against increasingly powerful settler regimes, until they were in a position to stand on their own feet. Implicit in this was first use of the concept of separation, or segregation, which, in theory, offered the opportunity for blacks to live and develop according to their own pace and inclination. However, in practical terms, this simply quarantined the bulk of 'tribal' blacks out of mainstream economic development, cracking the door only wide enough to admit those numbers necessary to satisfy the labour requirements of the colony.

This, of course, is an oversimplification, for only a handful of European colonies in Africa were comprehensively settled in this way, with a majority only either of strategic or prestige interest. The principle, however, became widespread and pervasive, and although each European power had a different policy and ideal of native administration, in general, as the century advanced, the age of idealism floundered on a practical and fundamental incompatibility. In the end, the Sacred Trust translated simply into the institutionalized separation of blacks, and the subversion of their interests in favour of those of the settlers.

This, therefore, was the background to the Glen Grey Act. In the Cape Colony, however, things were a little different thanks to the much-storied, colour-blind Cape franchise, and the fact that contact between native and colonists in the Cape was so much older. The non-racial tradition of the colony began as early as 1828, five years before abolition, with the promulgation of Ordinance 50. This freed the Hottentots, or non-whites in general, from forced servitude, indenture, apprenticeship or pass laws. By 1836, non-whites had begun to freely participate in municipal elections and, in 1853, with the introduction of a constitution, all limitations of colour and ethnicity were swept away. This opened the way for the legal franchise of all men over 21 years of age, regardless of race, who owned property worth £25, or earned a minimum of £25 per annum.

The first blacks to access the vote were the Fingo, or Mfengu, who were classed as refugees from the earlier predations of the Zulu. The Mfengu were somewhat allied to the Xhosa through language and tradition, but they were not Xhosa. Settled generally around the village of Victoria in the Eastern Cape, the Mfengu formed something of a buffer between the white settled districts of the eastern frontier, and the more remote Xhosa heartland. In due course the Mfengu would emerge as a progressive peasant community, accessing their voting rights to quite a considerable extent. The success of this process was confirmed by occasional admissions from successful white parliamentary candidates that they had found it necessary to be sensitive to the interests of registered black voters.

In general, however, during the early phases, blacks did not avail themselves of the franchise in significant numbers, and early political activity was focused mainly on encouraging them to do so. It was not until the last of the Frontier Wars was fought in 1878, followed a year later by the crushing defeat of the Zulu, that the futility of armed resistance became clear, creating a greater awareness and interest in politics. African quasi-political organizations began to appear at about this time, as did native newspapers and periodicals.

In general, the tone of black political activity was moderate, and across the spectrum it was supported by the white political establishment. Educated black society, nascent and entirely unthreatening, acknowledged white superintendentship with a degree of humility that might with hindsight seem misplaced. However, the emerging black political class complied with European increments, remaining loyal to traditional institutions, but defining a new class of 'civilized natives' under benign but robust British protection.

However, coinciding with Rhodes's entry into politics, and his steady rise to the premiership, a certain amount of partisanship began to take root within the white political establishment. The steady, grassroots rise of black political engagement began to manifest in local councils and parliamentary candidature in the Eastern Cape falling into black hands. Bearing in mind the rapid increases of black population in the Eastern Cape, Malthusian predictions of an overwhelming mass of black voters dominating the electorate began to surface in political discussion and, soon enough, small items of corresponding legislation began to appear on the table.

The first of these was the Cape Parliamentary Voters Registration Act, which specified that the property qualification necessary for voter registration no longer included what was termed 'Tribal Tenure', meaning land occupied according to customary allocation, or communal rights. The logic of this was to limit access to the franchise of voters with traditional title to land, but without corresponding standards of education and literacy. As a result, some

20,000 voters were struck off the register, no small number of whom were white, but the vast majority, of course, were black.

This was followed in 1892, two years before the tabling of the Glen Grey Act, by the Franchise and Ballot Act – debated under Rhodes's premiership and substantively supported by him – that successfully increased the property qualification from £25 to £75, further disenfranchising large numbers of blacks and poor whites.

However, the influence of black voters in the frontier constituencies of the Eastern Cape remained a live political factor. An example of this would be the 1884 parliamentary campaign of James Rose Innes, a locally born, English-speaking lawyer rooted very much in the Cape liberal tradition. For the sake of context, Rose Innes was the 29-year-old son of a Scottish liberal who immigrated to the Cape to become one of the colony's first native administrators. He was born in Grahamstown, and stood unequivocally upon a platform of racial parity at every level. Perhaps his most famous utterance in this regard was the following, made during a parliamentary speech: 'The policy of repression has been tried, and it has failed. What the country requires is that the existing laws should be fairly and equitably administered, and that the Natives should cease to be the subjects of rash experiments in the art of "vigorous" government.'[2]

Rose Innes's campaign centred on the Victoria East constituency, in the very heartland of the native political movement, including the town of Alice, later to be the home of Fort Hare University.[3] The native vote was mobilized on his behalf by one of the first mainstream black political activists of the age, newspaper editor John Tembo Jabavu. Thanks to Jabavu's marshalling of the black vote, Roses Innes succeeded to the Cape parliament, commencing a liberal political career that would culminate in his appointment as Chief Justice of the Union of South Africa between 1914 and 1927.

This represented the acme of plurality and political engagement at work, and one can imagine that at this pace of development, blacks would indeed begin to appear on the backbenches within a generation, and on the frontbenches soon after that. An ordered, peaceful and progressive development of black political organization in the colony would have resulted inevitably in a black prime minister, and a representative political institution that might, in practical terms, have led the world in the integration of the many races and cultures now intermingling and flourishing under the light of Britannia.

Forces less sanguine than this, however, were also at work. It is perhaps true that free access to the political process for non-whites in the Cape was the ideal until it began to influence the practical direction of matters.

Seated in the public gallery, and listening to Rhodes furiously defend the Glen Grey Act, was Jan Christiaan Smuts. The act had passed parliamentary muster, and had been granted the necessary royal assent, but so embittered was the liberal element that Rhodes was pushed into a corner, and forced frequently, both in the press and in debate, to defend his actions.

And what were the fundamentals of this controversial law?

The Glen Grey district of the Eastern Cape was a region of predominately native occupation in the vicinity of present-day Lady Frere, and north of the politically active settlement of Queenstown. It was this area that was chosen by Cecil John Rhodes, in his capacity as head of the cabinet and leader of government, to impose an experimental system of land tenure and taxation that was intended to fashion and influence native responses to modern life.

At that point Rhodes's perspective on the 'native problem' tended towards the paternal, articulated somewhat in one of his most oft-quoted comments on the matter, spoken seven years earlier on the self-same floor where he now defended his Glen Grey Act: 'The native is to be treated as a child and denied the franchise. We must adopt a system of despotism, such as works in India, in our relations with the barbarism of South Africa.'

This comment, the product of a very young and opinionated Cecil John Rhodes, nonetheless defines the common ideal of the Sacred Trust as well as any, and the key word is 'child'. Almost universally at that time, indigenous Africans were regarded as children, or child-like in terms of development and capabilities. On a scale of rational development, the black man of Africa was thought to belong in the Eden of life, in some as yet unidentified evolutionary niche, to be protected, and guided forth at the discretion of the civilized races.

The Glen Grey Act was a precursor to segregation, itself a precursor to apartheid, and premised on the notion that an overhasty inclusion of native Africans at the forefront of modern life was unwise, and a danger to European civilization. It stood to reason that, so recently liberated from primitive origins, the indigenous African would be far better served by a system of separate development that would not interfere unduly with traditional systems of life, law and government, but which would at the same time offer a phased and controlled entry into modern life.

An additional problem that Rhodes sought to contain through the terms of the Glen Grey Act was the rapid growth of the native population to a point where the capacity of land under communal occupation could no longer support it. He therefore proposed a taxation to be placed on each individual household that would force the non-productive members off the land and into the cash economy, in order to earn the coinage necessary to pay those taxes. At the same time, it was assumed that this would provoke a rapid embrace of consumerism, generating an increased need for money, and in consequence a greater movement away from the land and towards formal employment. The diverse effect of this would be to ensure a more rational and scientific use of the land, the creation of a black working class and a greater supply of labour to white farmers who could arguably make best use of it.

In the promulgation of the Glen Grey Act, Rhodes and a growing section of the parliamentary right wing sought to challenge the established liberal tradition, but were in general surprised to encounter such resilient opposition. The Glen Grey Act, therefore, was proposed just as an experimental constituency on the distant frontier as a template for this process, but should it prove beneficial – and who, indeed, was to be the judge of that – then inevitably it would be applied more widely. This was an ominous moment indeed, for a precedent was set, and an era of separation announced. It would seem that each time blacks knocked on the door, the door was fastened just a little tighter.

Is it possible that Jan Smuts sat in the public gallery and listened to all of this and failed to identify the obvious contradiction? Evidently this talk of unity and reconciliation across the racial divide did not apply to the natives. His essential philosophy required of him an acknowledgement that man and nature existed in a creative, evolutionary process tilted towards ultimate unity, and yet, instinctively, he was positioned to the right of these debates.

Although he could not as yet identify it, he nonetheless accepted the fundamental incompatibility of black and white. In common with many on the intellectual right, he was sensible to a superficial advance in black society – certainly some successes in education had been achieved – and a certain grasp of higher political concepts, but this need not be taken as a condition of the whole.

To Smuts, the evolution of the personality lay at the heart of the matter, and to understand how the native thought, Smuts would need to determine precisely what the native was. To him, the human personality was an actively evolving entity in search of perfect equilibrium and merger. A human being could be taught to speak words, but to understand those words, to absorb the philosophy of politics and law, the passion of beauty and art and the infinity of time, these came about as a consequence of character, and personality, and it was here, in his opinion, that the black man, no matter how educated, remained a child.

There is no evidence anywhere in the chronicle of Smuts's life to suggest that he ever held a serious discussion with a black man, and certainly not an African black man. How, therefore, he felt himself able to achieve an understanding of the black man it is impossible to say, but much of what he heard Cecil Rhodes say, he believed, simply because Rhodes said it. And what Rhodes said, in many permutations, was 'equal rights for all civilized men'.

At some point late in 1895, Smuts toured the republics, travelling for the first time to the Transvaal and the Orange Free State. The experience, of course, was educational, and although in no position to influence matters, he advocated passionately on Rhodes's behalf. On his return, he was invited by the De Beers debating society to address a meeting held in the Kimberley town hall, specifically to argue on Rhodes's behalf the merits of the Bond alliance, but inevitably he touched on the Glen Grey Act. 'The theory of democracy as currently understood,' he observed,

> and practised in Europe and America is inapplicable to the coloured races of South Africa … You cannot safely apply to the barbarous and semi-barbarous natives the advanced political principles and practices of civilization. Too often we make the mistake of looking upon democracy as a deduction from abstract principles, instead of regarding it as rather the outcome of practical politics.

One can imagine that in later years Smuts would have regretted deeply those utterances, but they nonetheless spoke very well to the right wing, and certainly they would have sat well in the republics. To him the capacity to exercise political responsibility was a matter of abstract personality, and he doubted sincerely, and continued to doubt, that under the superficial veneer of civilization, the native personality was capable of such an advance.

This sort of thing, however, so candidly expressed, scandalized one particular woman in the audience who had of late become rather fond of Smuts. This was Olive Schreiner. A few months earlier, Smuts had written admiringly of Olive Schreiner's *Stray Thoughts on South Africa*, and in gratitude she made a point of meeting and thanking him. She had also been on very friendly terms with Rhodes in the past, but excommunicated him at the moment that the Glen Grey Act was gazetted. Smuts she granted only the lien of his youth against a similar banishment and, of course, the infuriating fact that even the most absurd conjecture, when processed by Smuts, yielded slants and concepts that not even she had thought to explore.

In Smuts's defence, however, it might be worth noting that his use of the word 'barbarian' was in the contemporary context, still defined by the *Oxford English Dictionary* as a member of a community or tribe not belonging to one of the great civilizations, and one can certainly imagine that Smuts was easily able to so classify black Africans. The British, of course, stood at the zenith of civilization, but others such as Greeks, Romans and Egyptians he also admired. However, no monument south of the Sahara was he aware of that placed any black African culture among the great civilizations.

However, some thirty years earlier, a German-American hunter and explorer by the name of Adam Render happened to stumble upon an extensive complex of stone-built ruins on the central plateau of Mashonaland that proved, upon examination, to be the remnants of some great and ancient civilization.[4] The following season, Render guided German explorer and geographer Karl Mauch to the site, who made public the discovery, speculating, in the absence of any reasonable explanation, that the site was of biblical origin.

Obviously Mauch was entirely unable to embrace the possibility of an indigenous African society being capable of such architectural prowess. The native population of Mashonaland at that point comprised a politically fractured language group known as the maShona that appeared, on the surface, to be extremely primitive. The regionally dominant amaNdebele, a Zulu offshoot, on the other hand, although a powerful military nation, manifestly lacked even the basics of an advanced civic or artistic capability. Attempting to suggest that either group might have been responsible for this architectural masterpiece would have solicited such gales of defamation that there was none with the courage to attempt it.

Cecil John Rhodes, however, was fascinated by the discovery, and no sooner had his British South Africa Company occupied Mashonaland than he commissioned James Theodore Bent, an English archaeologist and explorer, to undertake a detailed excavation and archaeological analysis of what is now known as Great Zimbabwe. This unearthed a spectacular treasure trove of art and artefacts, many of which were absorbed into Rhodes's personal collection, and all of which alluded incontrovertibly to indigenous origins.

The entirety of this evidence, however, was ignored in favour of one particular wooden lintel thought to be of Lebanese origin, which was taken as incontrovertible proof that the original city had Semitic origins. Indeed, Bent theorized that this construction was a replica of the palace of the Queen of Sheba, and that the lintel in question had been imported by the

Phoenicians, and that the wealth that underwrote the emergence of such a city came from King Solomon's Mines.

Suffice to say, the maShona peoples did belong to an ancient and highly accomplished society, peaking during the seventeenth century, and declining thereafter. This society, known in part as the Kingdom of the Mwene Mutapa, the direct successor to the empire of Great Zimbabwe, was contacted and traded with by the earliest Portuguese explorers, but had largely disappeared by the time the first generation of modern Europeans arrived.

The point of this lengthy aside, however, is simply to illustrate the inability of nineteenth-century intellectuals and scholars, Jan Smuts among them, to equate great achievement with native African competence, and so therefore, the term 'civilized' tended to exclude blacks in the majority.

Chapter 13

The Great Betrayal

'I admire him, I frankly confess it; and when his time comes I shall buy a piece of the rope for a keepsake.'
—Mark Twain on Rhodes, *Following the Equator*

Having disposed of the Natal franchise, Joseph Chamberlain now turned his attention to the Transvaal, and the slow-boiling Uitlander crisis. The Uitlander crisis was the name given to an elaborate conspiracy that had its tentacles in Cape Town, Johannesburg and London, and which sought to hurry along matters, and influence the inevitable in the Transvaal.

The Uitlanders were the British and colonial outsiders, and although as colonial secretary, Chamberlain had no direct interest in their welfare, he was deeply interested in what their discontent could achieve. The Uitlanders were agitating for a curbing of official corruption in Pretoria, a loosening of state monopolies and political representation. To the right man, and under the right circumstances, a situation like this might represent a valuable opportunity.

It so happened that Cecil John Rhodes thought exactly the same thing, and although one might assume a commonality of interest, in fact both men were deeply suspicious of one another, and mistrustful of each other's motives.

Although of similar personality, Chamberlain nurtured no particular affection for Rhodes, and finding him brash and irresponsible, was disinclined to trust him. Their respective visions for South Africa differed too fundamentally. Chamberlain saw South Africa as a constituent of the world while Rhodes seemed now to see it *as* the world. Rhodes was driven by an almost religious vision, underwritten by pseudo imperialist objectives that, although for the most part legitimate, were not entirely removed from the secular implications of private control of the goldfields. He was perhaps too mesmerised by his own power, too certain of his own righteousness and too clear in the virtue of his objective. He lacked both Chamberlain's clear-sighted, long-term political gamesmanship and his global perspective. He had become irrational, driven and unpredictable.

Rhodes, however, was on the ground, and he had an organization, so clearly he had the jump on Chamberlain. Chamberlain took office on 29 June 1895, by which time rumours had already begun to circulate of a coup d'état of some sort building on the Rand.

In fact, the conspiracy was no secret at all. Between acts at the theatre, over bridge at the Rand Club or between polo sets at the gymkhana, discussion centred on little else. The scheme was hatched by Rhodes and his brother, Colonel Frank Rhodes, to include eventually a number of important commercial and political figures both in Whitehall and on the Rand.

From the moment that Joseph Chamberlain's appointment took effect, he began to field reports detailing Rhodes's indiscreet yarning on what precisely his solution to the Uitlander crisis would be. He spoke quite candidly of a filibuster, with very little attention paid to discretion, and most of his subordinates did likewise. The result was that the Transvaal government very quickly became aware that some sort of a coup d'état was in the planning.

A central player in the conspiracy was a man by the name of Leander Starr Jameson, an unlikely character to take to the stage of an imperial adventure such as this. He had been Rhodes's one-time physician and friend, later a frontier diplomat in the founding of Rhodes's territory of Rhodesia, and later still the ad hoc general who led a volunteer force to break the amaNdebele nation.[1] Like Rhodes, Jameson was bristling with hubris but, unlike Rhodes, he was well in body and, like a whippet, fixated only on the rabbit in his field of vision.

The fundamentals of the plot were simply to make use of Uitlander discontent to facilitate an armed seizure of the goldfields, followed by the installation of a temporary government in Johannesburg. This would precede annexation, with due recognition given to the private resources and capital of Cecil John Rhodes.

Drawn into the planning was Rhodes's inner circle of secretaries and administrators, mostly educated young men, who gaily fetched up the conspiracy and ran with it. The uprising was codenamed 'The Flotation', Jameson 'The Contractor', the many conspirators 'The Subscribers', the British high commissioner 'The Chairman' and the supply commissariat for Rhodes's private army 'The Rand Produce and Trading Syndicate'.[2]

Central to the scheme was the deployment of a large force of men loyal to Rhodes and his syndicate to some point close enough to Johannesburg for a lightning raid. A local base of operations was necessary for the sake of speed, and it was in regards to this that Chamberlain received his first official indication that something was up. Chamberlain heard a number of formal requests from Rhodes's people for administrative control of the Bechuanaland Protectorate or, failing that, the grant of a tract of land close to the Transvaal border for some purpose as yet unspoken.[3]

Chamberlain, of course, deduced easily that the objective was to garrison a small force of armed men – Jameson initially predicted 1,500 men – in readiness for a rushed takeover of Johannesburg. He eventually teased the facts out of his various visitors, and although officially he was obliged then to immediately distance himself from the scheme, under the table he asked to be kept informed and, making available a tract of territory in Bechuanaland, he covertly encouraged the conspirators to continue.

In the meanwhile, an amateur corps of clerks and secretaries went about the business of organizing the coup with the cheerful abandon of schoolboys at a midnight feast. Rhodes was by then so reduced by illness and fatigue that he allowed himself to be mollified by the assurances of men who had no idea of what they were taking on. Jameson, for example, a rather loosely packed and undisciplined character, airily declared on more than one occasion that a hundred men armed with *sjamboks* could carve a gap through a phalanx of Boers.[4] He had broken the back of a native kingdom, he had conquered a nation: why should he not take Johannesburg?

Sometime during this phase, Rhodes was visited in the Cape by British journalist Francis Younghusband, a name better remembered for soldiering and exploration. With the uncluttered view of an outsider, Younghusband identified a bewildering raft of flaws in Rhodes's planning. When he questioned Rhodes on the rumours afoot Rhodes was content to corroborate them all, without any attempt at evasion. Younghusband warned him that the conspiracy was bound to fail, for to his knowledge, there was no genuine appetite in Johannesburg for an uprising. In the midst of a financial boom, where every clerk, magistrate or administrator might well be a millionaire, what chance really would there be of enticing men to risk their lives in a pointless coup d'état? What was demanded by the majority of Uitlanders was simply a reform of the republic, not the revolution that was Rhodes's pipedream.

The long and the short of the Jameson Raid was that Rhodes got the jitters, realizing towards the eleventh hour that it would fail.[5] By then, however, it was too late, for Jameson had the bit between his teeth. Having recruited and assembled his army, he was poised on the border of the Transvaal and eagerly anticipating the call to arms. At that point he most certainly had no interest in calling the whole caper off.

Chamberlain, in the meanwhile, having made available a facility in British Bechuanaland for Jameson to base himself, then sought counsel on what precisely was taking place. A private coup d'état might ultimately be beneficial to the British, but whatever was going to happen, it needed to happen quickly. The Transvaal government had dispatched a deputation to Europe to highlight British predatory intentions in southern Africa, while in mid-December of that year, the United States, under President Grover Cleveland, threatened war with the British over a boundary dispute between Venezuela and British Guiana. For the time being, the Colonial Office would be able to deflect foreign protest at any unconstitutional action in South Africa, but should Europe organize in favour of the Transvaal, and Germany cement a US-backed alliance with Pretoria, the moment would be lost.

Ultimately, Jameson would ignore both the obvious dangers and the cables from many sources pleading him to postpone. He was poised at the head of a capable force, ample to invade and secure Johannesburg, and despite Rhodes gnawing his fingernails, he was determined that he would succeed. Selecting the advice that suited him, he and his men cut the cable lines, spurred their horses, and on New Year's Eve, 1895, rode valiantly across the open veld toward Johannesburg.

At the city gates, however, Jameson was astonished to encounter a full mobilization of the Transvaal civil defence, entirely forewarned by a catastrophic indifference to secrecy. His force of 600 was fought to a standstill within sight of the turning headgears, silhouetted against the dawn of the new year, and taken into custody without the mobilization of a single Uitlander militia to their aid.

When the news reached Rhodes later that day, he buried his head in his hands, and saw passing before his eyes the work of a short lifetime. His culpability was inescapable. Julius Caesar had once remarked that if a man must break the law, do it only to seize power, and in all other instances obey it. Rhodes had failed to seize power, so he had simply broken the law.

Chamberlain denied, and denied again, while Jameson shrugged his shoulders and entered the gates of the Fort prison with an air of tragic resignation. It had been a fair effort, and nothing inspired the British sense of heroism quite like the triumphant failure of amateurism. The news, however, immediately reverberated around the world, but apparently reached Jan Smuts only a few days later, as he lingered at his parents' home in Riebeek West for the last few days of the New Year holiday. A lengthy cable was delivered to him, perhaps through the offices of the Bond, of which he was by then a member, and perhaps bearing the signature of Jan Hofmeyr.

119

To these two men, and to Hofmeyr in particular, the grumbling discomfiture of the British political establishment meant nothing. The extradition of Jameson and his cohort to stand trial in Britain did not matter at all, and nor did the lengthy inquest that ultimately held no one to account. To them it was the utter disbelief struck by Rhodes's betrayal, followed by the humiliation of being among those few Cape Dutchmen who had most vocally supported him, and sworn to his integrity.

How was it possible that Rhodes, the Colossus, the man who stood at the Cape of Good Hope and cast his shadow north across the Zambezi, could have fallen so abruptly, and so far?[6] Why, after so many years of careful consensus-building and the care taken to cultivate trust and win friends, would Rhodes simply toss it all away on such a reckless throw of the dice?

The answer was simply the hand of death that lay heavy on his shoulder. If not now, then when? In two things Rhodes believed as a simple article of faith: strength in unity, and the God-given right of the English-speaking races to rule. In his mind there was no shred of doubt that once included in the Pax Britannica, the citizens of the Transvaal would rejoice.

And this might well have been so, but the cards did not fall that way, and he was disgraced. He was forced to resign his directorships, and step down as premier of the Cape Colony. Soon afterward he sailed to London to face the music, to return only when the yeast of his actions had risen, and the two races of South Africa did indeed stand on the threshold of war.

For the time being, however, Smuts remained in the Cape and pondered his future. His first lesson in politics and humanity could hardly have been more bitter. It would be a year or more before he could bring himself to speak again in public. In the meanwhile, he applied himself to burying his innocence in a deluge of written invective, condemning bitterly all that he had earlier supported.

We lift our voices in warning to England so that she may know that the Afrikaner Boer still stands where he stood in 1881.[7] If England sends Rhodes back to us the responsibility will be hers. The blood be on England's own head.

These were fighting words, spoken in recognition of a fight that was now inevitable. Rhodes had smashed the bridges, and the delicate trust that had taken root between Boer and Briton in South Africa had been obliterated. The sides separated, and war did indeed loom more clearly then than it ever had before.

Yet Smuts could not entirely release himself from the spell under which he had been cast. He did not forgive Rhodes – only much later would he do that – but he held firm to what Rhodes had taught him. Most men are content to settle into their yokes and tread their God-given number, but Rhodes was among the few who had done better. He had dreamed, and then stumbled and fallen, but he had dreamed no less.

Indeed, Rhodes's error could not erase their shared belief. In an empty office Smuts laboured furiously on his inner purging. He did not encourage visitors, nor solicit briefs. That part of his life was over. While the likes of Olive Schreiner and Betty Molteno were quick to say 'I told you so', Smuts wrote, while Hofmeyr buried his own humiliation in a furious moral assault against Rhodes. Nothing would pass between the two men until Rhodes's funeral six years later, on which occasion Hofmeyr put pen to paper only to write his condolences. On that same occasion, however, Smuts was moved to write of Rhodes that: '[He has an] amplitude of mind which throws a glamour around itself and draws men and undermines their independence in spite of themselves.'

Then, in something of a fit of pique, Smuts abandoned his British citizenship, turned his back on the Cape and threw his lot in with the republics. He was determined to abandon politics altogether, and concentrate on law. In September 1896, he placed on record his application for admission to the Transvaal Bar, establishing thereafter a practice in Commissioner Street, Johannesburg, but occasionally also lecturing in law just to pay the bills.

In the meanwhile, President Paul Kruger, now in his seventies, continued to rule the republic in the style of a biblical patriarch, presiding over a political system that Smuts would have found parochial to say the least. Johannesburg itself was undergoing rapid growth, awash with capital and transitioning briskly from the gold-rush economy of yore to a capital centre of global significance. Its English-speaking aspect did not endear it to Kruger, who in fact refused under any inducement to visit the city.

In Pretoria Kruger and his inner circle presided over a primitive system of government, characterized by informal administration, a pervasive cult of personality and institutionalized corruption. Kruger was a storied nepotist, and he ruled more or less by decree, acting often with questionable legality, and freely interfering with the judiciary.

Smuts, however, was asked one day to write a legal opinion on a particularly egregious transgression of this sort, which he did, coming out in favour of Kruger, who probably never read the judgement, but took notice of Smuts immediately. When the office of state attorney fell vacant, Kruger appointed Smuts to his first government position. The appointment met with some resistance, because Smuts was only 28, and unqualified under Transvaal immigration laws to hold a government position at all. Kruger, however, knew that a war was pending. He knew too that he would soon be dealing with some of the sharpest and most predatory minds of the British empire. At his side he wanted a man of intelligence and character, an English-speaking Boer who understood the British, but who hated them too. Men like Smuts were a rarity in the republics, and Kruger recognized in him the same value that had Rhodes before him, but arguably, he made better use of what he saw.

Chapter 14

The Disposition of God

'A larger number of men is of course required, but I take it that on the occasion of a great war men are both more easily obtained and fed than are transport animals.'
—George Henry Makins, *Surgical Experiences in South Africa, 1899–1900*

On 11 October 1899, the Boer republic of the Transvaal declared war against the British empire. With military garrisons deployed only haphazardly in the northern Cape and Natal, and despite lengthy sabre-rattling, British imperial forces were in the end taken largely unprepared. The Boers, on the other hand, had for months been quietly arming, introducing German personal and field weapons and priming the various district commandos to prepare for mobilization.

As a largely rural and pastoral society, the Boers valued community no less than they valued individualism, and with the skills of riding, hunting and field-craft integral to their culture, civil defence existed almost as a natural function of daily life. As a result, the raising and deployment of district commandos tended to be quick and relatively easy, and when war broke out the Boers were prepared, in the saddle and in the field long before the British.

Between October and November 1899, Boer commandos launched a series of lightning raids into Natal and the northern Cape, adopting almost from the onset a poorly planned siege strategy focused on the three British garrison towns of Ladysmith in Natal, and Kimberley and Mafeking in the northern Cape. In the extensive scholarship applied to Anglo-Boer War in the years since, the general conclusion has tended to be that an ageing Boer leadership embarked on the campaign without innovation, repeating the tactics of old wars and ignoring the suggestions of younger men who perhaps had a clearer sense of what was afoot.

Jan Smuts was one of these. He was no military man, of course, but in the tense preamble to the declaration, it was he who had presented the most coherent blueprint for the initial phase of the war. He proposed a rapid seizure of the main ports on the east and south coasts in order to halt, or at least inhibit the inevitable landing of a British expeditionary force. The republican Boer might then relatively easily have allied with the Cape Dutch, after which, with the combined weight of three allied territories, and with its ports secured, the Natal colony would have fallen relatively easily.

Thereafter, a negotiated accommodation with the British would have introduced far more advantageous terms of settlement, and the grand republic would have come into being. The British, however, made up for a lack of manpower with guile, manipulating the simplicity and paranoia of the Boer leadership with a feint tactic. Two minor British colonial regiments (the Rhodesia and Protectorate regiments) were formed and deployed as a decoy along the northern frontier between the Transvaal and Bechuanaland, which immediately ignited a fear within the Boer high command that a repeat of the Jameson Raid was underway. This deflected energy and attention away from the wiser strategy, resulting in the wasting of time and resource on the fruitless sieges of Mafeking and Kimberly, and likewise, the rather pointless Boer obsession with holding the siege of Ladysmith.

Two major actions, however, were fought in Natal before the closing of these sieges – the battles of Talana Hill and Elandslaagte – which, although tactical victories for the British, were fought at the cost of a great many British lives, and not necessarily followed up to any particular advantage. Nonetheless, the atmosphere in Natal at the time, and in Durban in particular, was tense, with mobilization and military preparation absorbing the entire energies of the white political and military establishment. A great many refugees from the interior of the colony found their way into Durban, and to satisfy their needs, and the general requirements of the military commissariat, Indian merchants and tradesmen found themselves enjoying a considerable economic boom.

In all of this hubris and upheaval, however, Gandhi identified what he felt was a unique opportunity, mixed in with which was also something of a conundrum. His perennial argument then, as it remained throughout his campaign in South Africa, was simply that, as subjects of the British empire, Indians were owed the same fundamental rights and privileges as white subjects of the same empire. This was an issue upon which, time and again, he made a principled stand. However, he was sensible also to the fact that with rights there came responsibilities, and if Indians demanded equal treatment, then they ought by extension to be prepared to accept equal responsibility. Thus, if Britain was preparing for war in South Africa, it was incumbent on the Indians to declare loyalty to the Crown, and to volunteer for active service.

One of the chief criticisms levelled against Indians at this time, in particular by the pathologically anti-Indian *Natal Mercury*, was the tendency of Indians to be clannish, insular and hoarding of their capital. It was often stated that the military relationship established between black and white in Natal gave each a right to title, but the Indians were inclined to equivocate, to keep to themselves and to export their wealth against the day when they would inevitably return home. Indians, it was claimed, were parasitical, and apt at the moment of crisis to take to transport ships and flee the colony for fresh pastures elsewhere.

This position was difficult to deflect against the steady arrival in Natal of large numbers of Indian merchants and traders decamping the Transvaal at the moment that shots were fired. Most took refuge under British protection, but many also dispersed to Portuguese East Africa, Kenya, Zanzibar and India. The British commercial and capital element, on the other hand, held firm, or formed improvised imperial units that were coalescing across the two colonies. Johannesburg and the Witwatersrand declared more or less openly for the British, and for the time being at least, the mine headgears continued to turn.

The opportunity, therefore, was for Gandhi to find a way to incorporate Indians into the defence of the colony, in order to illustrate under challenging circumstances that Indians in the colonies were loyal to the Crown. The conundrum, however, lay in the fact that the independent Boers were staking life and liberty in a struggle against the same bellicose British imperialism that inspired Indian resistance. Of all the various claimants and stakeholders in South Africa at the time, the Boers were alone in their commitment to the soil upon which they fought. The British, of course, saw South Africa only in the context of global empire, and Indians maintained above all an Indian identity, but the Boers regarded themselves as African, as sons of the soil, and they fought for no higher or alternative identity than this.

Gandhi thus found himself in rather a quandary, complicated even further by the fact that the Boers did not invite Indian sympathy, and in fact tended to be even more instinctively prejudicial towards Indians than the British. Other than in the alliance of a common enemy, there was nothing to bind Boer and Indian in common cause at all. The British, on the other hand, in the preamble to the war, had listed the assault against British rights and privileges in the Transvaal republic (the Uitlander Crisis) as their principal reason for provoking war, and lumped together with the general British population in the Transvaal were Indians. It was generally perceived, not only by Indians, but blacks too, that a British victory would see the Cape system adopted territory wide, as a minimum British standard, and so in general the black spokesmanship in the rural and urban areas urged support for the British, which might perhaps have lent Gandhi some encouragement.

There was, nonetheless, and not for the last time, some ideological inconsistency in his position, but he adopted a pro-British stance in spite of this, perhaps masking a slight odour of hypocrisy with the assurance, to himself at least, that under a fair and equal British dispensation, the Boer would enjoy the same high standards of liberty and equality as blacks and Indians. Naturally he disregarded the nuances of Boer history in this regard, and undervalued political independence as a motivation for resistance, temporarily placing the Indian demand for precisely that lower down on his scale of moral priorities.

On 17 October 1899, a week or so after the declaration of war, he called a meeting of senior members of the Natal Indian community, including a handful from the Transvaal, which was held in a community hall at the Juma Masjid mosque on Grey Street. To these men he proposed a motion that the combined Indian communities of South Africa throw their weight behind the British, and freely volunteer their resources and manpower to the imperial war effort. He did not go so far as to support a call to arms, but suggested instead the formation of an Indian ambulance detachment that would satisfy the non-violent principles of the movement, but at the same time illustrate in clear terms Indian loyalty to the imperial cause.

Gandhi was then just 30 years old. He had been resident in the Natal colony for five years, and in that time he had established himself as spokesman for the Indian movement, but was not yet its leader. His popularity and support were not universal, and there were quite a number among those influential members present who felt that he had already been responsible for more trouble than he was worth. The politically active elements of the community were in general the younger and less propertied members, whose voices often tended to be more audible, but whose influence was also minimal. The real power of the community lay in its wealthy members, and its religious elite – those traditionally conservative elements – and there were men among the former who were certainly very wealthy indeed.

In his later memoirs and chronicles, Gandhi has tended to paint a picture of this moment as one of unanimity and commitment to the struggle, and solidarity under his leadership, but this was by no means the case. He fought an uphill struggle to convince the wealthy elite of Durban that this was a wise course of action, and in fact in this regard he largely failed. The argument against him was simply that the advantages of political parity and equality under the law had been overstated, and were generally a matter of principle rather than tangible advantage. The elite among Indians were not disadvantaged; they commanded between them comparable wealth to the white community, and in a few cases much more, and so long as conditions for trade and business in the colony remained robust and secure, there was no reason under the sun to assume any posture other than one of absolute ambivalence.

What, the question was asked, would happen if the Boer emerged from this war victorious, how would the partisanship of the Indian community then be regarded? A neutral position was the wisest course of action, to which Gandhi threw up his arms in despair. That, he argued, would simply confirm British prejudices that the Indians were simply in it for themselves, and would cut and run at the first hint of danger. Indians were demanding equal rights not only in Natal, but elsewhere in the empire too, and such a demand had to be balanced by the same degree of commitment. The Indians, he insisted, were duty-bound now to commit to the war on the side of the British.

In the end the meeting broke up without unanimity, and it would be only Gandhi's more radical associates, and various volunteers from among the lower-caste Tamils and Telugus that would make up the core of the proposed ambulance corps. To soften what might have been construed as a defeat, and to present the wealthy elite with a more equivocal option, Gandhi established a Patriotic League, to serve as a receptacle for cash donations, a vehicle for fundraising and a means of supporting the families of volunteers.

Having established a degree of Indian willingness to cooperate in this scheme, Gandhi then faced the difficulty of persuading the military and civil authorities of Natal to allow an Indian ambulance corps to serve at all. He lobbied Harry Escombe, who had by then joined his ever-widening circle of European friends, and who had served briefly a few years earlier the office of premier of the Natal colony. It might be wrong to claim that Harry Escombe had become a friend of the Indian civil rights movement in South Africa, but his position had certainly been softened considerably by his acquaintance with Gandhi, and he was certainly sympathetic to Gandhi's interest in presenting the Indians as loyal subjects of the Crown.

A traditionally implacable enemy of all things Indian in Natal was ex-premier John Robinson, editor and owner of the *Natal Mercury*, who made it his business to lampoon and decry the Indians at any opportunity. However, even he softened his position somewhat, reporting the heroic role played by Indians in the two opening battles of Talana Hill and Elandslaagte.

Both engagements had been attended by a detachment of professional Indian Army stretcher bearers, otherwise known as *dhoolie*-bearers, who were typically included as an element of any major British expeditionary force of the period.[1] Of these men Robinson had this to say:

> [Their] courage and fidelity have been of the utmost value. At the Talana Hill battle, during the heaviest fighting, when bullets were scouring the air, and men were falling dead and wounded in terrible numbers, these stoical and stolid Asiatics went about their business with heroic indifference to the leaden rain. It is due to them very largely that so many wounded were not afterwards numbered among the killed.[2]

The success of this detachment of Indian ambulance men prompted a call for volunteers from among the ranks of the Indian indentured workers of the countryside. This call was not made to the Indians themselves, of course, but to their employers, who committed the services of their contracted workers on the basis of hours and wages. Here, however, Gandhi saw another opportunity, and presented himself and his better educated colleagues as the obvious leaders of this body of men. Thus he marshalled together a respectable corps of prospective ambulance men, and arranged with the head of the Anglican Indian Mission to Natal, the Reverend Dr Lancelot Parker Booth, a brief but comprehensive course of medical training.[3]

Thus fortified, both Gandhi and the Reverend Booth travelled to Pietermaritzburg, the territorial capital of Natal, and there presented themselves before a panel consisting of the governor, the colonial secretary and various senior medical officers. Gandhi explained that, having with some difficulty gained the acquiescence of his community, and placed it in a state of readiness, there would be great disappointment if the Indian offer of assistance to the war effort was rejected.

Although not insensible to the obvious political overtones of this proposition, the panel in the end conceded in the face of ongoing and urgent appeals from front line medical services for fresh orderlies and bearers. On many levels this was a moment of triumph for Gandhi, and in conclusion there were handshakes and congratulations, and numerous mutual expressions of apparently genuine goodwill and gratitude. Obviously this alliance of Indian and white would be temporary, and would not long survive

128

the war itself, but there was without doubt the achievement of a far greater degree of understanding, and a meeting of minds that could hardly but have influenced matters then, and into the future.

Prior to their departure for the battlefield, Gandhi and the leaders of his first batch of Indian volunteers attended a civic reception at the home of Harry Escombe. The Indian effort was commended on behalf of the empire, and various civic dignitaries, John Robinson among them, gathered to thank them, and wish them god-speed. To this Gandhi replied, not without some ironic humour, that the martial credentials of his countrymen would have been better served had a division of Ghurkhas or Sikhs been imported, but he nonetheless expressed the hope that his humble detachment would do their duty. With that, the party broke up, after which various first-, second- and third-class railway tickets were issued in order that volunteers might travel to the front lines in degrees of comfort appropriate to their castes.

The Natal Indian Ambulance Corps saw action in two key battles – Colenso and Spioen Kop – both of which were bruising defeats for the British. The volunteers arrived in the midst of the former engagement, marching onto the front lines from a nearby railway station, and beginning immediately to transport wounded from dressing stations to the railway station, and from there to various field hospitals.

This was the commencement of a harrowing few months for Gandhi, who remained at the head of the volunteer force throughout its deployment. His account of the experience makes no mention whatsoever of his own discomfort or trauma, which can hardly be understated bearing in mind his nature, and his frail, protein-starved physique. Much, however, is recorded of his disappointment in observing that his men were consistently treated on the battlefield as second-class servicemen. They were relegated to the rear of the queue in matters of rations, supplies and transport, and when no tents were issued they were forced to sleep in the open during the wet season when rain and humidity were constant.

Colenso was followed by the battle of Spioen Kop, fought over 23/24 January 1900. On this occasion, however, the Indians were pressed into the firing line, ferrying British dead and wounded under active fire across open ground, registering occasional shots directed at one or other of their number.

By the end of their deployment, over 1,000 Natal Indians from various origins had been active on the field. Spioen Kop was the last major battle in Natal, and soon afterwards the siege of Ladysmith was lifted, and for all intents and purposes the war in Natal was over. The Natal Indian Ambulance

Corps was disbanded soon afterwards, and 34 of its members, Gandhi among them, were awarded the Queen's South Africa Medal.

Concluding this episode, however, it might perhaps be worth noting that Gandhi was saddened by a snub delivered to the Indians that might on the surface appear rather trivial, but which has nonetheless has lingered in the memory of the Natal Indian experience. In the aftermath of Spioen Kop, an issue of chocolate was made to all the men who had taken part. This was a highly prized limited edition of 'Queen's Chocolate' packed in a gold-embossed tin case, inscribed with the field of battle and decorated by a cameo portrait of Her Majesty. Inside each tin was a note wishing a happy new year to each soldier on behalf of Victoria Regina.

This gesture, however, was not extended to the Indians, nor any of the black orderlies and labourers present at the battle, and when Gandhi queried this oversight, it was explained to him that the chocolate had been intended only for the fighting ranks. Gandhi nonetheless accepted his award of the Queen's South Africa Medal, which he kept until 1920 when it was returned to the British authorities alongside various other civic service awards that he received as a consequence of his humanitarian work in South Africa. This was in compliance with his attitude of non-cooperation with the British government in protest at its continued occupation of India. Gandhi's medals are now part of the collection held by Nehru Memorial Museum & Library in New Delhi.

Chapter 15

Of Passive and Violent Resistance

'[T]hat they will raise India with them rather than rise upon its ruins.'

—Gandhi, 1901

The century changed, and the world turned. By the end of 1900, it had become clear that the British would prevail in South Africa. The Boers were in retreat. Those early victories at Colenso and Spioen Kop, and the closure of the sieges in Natal and the Cape, were turned back as soon a major expeditionary force made landfall at the Cape. By mid-March of that year, Bloemfontein had fallen and, finally, on 5 June, Pretoria was occupied.

Until then, Jan Smuts had spent no time at all at the front, but had remained in office in Pretoria, almost single-handedly maintaining government function as the tide of war turned. With the collapse of the Orange Free State, however, the fate of the Transvaal was sealed, and President Kruger and his cabinet took to a train carriage and fled in the direction of Portuguese East Africa. At various points along the way, a style of government was briefly sustained, before inevitably the administration disintegrated, and the decision was made to move the ageing Kruger across the frontier and into Portuguese East Africa.

At that point, the British might well have concluded that the war was over, and by conventional reckoning it was. However, as the military commanders settled into occupation, and readied themselves to receive the surrender, to their utter astonishment the Boers simply abandoned the capital, broke up into commandos and dispersed into the hinterland from where the long and bitter guerrilla phase of the war began.

Here Smuts embarked on an unexpected transition. During the initial planning phase of the war, he submitted to the military leadership a blueprint for a strategic deployment that would have seen a greater emphasis on securing the seaports. With the collapse of the conventional defence,

131

however, and upon the determination of the rank and file to see the struggle through, it was he who composed the basic guerrilla strategy that would carry the war to its next phase.[1] In its simplest terms, his strategy required the engagement of the Cape Dutch community in the war on the side of the republics. If this could be achieved, the basis of British control of the capitals might conceivably be undermined, and even at that eleventh hour, a reverse effected. Upon that, he exchanged his quill and chambers for a rifle, and taking to the saddle, he joined the commandos in the field.

Initially he was placed under the command of an ageing but competent field commander by the name of Jacobus 'Koos' de la Rey, assuming a junior command position primarily because of his civilian status. Very quickly, however, and rather to the surprise of his superiors, this retiring and introspective technocrat began to display an aggressive and intuitive instinct for command. Under the patronage of de la Rey, he quickly grasped the essentials of strategy and leadership, to the extent that before long he was granted his own sectoral command, and was thereafter elevated within the informal hierarchy of the commandos to the rank of general.

It is worth pointing out that few if any Boer commando leaders had undergone formal military training such as the British would have understood it, so the evolution of tactics tended to be extemporized and rather informal. The award of titles and accolades was likewise, and if the ranks chose to refer to a man as general, then general he became. And even though Smuts by his nature was aloof, typically to be found alone, his hands more familiar with the pages of Kant's *A Critique of Pure Reason* than the mechanism of his rifle, he was blessed with the unforeseen virtues of courage, charisma and luck.

Smuts's war record is now the stuff of military legend, and this unanticipated introduction to war set in motion one of the most startling and brilliant military careers of the age. For the purpose of this narrative, however, just two episodes might suffice to sketch a brief portrait of Smuts the military commander.

During the last year of the war, Smuts was named to lead an extended commando raid into the Cape Colony. He had argued, and it was generally agreed that if the Cape Dutch community, which had throughout the war remained neutral, could be brought actively into the conflict, the balance of victory, even at the eleventh hour, might be tipped.[2]

Although the greater strategic objective was not achieved – the Cape Dutch remained out of the war – the Cape raid was nonetheless a remarkable tactical success insofar as some 350 mounted men successfully remained at large in the colony until the war was eventually concluded by treaty. Although hounded relentlessly by British and loyal columns, it succeeded in remaining operational, at times penetrating to within 150 miles of Cape Town itself.

The most authoritative account of this chapter of the war is that recorded by notable South African soldier and memoirist, Deneys Reitz, writing in his celebrated *Commando: A Boer Journal of the Boer War*. A sobering episode is recounted of General Smuts dealing with a traitor, a man by the name of Lemuel Colaine, a Cape colonist who had been received in Smuts's camp upon a tale of escaping from the British, and wishing now to take up arms against them. However, Colaine proved to be a spy, and when captured was subject to a short tribunal before being sentenced to death by Smuts himself, and shot shortly afterwards at the end of a shallow grave.

Although more has been observed and written by others about this episode than Smuts himself, he on occasion verbally disputed Reitz's version, claiming that Colaine had been granted a correctly constituted military trial, given representation and, upon a detailed examination of his case, was duly convicted and sentenced by committee. Reitz, however, stood by his version, and although salutary killings and executions were common on the front – Boer combatants were shot immediately upon being discovered wearing items of British uniform – this was the only incident of its kind on Smuts's war record.

Often in pursuit of Smuts and his Cape commando was British colonel John French, a cavalry officer of the old school with a record of imperial service that included Sudan and India. French developed a tremendous admiration for Smuts as he commanded British pursuit operations, turning up frequently with a mouth full of proverbial feathers as Smuts and his men galloped over the distant horizon.

In the years following the war, French was frequently heard to relate the anecdote of his grant of permission to a small group of Boers who approached his garrison under a flag of truce, to be allowed to bury their dead. The Boer party was held briefly during the conduct of operations before being released with the Christmas gift of a small box of cigars and a bottle of whisky for its commander, Commandant Christiaan Frederick Beyers. Beyers, touched by this gesture, responded by releasing two British cavalrymen who had been captured a few days earlier, returning them to their camp mounted and with full kit.

Smuts, when many years later the tale was told to him by French, is said to have contemplated it for some time, before remarking that Beyers had made improper use of property that belonged not to him but to his country, and ought, by rights, to have been disciplined.

The conventional phase of the war was substantively commanded by Field Marshal Lord Frederick Roberts, who relinquished command as soon as the capitals were occupied, handing over to his chief of staff Lieutenant-General Lord Kitchener, who was then left to deal with the very messy business of mopping up.

Kitchener, despite emerging as one of the most celebrated British career soldiers of the era, was generally regarded among those who knew him as being rather unimaginative, and tending to compensate for a lack of original strategy with a surfeit of arrogance and no small amount of ruthlessness. Thus, when confronted with the mercurial tactics of the Boers, at liberty to range freely over a battlefield of their choosing, he responded with mass infantry sweeps, scorched earth and the arbitrary containment of the rural population.

The result of this was the obliteration of Boer production, the shattering of the pastoral community and an assault on the core values of Boer society. Women, children and the elderly were gathered and contained in camps, the first institutionalized use of concentration camps as a weapon of war. This experience defined the darkest aspect of the Anglo-Boer War, and has troubled the British imperial legacy ever since.

Ultimately it was public disquiet in Britain over the horrific conditions in these camps – some forty-five in total – that swung metropolitan opinion toward a settlement. It had been the work of an early generation of primarily female social activists, Emily Hobhouse principal among them, that had alerted the British public and liberal establishment to what was taking place. This prompted, among others, leader of the liberal opposition Henry Campbell-Bannerman to criticize Kitchener by asking what kind of legacy was being created in South Africa by such barbarity as this.

Kitchener was apt then to fulminate against Campbell-Bannerman in private, and about Emily Hobhouse very much in public, famously referring to her as 'that bloody woman', which became her epithet, and one that she wore from then on with considerable pride.

Smuts made the acquaintance of Emily Hobhouse during the period of reconstruction, and granted her the recognition of the Boer people for the work that she had done, not only directly in administering to the ill and starving in the camps, but in the relentless campaign of awareness that she fought. Others contributed to this too, among them Olive Schreiner, activist and explorer Mary Kingsley, Florence Nightingale and the Quaker sisters Margaret Gillett and Alice Clark.

In the meanwhile, peace, when it came, came abruptly. Smuts was summoned to a meeting of the Boer leadership that the British convened for the purpose of negotiating an end to the war. He and his entourage were escorted from their camp in the northern Cape to Port Nolloth, then aboard a troop ship to the Cape, and from there by train to the Transvaal.

Smuts had just turned 31, and the experience of war had hardened him considerably. Sunburned and bearded, there seemed to be little remaining of the fair-skinned youth of yore. He was a man now accustomed to command, and unintimidated by the likes of Lieutenant-General Kitchener, when the two met. Kitchener, indeed, arrived alongside Smuts's train for a brief consultation mounted on a black charger, and escorted by a company of Pathan troops in full ceremonial dress.

The two men were formally introduced, after which Kitchener seated himself opposite Smuts, his blue eyes hooded, his black hair parted slightly to the left and his polished boot tapping on the linoleum floor. The Boers were finished, he told Smuts with a minimum of preamble, the war could go on, of course, but the ultimate conclusion was now self-evident. If the Boers would agree to lay down their arms, the language of defeat might be tempered by an agreed peace, after which the British would be found neither unreasonable nor ungenerous.

It is easy to imagine the titanic confidence instilled in a man like Kitchener, by the weight of his command, but also by his arrogance, supported by the institutions of His Majesty, and further reinforced by the tide of history. All of these, however, would have been considerably unbalanced by the expressionless appraisal of a young General Smuts, candidly measuring his opponent, revealing nothing, but hiding also none of the utter loathing that the presence of his enemy inspired.

This Kitchener would have felt keenly as he left that meeting, remounting his horse and trotting off with the burnish of his pretension tarnished by he knew not what. Kitchener could claim a respectable standard of intelligence, polished to the extent that it was possible at the Royal Military Academy of Woolwich, and then let loose upon an institution that seldom rewarded brilliance, but he had nothing with which to answer Smuts, and he knew it.

A more pleasing visit for Smuts was that of General John French, far more inclined than Kitchener to reward his opponent for a race well run. He arrived aboard the train with a ramrod-straight deportment, a stiff military salute and a keen, clear-eyed smile that reflected the pleasure of a man who had long anticipated this meeting.

French had no mandate to soften his opponent up for the knife. Nothing of the sort. His was the simple task of liaison, to put Smuts at his ease, and one can easily imagine his ringing laughter as Smuts informed him that a little over a year earlier, the two men had passed within feet of one another as Smuts and his men had attempted to derail a British military train with faulty explosives. As the train had sped by, Smuts had glanced up, and briefly observed French seated in a first-class compartment.

By this visit Smuts was touched, and some of his old admiration for the British was rekindled. However, the tide of history moved on, and as cordial to one another as these erstwhile enemies were, matters returned to the question of politics and diplomacy, and the necessity to balance the pride of a defeated race with the expectations of victory. And haste was necessary, for already the British imperial establishment had begun to glance over its shoulder at the quickening pace of armament in Europe, German naval advancement and the growing militancy of the Central Powers.

Chapter 16

Peace

'A mind all logic is like a knife all blade. It makes the hand bleed that uses it.'

—Ravindranath Tagore

Responsibility for negotiating on behalf of the British empire fell to two men. The first was Lord Kitchener, a military man, and although an imperfect diplomat, he had at least been present at the finish. His clear-sighted and uncomplicated perspective balanced out the profound emotion of the Boers, and also, perhaps, the rather narrow, ideological approach of his partner, and ostensible senior, a man by the name of Alfred Milner.

Alfred Milner, a name resonant in South African history, was a man loved neither by the British nor the Boer. He already had some history in South Africa, departing the territory prior to the outbreak of war as British high commissioner, and returning in the aftermath as governor-general, the roles in this instance being somewhat interchangeable. It was his official responsibility to craft the peace, but it was his ideological obsession to ensure that that peace favoured the British, and that South Africa be re-forged as a British colony with an indelible British complexion.

On the Boer side, a committee of military commanders and community elders represented the extremes of attitude – from the 'bitter-enders' determined to fight on to the death, to those who argued for peace with honour. All were guided by the technical expertise of Smuts, and no less his unemotional, legal perspective that bridged the inconceivable reality of defeat with a pragmatic sense of what was possible in the future.

Milner was a name already well known to Smuts, and vice versa. The former's earlier mission to South Africa – as British high commissioner – had been largely to pick a fight with the republics upon the general advice and guidance of Joseph Chamberlain. The British establishment at that point realized that a solution to the South African crisis was urgently required, and if war was that solution, then let it be so. Milner arrived in South Africa with the expectation that he would be dealing with an uneducated corps of rural burghers, around whom he would easily run circles, but instead he encountered the 29-year-old state attorney, Jan Christiaan Smuts, whom he very quickly came to despise.

In the winter of 1899, these two protagonists met for the first time in a freshly painted office of the Railway Department headquarters in Bloemfontein. In diplomatic terms, Milner was meeting the president of the republic, Paul Kruger, but in practical terms it was Smuts who represented the face of the republic. Milner, crisply attired, square-jawed and high-browed, could hardly have contrasted more sharply with Kruger, who sat sunk in the embrace of a stinking frockcoat buttoned to the neck, unwashed and saturated with the smell of heavy shag tobacco. Beside him, however, sat Smuts, dressed as he always was, his pianist's fingers nervously tapping the table top, his intellect discharging and quivering with the disciplined energy of a whippet.

Milner, however, although perhaps not his intellectual equal, was certainly Smuts's professional superior, and not by any means was he in a mood to be trifled with. It irritated him immeasurably that this over-empowered presidential understudy presumed to glare at him with those steel-blue eyes, and threaten him with barbed innuendo, and flashes of incendiary brilliance. Smuts might have impressed his opponent in an abstract way, but Milner was neither moved nor overawed.

Smuts and Kruger were representing a weak republic on the ropes, while Milner stood proxy for a global empire at the zenith of its powers. The question remained fundamentally the Uitlander franchise supported by a handful of other smaller issues. Kruger grumbled, dabbed his ailing eyes with a handkerchief and conferred with Smuts in whispered Dutch so colloquial that neither of Milner's official interpreters could make head or tail of it.

It was an unequal contest, however, and as Kruger yielded, so Milner advanced. In this tournament of degrees, Smuts either could not, or simply would not display his customary tact and restraint. He was young and arrogant, and of course profoundly enraged. Milner ignored him, and while clearly bristling with hatred, maintained his composure, enraging Smuts with a refusal to engage.

In the end, of course, the inevitable occurred. Kruger was goaded to the point of an ultimatum, demanding that the British remove all forces from the borders of the Transvaal. This caused the British delegation to snigger into their mitts, and the political establishment at home to double up in mirthful derision at the sheer audacity of it.

Kruger then left Bloemfontein, and in many respects the political stage, returning to Pretoria deeply resigned. He was 74 years old, and age had been unkind to him. Smuts accompanied him, returning the old president wearily to his home before repairing to his offices on Church Square, were, as the hours of the ultimatum slipped by, he immediately took control of the non-military affairs of government.

Smuts's sheer ability, and the almost limitless faith shown in him by the president, left him at liberty to unleash his energy on every department of government, which he freely did. He had by then acquired the nickname of Slim Jannie. The word *slim*, translated directly from the Dutch means clever or smart, but in the idiom-rich Afrikaans language, it might also be taken to mean sly, crafty or cunning, and certainly Smuts had the capacity to be all of these. Indeed, an interesting series of tit-for-tat actions between the British and Transvaal governments gave an early and unexpected glimpse into the inner working of both his and Milner's minds.

Milner had, of course, complained loud and frequently that Smuts was far too absorbed in his own intelligence to be taken seriously, and that he could not be trusted, which was in both instances a blatant case of the pot calling the kettle black. Milner was himself, among other things, a shrewd card player, perhaps even a card-sharp. He tended to play fair only when he had a fair hand to play with, and crying foul against Smuts, who at that moment held a bust, was uncharitable at the very least.

Smuts's problem was the Uitlanders, the wild card in the British pack. He took note of the fact that the Uitlanders had been unusually quiet during the tense weeks of negotiation, but, now that a declaration of war was inevitable, there was evident in Johannesburg an air of strutting and insolent confidence. Who controls the purse controls the destiny, and it bothered Smuts that the Uitlanders held that particular card.

He determined to intimidate the British in Johannesburg by ordering the arrest of a number of senior British military officers on spurious charges of spying. One can presume that he hoped to provoke an outcry from the British in the Cape, gambling perhaps on Milner demanding their unconditional release, upon which he could point to the bullying tactics of the British. Milner, however, insisted on a trial, to which Smuts responded by ordering the further arrest of the editor of the pro-British *Transvaal Leader*. This proved to be a step too far, however, prompting such a terrific uproar among British both in South Africa and at home that Smuts immediately retreated, issuing a public statement that cleared himself and blamed a subordinate.

Three years later, with the war now behind them, Milner and Smuts found themselves once again on opposing sides of the table, this time over the process of surrender. For a long time prior to this Jan Smuts had meditated, and written widely on the picture forming in his mind of a future South Africa. His inclination was to state powerfully the commitment of the *volk* to the land. Those urban, English-speaking capitalists and invaders held only a temporary tenancy of the ground underfoot. It was the Boer alone who owned the country, and who belonged absolutely to that abstract object of homeland. He was bitterly condemnatory of the British, and insistent that the independence of the Boer was sacrosanct.

Milner, however, pictured an entirely different future. Surrender and independence were inimical. There would be no question of Boer independence under a vague acknowledgement of British hegemony. Full and absolute British sovereignty, and English as the language of state, was Milner's minimum negotiating position.

It is therefore fortunate, perhaps, that initial negotiations were conducted by Kitchener, who was entirely disenchanted with a war that gave him no credit, and which obstructed his appointment to India where his immediate future lay. He was prepared, therefore, to concede a little more than Milner, but certainly not Boer independence. Annexation of the republics had taken place, and each was already under military administration, pending full colonial control as soon as the way was clear.

On the sidelines, however, Kitchener took Smuts to one side, and reminded him that an electoral victory for the Liberals was just around the corner, and why not wait until then before bringing up such challenging questions as responsible government and home rule. The Conservatives, after all, had presided over a costly war, so allow them at least the savour of victory before expecting them to return the country to its owners.

By the time Milner fetched up the baton, Smuts and his colleagues had come to accept the inevitability of British rule. Smuts, in his concluding speech – he had been a key adviser, but only latterly a practical negotiator – made the point that the war could go on, for with 18,000 salted veterans still in the field, any amount of mischief could still be done. But was the preservation of the Boer republics really worth the obliteration of the Boer people?

And of the native issue, and by extension the Indian issue, or any issue for that matter outside of the interests of the two combatant races, Slim Jannie played his hand well. In Milner's original draft proposal, it had been stated that the franchise 'would not be granted to the native until representative government had been achieved', which Smuts altered to read that

Gandhi, the Transvaal lawyer.

Gandhi in about 1894.

Gandhi in 1908.

With the Stretcher-Bearer Corps,
15   Zulu Rebellion

Gandhi during the Bambatha Rebellion, 1906.

Gandhi during the visit of Indian political leader Gopal Krishna Gokhale to South Africa, Durban, 1912. Below row, center, from left: Dr Hermann Kallenbach, Gandhi, Gokhale, Parsee Rustomjee.

Gandhi with Sonia Schlesin and Hermann Kallenbach, 1913.

The Great March.

Dadabhai Naoroji.

Jan Smuts, 1916. (Courtesy of Chris Cocks)

Jan Smuts, 1900. (Courtesy of Chris Cocks)

Lord Salisbury.

Cecil John Rhodes.

Elizabeth Maria Molteno.

Olive Schreiner.
(Courtesy of Chris
Cocks)

Paul Kruger.

Smuts in about 1914.

Joseph Chamberlain. (Courtesy of Chris Cocks)

General Lord Kitchener. (Courtesy of Chris Cocks)

Jan Hofmyer.

John Dube.

Leander Starr
Jameson.

Henry Campbell-
Bannerman.

Lionel Curtis.

Louis Botha.

William Phillip
Schreiner.

John Merriman.

THE CHINESE PAUL PRY

CHINESE LABOURER. "I hope I don't intrude?"
BRITISH COLONIST. "Yes, you *do*. Get out!"

(*December 16, 1903*)

Punch Cartoon.

James 'Barry' Munnik Herzog.

Smuts at Cambridge.

Alfred Milner. (Courtesy of
Chris Cocks)

Emily Hobhouse.

'consideration to the native franchise would be given only upon representative government'. This cast an entirely different complexion on both matters, virtually ensuring the exclusion of blacks in any meaningful determination until such time as the ruling minority saw fit.

Milner witnessed this, and allowed it to pass, burying the question in the interest of an agreement between the white principals. Whether upon direct instruction, or simply because of the blindness of the bureaucratic animal, the race statues and conventions of the two ex-republics remained intact, and were enforced by the successor administrations of both without let or alteration. Equal rights of British subjects overseas were subordinated to the wider strategic interests of peace in South Africa. No relaxation of restrictions against Indians in Natal was noticed, and, indeed, Indians moving between the two colonies of Natal and the Transvaal took note of a more diligent enforcement of old laws. Things did not grow easier for them, but a great deal more difficult.

Chapter 17

Transitions

'As regards the extension of the franchise to the Kaffirs in the Transvaal and Orange River Colony, it is not the intention of HMG to give such franchise before representative government is granted to those Colonies; and if then given it will be so limited as to secure the just predominance of the white race. The legal position of coloured persons, will, however, be similar to that which they hold in the Cape Colony.'

—British peace proposals, 1901

It was the dawn of a new century. The British empire now covered more than a third of the globe, British foreign service officials were deployed on every populated continent, and an English-speaking person might contemplate any corner of the world with a view to choosing a field of endeavour. The world to those English-speaking persons was now richer in opportunity than ever before, and India, more than ever, represented the power and prestige of the greatest empire known to man. Victory in South Africa, the death of Victoria and the coronation of Edward VII generated a pitch of nationalism and patriotism that the kingdom had never before witnessed. British power was almost inconceivably vast, and British industry, capital, art, science, philosophy and literature predominated. It was the age of the British empire, sublime in its majesty, and divine in its purpose.

The dawn of this new century, so brilliant, was marred for those with a mind to see it by the publication of an unusual, and quite brilliant, book. *Poverty and un-British Rule in India* was the culmination of a decade of exhausting scholarship by Dadabhai Naoroji, and in the summer of 1902 it was published to great acclaim, but also some uncomfortable introspection.

Un-British Rule, as the book came to be known, presented for the first time, and in naked fact, the economic misuse of India by the British. Through some 700 pages of exhaustive and precise detail, Naoroji laid bare a cold and factual economic analysis of three centuries of British rule, exposing the impoverishment of one people for the sake of the enrichment of another.

This, in and of itself, was an enormous achievement, but the title of the book hinted at a gentler criticism that Naoroji, and indeed Gandhi too, had long levelled against the British. The term *Un-British Rule*, deceptively simple, nonetheless called the British out for a betrayal of the very principles of their own empire. What the British empire represented in principle against what it represented in fact amounted to a shameful deficit that was undeserving of the greatest race on earth.

The book opened with a short statement on the benefits of British rule – the abolition of infanticide and the practice of *sati*, the introduction of English standards of education, culture and democracy, great advances in science and industry and the many vast and impressive infrastructural developments implemented by the British.[1] None of these, however, could justify the wholesale looting of Indian productive capacity through rapacious economic practices. Naoroji went on then to define his Drain Theory, immensely complex, and supported by unassailable sources, but in its essence illustrating the simple siphoning of economic wealth from India to Britain, and by extension the calamitous effects of British colonization on the sub-continent.

It took some time for the facts of this ground-breaking work to sink in, but once they had, a ripple of indignation in Britain soon washed up on the shores of India. What many had long suspected was now incontrovertibly proven, and born in its wake was the Swaraj movement. In simple, idiomatic terms, *swaraj* implies home rule, or absolute independence. It was a complete departure from the established Congress tenets of gradualism and the incremental inheritance of power, demanding instead a complete overthrow of British rule in India.

These were the first notes of authentic Indian nationalism, and although still faint at the turn of the century, Gandhi was listening. The establishment and disbanding of the Natal Indian Ambulance Corps had fomented something of sea change in British attitudes in Natal, and for a while the sharp edges of hostility were hidden behind respectful press reporting and a handful of honourable mentions. The inevitability of British victory, and the frenzied pace of trade and commerce in the war economy of the colony, engendered a feeling of wellbeing that affected the entire community. The prospect of British rule promised a revision of current race legislation, and ignoring the obvious contradiction of his belief in future British integrity against his knowledge of past British duplicity, Gandhi considered his work in South Africa complete.

In October 1901, he and his family set sail for India, pausing briefly in Mauritius where they were greeted and publicly honoured by the large Indian community. Several weeks later, however, the family landed in Bombay to an unexpectedly muted reception. Gandhi was not immediately welcomed into the Congress leadership, as he had expected, and, moreover, he was disappointed to discover that the South African struggle enjoyed almost no exposure or interest in the movement at all. He was forced to enter Congress as a simple member, without recognition for his role on the executive of the Natal Congress, and nor for his political work in South Africa. It was, on the whole, very disappointing.

Traditionally, Congress held its annual general meeting in December, and that year it met in Calcutta under the presidency of Sir Dinshaw Edulji Wacha, a middle-aged Parsee who, although one of the founders of Congress, was not among its most dynamic members. Gandhi attended as a low-level activist, attempting unsuccessfully to introduce a resolution on South Africa, returning obviously to a point of strength for him, and sensing, as he clearly must have, that there was no place for him at the centre table on any other agenda.

He seemed also to find his fellow delegates parochial and clannish, and in his memoir he comments on the fact that ablution facilities at the venue were allowed to degrade under the tropical heat to unbearable conditions simply because there was none among the delegates of the appropriate caste to clean a latrine. One morning he took up a mop and bucket and cleaned the latrines himself. It was a demonstrative gesture, displaying his humility, his growing opposition to caste differentiation and a shrewd appreciation of theatre.

He went on in the same vein by making a point of calling on as many Indian Christian organizations as he could, in order to pass on the greetings of South African Christians with whom he had encountered no barrier in the way of friendship. He visited a temple during the festival of Kali Puja, and expressed his utter revulsion at the mass slaughter of sheep, encountering what he termed a 'river of blood' on a floor on which he could not bear to stand.

'The more helpless a creature,' he later wrote, 'the more entitled it is to the protection by man from the cruelty of man ... I must go through more self-purification and sacrifice before I can save these lambs from this unholy sacrifice.'[2]

Clearly Gandhi had travelled far on his journey from the ambitious young Indian barrister towards the universalist, pan-religious Mahatma. The moment, however, was premature for this unique approach to politics to be understood, and accepted. He was regarded for the most part as a curious eccentric, and nowhere was he taken particularly seriously. The only member of the Congress establishment who made any effort to understand him was the eminent scholar and nationalist Gopal Krishna Gokhale. Gokhale, of whom more will be heard later, hosted Gandhi for a month at his home, but even he was bemused when Gandhi decided to enter upon a lengthy odyssey by rail across northern India, travelling third class for no greater purpose than to expose himself to hardship, and to familiarize himself with the peasantry of his nation.

He was, however, disappointed by this too. He discovered the masses uncouth, unsanitary and godless. In Congress he could find no place other than as a voluntary clerk, which he accepted with humility, but clearly he was disillusioned. It was obvious that India did not stand upon the cusp of self-realization as he had earlier imagined, but had just begun what would be a long, and perhaps even an eternal journey.

Sensing no alternative, he returned to Bombay, and there settled into a professional and family life that he found both arid and unsatisfying. Then, after almost a year languishing in Bombay, he received a short cablegram from the Natal Congress advising him of the pending visit to South Africa of the British colonial secretary, Joseph Chamberlain, and inviting him at his earliest convenience to return.

Within minutes a reply had been sent, advising the committee that he would indeed return to Natal as soon as he was in funds. Funds were quickly arranged, and Gandhi quit his chambers, lodged his wife and sons and made ready to sail. In his autobiography, he frames the summons as a challenge to his commitment to his family and his professional life, but there can be no real doubt that he seized upon this second chance with both hands.

Within a month of receiving the cablegram, Gandhi was once again standing on the teak boards of the Port Natal quays, having arrived in South Africa just a few days in advance of Joseph Chamberlain. Although well received by the Indian community, the white press, once alerted to his return, offered up just a few glum words of welcome. With little time to waste, however, he set about framing the enlarged list of Indian grievances into two separate petitions, one for Natal and the other for the Transvaal. A request was then submitted to the city of Durban for an audience with the colonial secretary, which was agreed to, and a date set by the mayor for the afternoon of 26 January 1903.

This, however, Gandhi noted as inconvenient, since it was a Friday, a day upon which the Muslims wishing to be present at the meeting would be indisposed by their religious obligations. He suggested instead the following day, a Saturday, which was obviously inconvenient to both Chamberlain and the various dignitaries of Durban. Gandhi, however, in his unfailingly cheerful manner, insisted, and eventually an hour was found for him and the colonial secretary to meet.

Chamberlain spent a little over a month in South Africa, touring the colonies and inspecting Milner's work in reconstruction. He also sought to build bridges with the Boers, who, in the aftermath of the peace, accepted the burden of British rule, but refused to play any part in it. The leader of the Transvaal Boers, General Louis Botha, was in Europe on a tour of friendly nations appealing for funds to aid the rehabilitation of his nation, which irritated Chamberlain enormously. His meeting with Smuts was conducted through interpreters, for Smuts, when he agreed to be interviewed at all, refused to speak English.

Chamberlain nonetheless established a confederacy with Milner over many issues, but in particular the questions of race and race policy. Milner's initial strategy was twofold: in the first instance to restart production on the mines as a matter of urgency, in order, quite obviously, to revitalize the economy, but also to attract the waves of English-speaking immigration that he hoped would underwrite his second policy. This was to establish English-speaking predominance throughout the region by encouraging the enlarged immigration of English tradesmen and workers to the industrial centre of the Witwatersrand. In support of this he sought to force upon the Dutch population the use of English as the language of government, administration, the judiciary and education.

To help him achieve this, Milner recruited a corps of Oxbridge technocrats who adopted the informal name of 'Milner's Kindergarten', and whose role was simply to populate the higher civil services with English blood, and reform the administration from the inside with English virtues. They were to create a dominion imitable to English interests, and English-speaking interests only, and reflective to the very last degree of English-speaking values.

Naturally this was unpopular with the Boers, and so deeply divisive that it made necessary the third initiative of his administration, which was to sweep pre-war promises of racial parity under the carpet. In the case of blacks, this was relatively easy, since there was no discernible pressure for change originating from that quarter. The Indian issue, however, was a different matter. Indians were regarded by both black and white in South

Africa as invasive and foreign, and were generally detested. The matter could be hidden behind whatever verbiage or political language suited the moment, but its essence remained a fear that, once unleashed, and under conditions of free movement, Indian immigration, by its sheer pressure of volume, would overwhelm the future dominion.

With all of this in mind, Chamberlain approached his meeting with Gandhi and the Natal Congress rather negatively predisposed, seeing in it not only a necessary but irritating formality, but an unwelcomed light shining on a rather shoddy domestic issue. He arrived at Town Hall in Durban some twenty minutes late, leaving just a few minutes to deal with the business at hand, much of which he then wasted in a lengthy appraisal of each waiting Indian through a clenched monocle. He listened to Gandhi's representation with obvious impatience, declining to take a seat and glancing intermittently at the clock on the wall.

Gandhi, aware that Chamberlain would unlikely be drawn on any specifics, and in the face of such obvious hostility, wisely moderated his representation, avoiding carefully the sensitive issue of franchise, arguing instead only for a relaxation of licensing laws, for the equal dispensation of law, for schools and facilities specific to Indians and for the rights of Indians to trade, live and invest without obstruction.

All of this Chamberlain listened to in silence, and when complete he allowed Gandhi to rest under his gaze for almost a minute before clearing his throat, glancing down at his notes and taking a moment to carefully frame his reply. When he looked up again, he fixed Gandhi with a penetrating stare, directing his reply specifically and only at him.

The imperial government, he began, was in a position to exert little if any influence over the legislative affairs of the self-governing colonies, and although the grievances expressed appeared to be genuine, the best advice on offer was for the Indians to avoid antagonizing the white community if it was their wish to live peacefully among them.

With that, he pocketed his notes, nodded briefly to the Indians and left the building. A few days later he returned to Pretoria, and there, to his further annoyance, he found Gandhi waiting for him, prepared this time to deliver a petition on behalf of the Transvaal Indian community. Chamberlain, however, refused to entertain him, based on the fact that he already had, and that as a Natal Indian he could hardly be expected to fully appreciate the particulars of the Transvaal Indian situation.

Little did Chamberlain himself appreciate, however, the extent to which Gandhi knew and understood conditions in both Natal and the Transvaal. As he travelled up from Durban to Pretoria to attend the meeting, he was surprised for the first time to encounter the question of a permit. This, of course, had always been mandatory, but had never, or at least very rarely ever been demanded. Indians had always been free to travel between Natal and the Transvaal as they chose, so long as they travelled second or third class. Now, under British administration, an Asiatic Department had come into existence solely as a means of enforcing the law as it applied to Asiatics in general, and Indians in particular.[3]

While entry permits were available at any port of entry, and were not as a consequence difficult to obtain, a fairly arbitrary vetting process offered the opportunity for individual border officials to act directly against Indians. Registration requirements for Indians included fingerprinting and detailed identification, coupled with a more rigorous enforcement of legacy bylaws restricting those applying for trading licences to specific locations or bazaars.

Gandhi was able to obtain his entry permit without difficulty through his connections in Natal, and to sidestep the scrutiny of the Asiatic Department based on an earlier period of residence in the colony. He was nonetheless alerted to an unexpected state of affairs. Although the laws of the old Transvaal Republic as they related to Indians and other Asiatics remained unchanged, under more efficient British enforcement the effects were infinitely more restrictive than they ever had been before. Gandhi was left, perhaps to his relief, with the realization that his work in South Africa was far from over.

Chamberlain, in the meanwhile, left South Africa early in February, 1902, in absolute agreement with Milner that South Africa would remain a predominately white country, and that no concessions in terms of government or administration would be made to any other race for so long as the weight of white opinion opposed it. He understood the need to defer the native franchise in the interests of peace, and for that reason he was prepared to look the other way over laws and statutes limiting the immigration and freedom of movement of Indians. This would be a small price to pay for the achievement of a stable South Africa, and, while a decade or so prior to this, such things would have stirred up a hornets' nest of domestic protest, times were changing, and he was reasonably confident that the imperial government would throw up no unnecessary obstacles.

Chapter 18

Fear and Labour

'God's soldiers sometimes fight on a larger battlefield than they dream of.'

—Olive Schreiner

The Anglo-Boer War reduced gold production on the Witwatersrand to a trickle. The mines, of course, had been a central strategic factor from the onset, and, as the line of British advance crept northward, a fierce debate between the hawks and the doves of the Transvaal cabinet raged over whether or not to destroy them before the British could reach them.

The urge to obliterate the dumps and the rolling headgear from the landscape of the republic affected the hardliners in a manner both visceral and irrational. Gold sat like a curse on the land. It was gold that had brought this catastrophe about, and British capital that had tempted and corrupted the *volk*, dehumanizing the community and introducing the virus of social contamination. An unregulated Babel seethed in the heart of the republic, and only its utter destruction could truly cleanse the soul of a nation that was, in any case, dying.

There were few who despised the British capital element with quite the same passion as Jan Smuts. To him, Johannesburg had become the Augean Stables of South Africa, and among his first actions as Transvaal state attorney was to challenge endemic lawlessness in an environment over which he enjoyed practically no control. In this regard, however, he was simply lashing out, for he did not at that point have at hand the rivers of Alpheus or Peneus to wash out the filth, and when such a tool did come to hand he was no longer of a mind to use it.

In his prolific correspondence with writer Olive Schreiner, Smuts lamented the paradox of the mines, the ubiquity of British capital and the powerlessness that he felt in the face of its resurgence. In reply she wrote a revealing paragraph: 'To me the Transvaal is now engaged in leading in a very small way in that vast battle which will during the twentieth century be fought out – probably most bitterly and successfully in America and Germany – between engorged capitalists and the citizens of other races.'

On the eve of occupation, however, it would be Smuts who would fight most passionately for the preservation of the goldfields. Beyond defeat, he argued, there would be victory, but implicit in that victory had to be the understanding that the old ways were passing, and resistance to that would not return the people to the innocence of yore. The past would be buried under the rubble of war, and the future would be financed by gold. As repulsive as the notion might be, it would be British capital that would ultimately underwrite reconstruction.

And indeed, under the rubble of war, with a pulse still faintly throbbing, lay gold. One of Alfred Milner's first and most urgent priorities was to restart gold production, and with his Kindergarteners in place, and the fundamentals attended to, he applied his mind almost exclusively to this. The difficulty, however, lay not with capital, since the British were in a position to supply a great deal of that, but labour.

South African gold was unique insofar as deposits were abundant and widely dispersed, but also locked in low-grade ore that lay at significant depths.[1] This, therefore, was not an experience of itinerate diggers and gold-panners, but of large investors and deep mines that depended on quantities of cheap labour, both skilled and unskilled, to function. The fortunes that were made were not made by happenstance, but by the evolution of production. And although sizeable fortunes were quickly made, they tended on the whole to be at the capital and investment level, or in allied industries and trade, with mineworkers themselves labouring on relatively low wages.

As an industry-wide prerogative the Transvaal Chamber of Mines established wage levels, and a certain perversity in the aftermath of the war saw a reluctance to raise wages in line with international standards. This in turn frustrated efforts to restart the industry, but also to attract the level of immigration from Britain that Milner had established as a priority.

During the war, what had been a healthy growth of unskilled and semi-skilled black labour had been diverted from the mines to wartime service by inflated wages paid by the British Army.[2] The native economy, therefore, was, for the time being at least, replete, and white labour was generally unavailable, and so with great caution, Milner and his Kindergarteners began to explore the political viability of imported indentured labour.

What was at once clear, however, was that any attempt to import quantities of Indian labour would provoke an immediate insurrection. The

Indian problem had by then become an object of morbid fear in the white community, whipped up by the press, and now so much greater than the sum total of its parts. A secondary consideration was that Indians were British, and could not wilfully as a consequence be exploited, or repatriated at the conclusion of their contracts.

The only alternative, therefore, was Chinese labour, no less abundant, probably cheaper and a great deal easier to procure. The British were influential in China but, apart from Hong Kong, held no territory, and pretended to nothing more than diplomatic predominance. A contractual arrangement with the British authorities in Hong Kong, therefore, utilizing mainland contractors to procure labour, would not be in any way as emotional or problematic as the involvement of the British government in India.

Behind closed doors, and in closed consultation with the Chamber of Mines and various industrial bodies, the matter was decided, and having made up his mind, like a terrier, Milner began to tear away at the sources of traditional resistance with a finely balanced strategy of propaganda and threat.

Among his Kindergarteners at that time was a heavily bespectacled, rather sun-starved and pipe-smoking technocrat by the name of Dr Patrick Leys. Dr Leys styled himself an expert in native affairs, and in 1902, he wrote and published an essay entitled 'Chinese Labour on the Rand'. This was obviously intended to soften up the critics of labour importation with something alluding to a scientific analysis, although in the end it proved to be little more than parody.

The author opened his narrative with the observation that the tribal African represented a poor potential labour resource for the simple reason of his fidelity, or lack of. It was the tendency, Leys wrote, for a Bantu male to labour intermittently only when cash was required, but after the acquisition of his required number of wives and cattle, to simply spend his days in contemplation of the transcendental and the combustion of tobacco.

'Now I venture to say,' Doctor Leys continued, in much the same tone,

and I may as well say it just once, that every one that has had personal experience of each and all of the different kinds of labour – Somali, Arab, Indian and Chinese – that it has been proposed to import will unhesitatingly affirm that, viewed solely from a commercial point of view, Chinese labour is by far the best. The Chinamen is not turbulent like the Arab, nor is he rebellious under pressure like the [African]; he is thrifty and economical like the

Indian, but, unlike him, he is not mean and hoarding, but, on occasion, can and does spend, and even gives freely. Doubtless he is more of an animal than either the Indian or Arab coolie, but he is by no means a semi-savage whose prehistoric days were yesterday ... he is neat and [compared with other coolies] intelligent in his work, while for patient, steady, persevering work ... he has few equals and no superior. He has, however, his limitations and his peculiarities ...'

Such comments offer not only an insight into the social and economic difficulties confronting the likes of Milner, but also on contemporary views and responses to race, which, although hardly venomous, were nonetheless patronizing. On the matter of how best to handle and contain an infusion of Chinese coolies, Dr Leys' advice was simply to ensure happiness and contentment by the provision of adequate fresh pork and vegetables, and the regular importation of chow-chow from China, 'all of which his soul loveth'. Leys was also able to calculate, based on past usage of Chinese labour in various colonial contexts that, all considered, Chinese labour in South Africa would prove to be a revenue saver to the extent of some twenty-five per cent per individual over the use of native labour.

This exercise in quack sociology and economics was accompanied by others to the left and right, gradually alerting the British and the various local factions to what was afoot. The Boer, mute over every aspect of administration, remained tight lipped in public, but nonetheless, private expression revealed a renewed horror at British determination to destroy the racial integrity of the land. The mine owners and various allied interests greeted the news with a combination of enthusiasm and relief, while white labour, sensing a conspiracy, erupted into a ferment. Indian labour was one thing, but Chinese, the much-storied 'Yellow Peril', was another altogether.

Chinese, of course, were no strangers to South Africa. A trickle of free immigrants had appeared in the territory consequent to the mining boom, but strict limitations on their access to mining licences had confined a majority to such menial occupations as barbering, laundry and portage. As immigrants, of course, they fell under the same ordinances as Indians, forming temporary communities in and around the Indian bazaars, and representing for the time being no particular threat to anyone.

The decision, however, once made, created an immediate ancillary need for a supporting framework of laws. In 1904, the Transvaal Labour Importation Ordinance was cautiously tabled and debated in the Transvaal assembly, clearing the way for the legal importation of Chinese contract labour for use in the gold industry. The law was carefully crafted to close as many doors as possible to permanent settlement and to limit Chinese access to skilled and semi-skilled occupations, specifically prohibiting Chinese inclusion in a total of fifty-five scheduled occupations.

To many, however, this did not go far enough, and to others, such as Smuts himself, the entire enterprise stank of a British conspiracy. In a letter written to Emily Hobhouse, Smuts rather naively vented his anguish over the matter, and was horrified when the letter was passed on to *The Times*, unedited, and subsequently published almost verbatim. In part he wrote:

> In the Boer mind, [there is] a fierce indignation against this sacrilege of Chinese importation – this spoilage of the heritage for which the generations of the people have sacrificed their all. Often when I think of what is happening now all over South Africa, my mind stands still – for the folly, the criminality of it all is simply inconceivable.

The publication of this letter provoked an outcry in Britain, and Smuts was heavily censured. He was deeply hurt that the letter should have been made available for publication without his permission, and it shook the foundations of his friendship with Emily Hobhouse, which survived, but not without some modification of its terms.

In fact, reaction in Britain was confused and rather refracted, and for the most part contrasting sharply with views expressed in the wider imperial diaspora. The British liberal element formed up for the third time around the banner of abolition, decrying the modern revival of slavery, which in turn excited cries of derision from the outer reaches of the empire, where past experience generated a solid backdrop of support for any exclusionary position.

White Australia, for example, felt the threat of a Chinese invasion particularly acutely, situated as it was in the heart of the Asia-Pacific region, and upon its statute survived a variety of past and present instruments to limit and control Chinese immigration. In the United States, and Canada too, strong measures had been implemented at various times to limit Chinese immigration, and even the Cape, staunchly liberal in matters of race and colour, hurriedly enacted a Chinese Exclusion Act as the Transvaal importation ordinance came into effect.[3] The object of this was to establish legal barriers against opportunist Chinese from the Transvaal seeking sanctuary in the Cape. This was, ironically, supported by the small Chinese trading community in the Cape, concerned by a potential influx of low-class compatriots seeking its protection.

An interesting corollary to the general labour discussion, and one that might bear some detailed examination, is the question of native labour, and indeed white labour, from where the entire labour debate in South Africa began.

By 1900, black labour had more or less been priced out of the market by a reduction of statutory wage levels intended to ensure that whites remained fixed in the higher trades, and that those trades were protected against contamination by any other race. Repeated reference at that time was made to the British Army's tendency to overpay native carriers, wagon drivers and such like, in order to attract as many as possible, rendering native society in the aftermath of the war so flush with cash that it was unwilling to consider the bleak conditions of subterranean toil.

This, at some point, would obviously change, and as the Chinese debate neared its conclusion, greater consideration began to be given to developing regional labour pools that were becoming available as surrounding colonies opened for business. Indeed, certain colonies – Mozambique, southern Congo and Nyasaland for example – built substantial pillars of their respective economies on the factoring and supply of labour, not only to satisfy the appetite of the Witwatersrand, but also to the Copperbelt in Northern Rhodesia, the nascent coal-mining industry in Southern Rhodesia and the emerging agricultural sectors of all the settled colonies.

The history of organized labour in South Africa is allied almost entirely with the history of the mining industry, and it is precisely there that the labour relationship between blacks and whites began. Dr David Livingstone's appeal for Christianity and commerce in Africa was honoured in small part for reasons of philanthropy, but in far greater part because of vast economic opportunities becoming available in Africa. Within twenty-five years of Livingstone's death, Africa would be under almost absolute European control, divided up into regional spheres of influence that were solidified into colonies and protectorates early in the new century.

Migrant labour would soon come to form a cornerstone of the South African segregationist tradition. A great deal of literature, scholarship and art has been created around the movement of itinerate labour entering and migrating within South Africa. Migrant labour during the critical years of the twentieth century can be credited arguably with constructing the infrastructure of the entire region, and laying the foundation of the economic might that would define South Africa in the new century, and indeed, separate it from a continent that nowhere else offered anything comparable.

The movement began with the first displaced natives arriving on the diamond fields of the northern Cape to seek work. For the most part these men worked only briefly, earning enough money to buy a gun or two before returning to a semi-nomadic, semi-pastoral life.[4] With the consolidation of the diamond mines in the late 1880s, however, and the movement from open-cast to underground mining in the gold sector, a more reliable and skilled labour force became necessary. By then a combination of taxation and a general movement into the consumer/cash economy had witnessed a growing interest in formal employment among young black males. That movement, however, remained transitory, and somewhat chaotic in nature, and it was Cecil Rhodes who founded the concept of the labour compound as an indivisible component of any mine complex. Here, under controlled conditions, tight restrictions could be exercised over the movement and activities of individuals confined within it.

Victorian social commentator and *Times* African correspondent Flora Shaw once described this system as a 'monastery of labour'. Here she alludes to the virtual confinement of black men into dormitory compounds with steeply restricted contact with the outside world, and stringent and highly invasive controls to limit the theft or illegal movement of diamonds. The system worked well, however, and while it had about it an uncomfortable aftertaste of slavery, it excited little notice or criticism, and continued to develop. In 1886, with the discovery of gold in the Transvaal, the system was taken up and further refined, until in due course labour compounds became a ubiquitous feature of the South African industrial landscape.

In 1896, the South African Chamber of Mines attempted to formalize and monopolize native labour recruitment through the establishment of the Rand Native Labour Association, which in 1900 became the Witwatersrand Native Labour Association. By then the colonies of Northern Rhodesia, Southern Rhodesia and Nyasaland had been founded, and were beginning to develop their own agricultural and mining sectors, as a consequence of which the regional competition for labour became intense.

It is perhaps also worth noting that the movement towards rearmament in Europe resulted in a massively increased demand for base metals and other raw materials, which in turn heated the bearings of non-ferrous metal production in Central Africa, in particular in Katanga (Congo) and Northern Rhodesia, as well as a vast increase in agricultural and timber production throughout the region. This placed yet further demands on African labour, generating even more competition and regional protectionism.

One of the great labour suppliers of the age was the Portuguese. It was they who pioneered the Atlantic slave trade, and the scars of that trade remain visible to this day. The Portuguese made permanent landfall in southern Africa centuries before competing European powers, and much of their early economic exploitation was centred on slavery. In both territories, the business of slavery lay largely under the control of a corps of established colonists known as *prazeros*, who, quite often, in particular towards the end of the nineteenth century, were either partial or full-blood Africans, perhaps with some Islamic or Indian influence, although speaking Portuguese, claiming to be Portuguese and owing allegiance to the Portuguese state.[5]

Prazeros were granted sweeping concessions of land or territory by the Portuguese Crown, somewhat in the manner of British and other European royal charters, which empowered and obligated landowners to productively administer those territories to the benefit of the Crown and the colony. With almost unlimited powers over their concessions, these men became the de facto authority on the land, and more profitable by far than to stimulate production was to sell labour as a raw material. Although the slave trade was abolished by the Portuguese at the same time as other European powers, slave ownership remained legal, and until 1888, the practice remained widespread in Brazil. And thus, for as long as there remained a viable market, Portuguese *prazeros* provided merchandise for export. David Livingstone made frequent and regular note of Portuguese slaving activities until as late as his death, and anecdotally, the last slave sold in Mozambique changed hands as late as 1902.

When full abolition did take effect, however, the *prazeros* simply reconfigured the obligations imposed on their native charges by creating a system of forced, or bonded, labour known as *chibalo*. By the turn of the century, as labour demands in both the south and west of the region created a market too tempting to ignore, a great many *prazeros* turned to the business of labour recruitment and began exacting *chibalo* through the export of labour south into the Transvaal, and less frequently west to the Rhodesias.[6]

Much of this, however, would reside in the future, and for the time being, native labour recruitment remained improvised. By the dawn of 1904, however, as Milner found himself grappling with the problem of reconstruction, many of those traditional sources of African labour had temporarily run dry, creating a vacuum of labour on the Rand that demanded immediate and decisive action.

And so it was that on 25 May 1904, the first consignment of 1,052 Chinese indentured workers arrived from Hong Kong aboard the SS *Tweeddale* which, like the SS *Truro* forty-three years earlier, rode at anchor across the bay from the port of Durban. A delay of two days followed before officials of the Foreign Labour Department arrived on board to discover that three passengers had died of beriberi en route, and that forty-three others were displaying symptoms of the same condition. These were promptly repatriated, allowing the remainder to be disembarked and, under careful supervision, held until they could be transported by train to the Transvaal.

Arriving at Johannesburg railway station in a specially chartered train, they were disembarked and marched through the city under careful supervision, carrying their miscellaneous bundles under the curious gaze of the local citizenry, arriving eventually in Krugersdorp where they entered the compound of the New Comet Gold Mining Company. There, under the no less careful supervision of police and interpreters – a special Chinese constabulary had been formed – they were marched into a compound secured by a chain-linked fence, and introduced to rows of Spartan concrete dormitory blocks that would be their homes for the duration of their contracted service.

Under the terms of the Labour Importation Ordinance, the lives and liberties of these men were to be carefully controlled. They were to be issued passes, were to reside in situ and remain in secure compounds, subject to periods of absence no longer that forty-eight hours. They could undertake no commercial activity other than that elucidated within their contracts, and were to be repatriated upon the completion of contract. Offences such as desertion, refusal to work, absenteeism or employment other than that stipulated would be punishable by imprisonment or a fine. Their day-to-day affairs were to be monitored and reported upon by the Foreign Labour Department that would provide officers and inspectors to monitor compliance, but also to regulate conditions of importation, work conditions, general treatment and complaints. The latter included the provision of adequate and culturally appropriate food, medical attention and qualified interpreters.

One can hardly imagine that Milner could have done more to satisfy all sides in this controversial effort and, initially at least, he won the approval and thanks of the Transvaal Chamber of Mines. The Chinese went to work with diligence and discipline, and despite minor issues of language and culture, experienced a reasonably smooth integration.

Opposition, however, was forcefully and immediately voiced elsewhere, in particular from the direction of white labour, both local and metropolitan. A secondary series of appeals originated from various aboriginal protection agencies, and multiple organizations and individuals with an interest in human rights.

The rallying cry of each was slavery or, more specifically, the condemnation of Whitehall for its support of a labour practice almost indistinguishable from slavery. Such had been the cry raised in condemnation of Indian indentured labour two generations earlier, but that had been in an age when the image of slavery remained close to the collective memory. That same image, however, was not quite so easily transferable to the picture of a Chinese coolie, generally portrayed as a contemptible character, already legally excluded from a number of British territories by race legislation unashamed of its intentions.

In this instance, the anti-slavery cry was confused, and confusing. White labour in the Transvaal, supported by white labour in Britain, cried slavery only in the context of the importation of cheap foreign labour consigning honest British workers on the Witwatersrand to slavery. There was certainly no sympathy expressed or implied towards the Chinese coolie himself, who was seen as usurping and devaluing local white labour.

At the same time, the international humanitarian movement in Britain found itself in a curious quandary. Modern abolitionists were mutating into an activism more widely configured than simply the ending of slavery. In March 1904, just a few weeks before the SS *Tweeddale* dropped anchor in the Durban roadstead, an organization named the Congo Reform Association was formed in London by two men who would found the great humanitarian movement of the age, Edmund Dene Morel and Roger Casement. The focus of their interest was the Congo Free State, a territory that would pass soon to the control of the Belgian parliament as the Belgian Congo, but which, since 1885, had existed as a private fiefdom of the Belgian king, Leopold II.

The story of Leopold's Congo has been chronicled comprehensively in recent years, and for the purposes of this narrative it need only be said that Leopold founded the territory ostensibly as an international vehicle to eliminate the last surviving remnants of the African slave trade, while reaping fortunes by the genocidal exploitation of the Congolese native population, and utilizing practices that differed not one iota from slavery, and in many instances a great deal worse.

This scar on the conscience of European Africa catalyzed the mobilization of organized humanitarian resources in Europe that had never been seen before. Mass media was deployed while luminaries in the fields of exploration, the arts, politics and academia were seconded to support and speak out on behalf of the Congo Reform Association. Ultimately this effort would succeed, and Leopold's excesses would be exposed, and the territory taken over and administered as Belgium's only colonial territory.

FEAR AND LABOUR

In the midst of all of this, however, the Chinese labour crisis erupted, diverting attention away from what many in the association felt was the essence of the anti-slavery movement – black slavery – and diluting its severity with the relatively mediocre plight of an unsympathetic clique of foreign workers. Morel, having launched a political career on the back of the Congo crisis, was recorded as commenting off the record to the press: 'Don't you think it is a great pity … that the suggestion of a parallel [between the Congo and the Transvaal] should be drawn between the Congo business and anything else in the world.'[7]

While the 'Congo business' had the effect of casting capitalism and monopoly as incompatible with ethical government, the Transvaal crisis appeared as just another example of precisely that. In a nutshell, it seems that those who upheld the true values of empire felt that the Chinese should be kept out of Africa for reasons not so much of their exploitation, but because their presence simply confused the clear lines of race politics. Some even went so far as to claim that the Chinese – conniving, depraved, comical and at times pathetic – would directly corrupt the vulnerable sensibilities of a race only just beginning to blink under the light of civilization. The white man, if right minded and morally aligned, had much to offer the natives of Africa, while the yellow man had nothing at all.

Approaching an election year, in the meanwhile, the British Conservative government, under Prime Minister Arthur Balfour, remained in a horrible dilemma over the matter. An accusation of countenancing slavery in the colonies, no matter what its motivation, was powerful political medicine indeed, and as such it was deployed with a ruthless resolve by the liberal opposition. Indeed, a restive domestic labour movement, beginning to find its feet, found encouragement from the opposition, and in solidarity with white South African labour, British labour now mass-marched and struck.

The Conservatives were reminded that the just-ended Anglo-Boer War had been sold to the British public upon the understanding that the Transvaal under the Union Jack would be an importer of British workers, welcomed into a lucrative and high-paying labour market liberated for the general good of the empire. Now it was becoming clear that war had been fought by Tommy Atkins and paid for by John Bull for the sake of the capitalists only, who could not care less upon whose sweat it was that their fortunes were built.

So much for white reaction, but where in this debate did Gandhi stand? Having lately applied successfully to join the Transvaal bar, Mohandas Gandhi obviously observed these turns of events with interest. So multifaceted were the implications, however, that it is hardly surprising that his public comments on the matter were few.

Neither his autobiography, *My Experiments with Truth*, nor his memoir of *satyagraha* in South Africa makes any detailed comment on the Chinese phenomenon at all. Numerous biographers, however, depending on the bias sought, have described Gandhi's relationship with the South African Chinese in general, and Leung Quinn, the unofficial leader of the community, in particular, as both fraternal and cooperative. This probably was the case, but another fact to be considered was that the Chinese were so disliked, in equal measure by whites, blacks and Indians, that even though they contributed to the later movement of passive resistance, Gandhi probably sought to avoid any risk of polarizing the struggle by awarding too much recognition to what was in practical terms a fifth column of outsiders.

This general antipathy obviously had much to do with the fact that Chinese cultural peculiarities at the time were just too peculiar, and too remote from the common understanding to be appreciated, coupled, of course, with the fact that the Chinese tenure in the struggle was brief. Nonetheless, the Chinese happened to be standing on the stage as the main act of Gandhi's South African drama began to play out, and so, in January 1908, when the Satyagrahis signed a pact with the Transvaal government, and as Gandhi at last began to be taken seriously, both he and Leung Quinn were co-signatories.

Chapter 19

A New Horizon

'They gave us back our country in everything but name. After
Four Years. Has such a miracle of trust and magnanimity ever
happened before? Only people like the English could do it.
They may make mistakes, but they are a big people.'

—Jan Smuts

All told, some 63,000 Chinese indentured labourers were imported into South
Africa, and then promptly repatriated as their individual contracts expired.
Very few were able to slip through the net in order to remain in the country,
and for the entirety of their experience in the Transvaal, their lives were
carefully monitored and controlled. The entire episode was ugly, divisive and
anachronistic, and its greatest value is that it painted the entire culture of
organized labour importation in such dark and unpleasant colours that it was
soon afterwards consigned to the dustbin of history. It was symptomatic
simply of a weak British administration, an empire in a momentary crisis of
direction and a nation emerging with a predisposition to warped perceptions
of race and colour.

For the Chinese indentured workers themselves, the experience was
without doubt an unhappy one, and once scrubbed off the modern face of
South Africa, memories of that brief six-year period remain only faintly
ghosted on the more elemental race pictures of the age. A majority of those
recruited came from the distressed northern and coastal provinces of China,
that had seen drought and poverty compounded by the traumatic effects of
the Boxer Rebellion and the Russo-Japanese War. Most were illiterate and
landless rural wage labourers, with a sprinkling of urban destitute, and if any
statistic were to reveal the underlying human condition, it would be the high
rates of medical rejection that ran to over half of the applications.

Nonetheless, in a curious way, this episode of South African history
appears in the long run to have benefited all sides. Chinese labour certainly

rescued the Transvaal mining industry at a crucial moment, which in turn defibrillated a moribund economy, setting the combined territories of South Africa on a trajectory of almost unprecedented economic and political growth. It was, however, so spectacularly unpopular, so divisive and so politically polarizing that it contributed to the collapse of a malingering Conservative administration, paving the way for a Liberal victory, which in turn signalled the moment that Smuts would finally emerge from the political shadows.

No thanks, of course, was offered to Milner for any of this. In the three years that this stoic and furiously energetic man had held the tiller of British South Africa, many miracles had been wrought, but also no small number of compromises and blunders. All the while, he had been aware of Smuts's hostile presence, biding his time in the wings, and as the tide of history began to shift, as it was bound to do, it began to occur to him that he had not done quite enough.

During those bitter months of 1899, he had been the dominant personality, riding the crest of the imperial wave, checking Smuts at every move, and ultimately forcing a declaration of the war that he, Chamberlain and the British establishment desired. However, in the aftermath of that war, Milner found himself unexpectedly denied the absolute victory that would have given him complete control – and who should he now find checking *him* at every move, but that quarrelsome young attorney Jan Smuts.

Smuts's decision to reject political office under Milner's administration, which had seemed at the time to amount to no more than the immaturity of a political amateur, now proved itself to be the genius of a man who had long ago predicted the advent of an imperial winter.

Alfred Milner's term of office in South Africa expired at the beginning of April 1905, after which he set sail for England, leaving behind him little regret at his departure, and a great deal to occupy his personal reflections. His policy of promoting English and encouraging English-speaking immigration had proved a failure. The post-war depression had seen more British nationals decamping the colony than arriving, and his Anglophile policies simply polarized the Boers and energized their political cohesion. In the years to follow he would wander the political wilderness, emerging only in 1919 as an older and wiser man, to finally accept, under Prime Minister David Lloyd George, the Office of Colonial Secretary.

In the meanwhile, as the ghost of Table Mountain disappeared behind a pall of early fog, he took to his desk aboard the SS *Umbria* and began to examine his correspondence. To his surprise he encountered a letter written in a familiar hand, causing him to frown slightly as he opened it. It was from Smuts, wishing him well and reflecting that, although things might have been friendlier between them, the rift between Boer and Briton would in the fullness of time heal.

'History,' Smuts noted, 'writes the word "Reconciliation" over all her quarrels.'

With Milner's passing, the imperial factor in South Africa began to fade, and with his enemy now gone, Smuts was disposed to greater charity. Less than a year later, a politically crippled Arthur Balfour, Conservative prime minister of Britain, crumbled, in no small part thanks to the Transvaal Chinese labour crisis, passing the baton to the incoming Liberal prime minister, Henry Campbell-Bannerman.

This instantly tilted the game in Smuts's favour, for the Liberals were not the party of the war, and in fact it had been Bannerman himself, as leader of the opposition, who had stood at the forefront of the anti-war movement. He was known to be favourably disposed to both Smuts and Botha, and he inhabited the same trusted inner circle of Emily Hobhouse's friends that Smuts did himself. Thus, a little muted trailblazing undertaken by Ms Hobhouse, among others, prepared the way for Smuts to at last feel comfortable enough to contemplate a visit to Britain.

This was the year 1906, and, at its near-zenith, the British empire consisted of multiple minor territories, protectorates and colonies, spanning virtually the entire globe. The German, French and Portuguese empires likewise stood at the apex of their global reach and, with little exception, the entire geographic scope of the earth lay to some degree or another under European control.[1]

In many cases, and this was certainly true for the British, the wider scope of the empire had been established less for reasons of practical economics than global strategy or inter-European rivalry, and a vast majority of overseas territories were neither productive nor attractive to settlement. There was no particular impediment to these territories achieving independence other than their strategic value, or their own lack of preparation to do so. Matters were complicated somewhat by territories such as Kenya or Rhodesia that hosted large settler communities alongside even larger native communities, but only the territories of Australia, New Zealand and Canada represented viable and permanent overseas British territories that would one day be dominions. The conversation between these three governments and Whitehall was of a federalized empire, a commonwealth of interested territories, loyal to the Crown, but neither bound to fealty nor subject to British foreign policy. Smuts desired, on behalf of South Africa, to join this conversation. The individual colonies of South Africa, however, did not qualify for inclusion in this club, but the combined territories, with a population of some 1.1 million whites, might.

In the order of things, therefore, Smuts sought responsible government for the two ex-republics, followed inevitably by a union of territories, after which, like Australia, New Zealand and Canada, the new dominion thus formed would seek to become a full and permanent partner in the federation of empire, autonomous in almost every respect, but bound by the common ties of empire.[2] His mission now, therefore, was to convince the new British government that the domestic political establishment in the Transvaal and Orange River colonies could be trusted, under conditions of independence, to remain loyal to British interests.

And indeed, it could. Smuts realized, even then, and despite his own unresolved feelings towards the British, that South Africa's inclusion in the present and future British empire, on full and equal terms, would place the new dominion among the foremost nations of the world. Moreover, he stood within a circle of men who had already begun to cast their minds beyond the age of empire, conceptualizing a world united – a league of nations no less – dominated by English-speaking interests, but with fair and equal dispensations of power and influences between the greatest and smallest of the world's nations. The integrity of the Whole, a greater human community in every respect than the sum total of its parts.

In the spring of 1906, therefore, Smuts set sail for London. There he addressed himself as a man for all seasons. What South Africa most needed, he argued, was political settlement and tranquillity. The colonies of South Africa, and the nation within, had reconciled themselves to a period under British annexation, but in return the time had come to place trust in the ability of the people of South Africa to govern themselves, and to do it well.

'There may be some danger,' he said, 'in trusting the people too soon, but there may be much greater danger in trusting them too late.'[3]

Somewhat doubtful of Campbell-Bannerman's cabinet, in particular the Liberal secretary of state for the colonies, Lord Elgin, Smuts bypassed the Colonial Office and presented himself directly to the prime minister, who he knew to be a fellow alumni of Cambridge. They met at Downing Street in an unofficial capacity, since Smuts at that moment represented no formal constituency, and while Campbell-Bannerman was perhaps a little overawed by Smuts in the beginning, the two men formed an almost immediate bond of understanding and interest. With the effusion of relief, Smuts's correspondence over the of the next few weeks was rich with praise for Campbell-Bannerman, whose greatest attribute, it would seem, was to agree entirely with Smuts at a time when Smuts had expected so much less.

And for his part, Campbell-Bannerman appears to have been mesmerized by the arrival in London of this extraordinary man from the outer perimeters of the empire. British intelligence reports, and the various press coverage of Smuts during the war, had painted a picture of an ice-cold and anarchic enemy of all things British; an over-educated Boer, contaminated by the liberal traditions of Cambridge, empowered by his membership of the British bar and over-enamoured of his own brilliance.

Instead, what Campbell-Bannerman, and others of the metropolitan political establishment encountered, was a man entirely configured for the moment. Smuts was thoughtful and rational, moderate and accommodating, but yet wise, intelligent and honest. In an age of pending imperial divestment, the British establishment could hardly have encountered a man more qualified to carry forward the concept of British South Africa.

Campbell-Bannerman would succeed to Herbert Asquith, who would in turn lead the empire into war. There were, therefore, few among the educated political elite in Britain, no matter on which side of the House they stood, who were immune to what was pending. Of paramount importance now was consolidating the empire in the face of war. There was only one colony of the empire peopled by white men who were not British, and few within the establishment, even those who lately had exchanged gunfire with the Boer, could say with certainty that they understood who this people were.

To meet, therefore, and to hear this rather subdued man, Jan Smuts, his accent curiously difficult to place, but his mind fruitful with practical ideas, proved to be a pleasant and unexpected surprise. Smuts presented South Africa in portions palatable to the British, and with a flavour that they found not in the slightest bit bitter, and in reply, he was rewarded with British affection, likewise unexpected, and no less pleasant on the tongue.

All of this was fortunate, for Smuts required much of the British. His manifesto amounted to little less than a request for a complete return of the country a mere five years after it had been conquered in war. It was an audacious appeal, premised on the simple assertion that the British could choose at a crucial moment between the Boers as friends, or enemies. Bearing in mind the geographic and ideological proximity of the Germans, Smuts was well fortified in his belief that the British would be certain to prefer the former. This petition was presented to Campbell-Bannerman in a private meeting held at No. 10 Downing Street, and having softened up the prime minister over several weeks of fruitful engagement, the result was almost a foregone conclusion.

'I used no set argument,' Smuts later wrote, 'but simply spoke to him as man to man, and appealed only to the human aspect which I felt would weigh deeply with him. He was a cautious Scot, and said nothing to me, but yet I left that room that night a happy man. My intuition told me that the thing had been done.'[4]

What Campbell-Bannerman asked nothing about, and about what Smuts himself ventured nothing, was the question of where in this equation of self-government the black majority of the region stood. While this was a test case of the future, for the time being both men were pragmatic enough to realize that no fruit could be borne in the short term from that particular tree. Smuts had promised Campbell-Bannerman the friendship of the Boer people, which he was not entirely certain that he could deliver, but if he brought home with him British demands for racial equality, that friendship would be forever denied. As for Campbell-Bannerman, he realized that white friendship in South Africa was of far greater value than black, and, moreover, that the Germans, given the opportunity, would make no such demands upon the uncommitted Boer.

The question of self-government for the ex-republics remained to be debated in the House of Commons, but Smuts returned to South Africa a week or so later satisfied that what could be done had been done, and that his efforts would be rewarded. And in general, the British establishment seemed to be in agreement. Before he left, and throughout his visit, Smuts had met with and been entertained by a great many establishment figures who drew from him great encouragement, and supported him because he offered Britain the continued loyalty of white South Africa.

One whom he did not meet, and who offered him no such support, was the now Lord Alfred Milner, who bore witness to the process from the wings, and saw in it perhaps the final consummation of his own failure. As the matter was under debate in the House of Commons, his voice was heard to utter in deprecation: 'People here – not only Liberals – seem delighted, and to think themselves wonderfully fine fellows for having given South Africa back to the Boers. I think it all sheer lunacy.'

Upon his return to Pretoria, however, Smuts was quietly congratulated, and he and Botha set about mobilizing the Afrikaans element of the Transvaal, and trench-building in preparation for what promised to be a bruising electoral battle. Het Volk (The People) was the first free-standing political party to be formed in South Africa around the Afrikaner movement,

166

and although not exclusively Afrikaner, it was in the first instance a tool to unite the *volk* in a single direction. The English and Labour constituencies formed their own bodies to support their own various interests, but the job of leading the people fell to Botha, and the job of fetching up the baton from the departing Kindergarteners fell to Smuts.

During those exhilarating months, a pro-British mood was tangible in the Transvaal, intermingled with a sensation that at last the colony, and the nation, was flowering after a long and at times bitter rain. This was Pretoria, but in Bloemfontein, capital of the Orange River Colony, there was less salutation and cheer. Here was focused a much more hard-line remnant, and a powerfully pro-Boer movement. This bloc, united under the Orangia Unie, was anti-British, and instinctively hostile to any liberal view of race.[5] Orangia Unie was led by a highly accomplished Boer diplomat and politician by the name of Abraham Fischer, not instinctively racist within himself, but certainly eclipsed in his liberal base by a much larger conservative wing. This was led by a firebrand, a Dutch-trained lawyer by the name of James, or Barry, Herzog.

Herzog's contribution to the movement until that point had been unremarkable, notwithstanding his echoing of Smuts at almost every key point of their careers thus far. He too was an alumni of Victoria College, a product of a European university and a general of the Boer army. He and Smuts had participated on more or less equal terms as architects of the Vereeniging peace, but a great deal of latent competition had also existed between them. Herzog, however, fell a few degrees short of that rare pitch of Smuts's intellect, and as a severe, somewhat humourless man, dark of complexion and with a shrew-like purse of the lips, he was eclipsed entirely by Smuts in the international constellation into which the latter was drifting.

In response, Herzog defined his agenda as strictly domestic, and more narrowly still, as Afrikaner. As Smuts argued for a more international role for South Africa, Herzog rejected internationalism and any sort of alliance with the British, and certainly no common defence pact that would see South Africa drawn into an international war on the side of the British.

Herzog, needless to say, was inimical to any discussion of equal political rights for blacks, and in fact argued for greater restrictions, with strong and verbal allusions to the fact that he intended with all of his might to oppose the Cape colour-blind franchise at the moment that he was in a position to do so.

Behind him was always audible a steady drumbeat of support. Smuts had been wise to keep the matter of race off the imperial agenda for the time being, and his fears for the future might just as well have been directed towards his own people as towards the blacks. Hertzog, and by extension the extreme right wing of the Afrikaner movement, announced their presence in February, 1907, as the two ex-republics went to the polls as British self-governing colonies. Het Volk emerged victorious in the Transvaal, and there the soul of the nation was born, but, more darkly, the victory in the Orange River Colony of the Orangia Unie hinted at a far more turbulent future than many at the present were prepared to acknowledge.

Chapter 20

Teach the Natives a Lesson

'[S]et no other excellence before their eyes; disturb none of their reverence for the past; do not think yourself bound to dispel their ignorance, or to contradict their superstitions; teach them only gentleness and truth; redeem them by example from habits you know to be unhealthy or degrading, but cherish above all things local associations and hereditary skill.'

—John Ruskin

On 23 January 1906, deep in Zululand's Valley of a Thousand Hills, a white farmer by the name of Henry Smith was speared and beaten to death on the veranda of his home by a group of disgruntled Zulu labourers. An hour or so earlier, he and a section of his labour force had returned from Pietermaritzburg, to where he had escorted them in order to ensure that their taxes were paid. A visit was made to the office of the local magistrate, where, under supervision, payments were made, after which the party returned to the farm in somewhat sombre mood. An hour or so later, as Smith lay dozing in a long chair in the heat of the afternoon, the same group approached, and the attack was launched.

Smith had no chance, and before he could draw his revolver, he had been stabbed several times and his head smashed in with knobkerries. The police were summoned, and those culprits that could be identified and apprehended were processed on simple, criminal charges. No initial link was made between this murder and a number of other similarly angry disturbances taking place at tax-collection centres throughout the district. A few days later, however, on the back of numerous similar reports of violence and indiscipline in the countryside, it began to dawn on local authorities that they had on their hands the beginning of a localized insurrection.

The roots of this situation lay in a by now familiar theme. A year earlier, a troubled period of internal discord and party political squabbling in Natal

169

introduced the weak coalition government of Prime Minister Charles John Smythe. Faced with, among other problems, a fiscal deficit, Smythe adopted as a partial strategy the imposition of a £1 poll tax on every male in the territory living under customary law. This, of course, was aimed at the native population in general, but specifically at a large and economically unproductive male Zulu population still living under tribal custom in Zululand.

In expectation of resistance, a phalanx of local magistrates, police and native administration officials was dispatched into the countryside in advance of collection to explain to the native population the details of the new tax code. These delegations were met in general by an ominous mood, but here and there too by overt displays of discontent and anger. As enforcement of the new tax took effect, rumours began to circulate that an organized rebellion was brewing, supported by anecdotal reports of millennial prophets and seers seen visiting the villages in the wake of magistrates, urging tribesmen to destroy all white chickens, all white pigs and any accoutrement of life attributable to white influence.

The administration and the white rural community were in general dismissive of these rumours, and tax collection in the countryside went ahead under routine police supervision. In a book published in 1966, popular South African history writer, Terry Victor Bulpin, well illustrates the enduring contempt and indifference afforded black superstition and fear at that time. The book was entitled, *Natal and the Zulu Country*, and in it Bulpin remarks of the preamble to the rebellion:

> Discontent spread from one kraal to another. The very mode of life of the tribal Bantu was given to the spreading of distortions. Having no newspapers, they depended on hearsay, and if the mood of the people favoured prejudice, then any rumour supporting that feeling was readily believed. All manner of mystics, village halfwits, witchdoctors and prophets found it profitable to spread stories of omens and signs of their ancestors' wrath at the burdens of the Bantu. Secret commands were whispered for all manner of preparations by rumoured order of such personages as the King of the Basuto, Dinizulu; or Mujaji, the Rain Queen of the LoBedu.

The wrath of the ancestors at the burden of the Bantu might have been easily dismissible, but that burden was real enough. In 1879, the Zulu were defeated in the Anglo-Zulu War, which marked the beginning of the end of the great, independent Zulu polity. The general and steady sequestration of Zulu land shrunk the realm to a fraction of its original size, compounded in the 1890s by

170

an epidemic of cattle disease that decimated the national herd, resulting in many instances of real hardship, and periodically of actual starvation. The decision, therefore, to impose a general tax on the population seems both draconian and insensitive, and it is hardly surprising that a people driven to the very edge of viable existence should fall upon traditional resources, and resist.[1]

Collection began on 20 January 1906, three days before the murder of Henry Smith. The responsibility for collection fell on local magistrates, and while many reported difficulties, for the most part the process went ahead without major disturbance. Then, early in February, in the magisterial district of Henley, just west of Pietermaritzburg, a group of armed men gathered to intimidate the tax-collection party, in response to which the local magistrate ordered a deployment of police. This resulted in a skirmish that in turn resulted in the killing of two white policemen.

This marked something of a point of no return, and what now appeared to be an orchestrated uprising spread throughout the district. In response martial law was declared, and an imperial force of some 1,000 men was raised and deployed into the affected area in order to isolate and quell the disturbance. The rebels, twenty-three in total, were rounded up with the help of loyal reserves of Zulu men, and thereafter tried, with twelve of their number sentenced to death.

The Office of the Governor, Sir Henry McCallum, received instructions from the office of the British colonial secretary, Lord Elgin, to challenge the death sentences, which it did. The effort, however, was generally unenthusiastic, and not surprisingly, it was unsuccessful. Sir Henry McCallum, although an imperial agent, had been locally recruited in Natal, and so his loyalties lay not with Whitehall, but with the local settler community. To quote Terry Bulpin once more: 'The twelve condemned men were publicly shot in Richmond on the 2nd of April after *some legal argument with the British Government* [author's italics] over the sentences had been settled.'

The details of that legal argument remain obscure, although in likelihood it amounted to a query from the colonial secretary into the legality of martial law, and a questioning of the actual necessity to execute men under the delicate circumstances of a native rebellion.

The remaining particulars of the rebellion are perhaps not strictly relevant here, although for the sake of context, the initial disturbances continued as simple resistance to the formal collection of taxes, spilling over here and there into displays and threats of violence. However, in the face of occasional exhibitions of force by local military detachments, tax payments were usually concluded without a repeat of the Henley disturbances.

171

However, in February of that year, a certain Zulu sub-chief by the name of Bambatha kaMancinza refused on behalf of his Zondi clan to pay any taxes. Bambatha was already known to the authorities for various petty acts of resistance and non-cooperation, and there had been some expectation of trouble when the business of tax collection arrived in his area. After a brief standoff, Bambatha was ordered to appear in Pietermaritzburg, which he refused to do. When a police patrol was sent to detain him, he fled with his wife and children north into Zululand, and thereafter became the central figure in the rebellion.

Prior to this, the disturbances had involved small bodies of farm workers and Zulu men in one way or another estranged from tribal law and custom. Bambatha however, entered Zululand where he began immediately to organize formal resistance. His calls to arms proved popular, and he and several other senior chiefs petitioned the Zulu king Dinizulu to throw his weight behind a general rebellion.

This placed the king in a difficult position. He was officially a salaried member of government, and technically ranked no higher than any other traditional chief seconded to the administration through the award of a government salary. The king of the Zulu was the British king, Edward VII, and all were subjects of the British empire. However, Dinizulu remained informally the leader of the Zulu nation, and to his people he owed leadership under these difficult circumstances.

He however adopted a pragmatic position, and although he sheltered Bambatha, and did not, as the law required, arrest and surrender him, he nonetheless admitted that under the circumstances there was nothing that he could do to aid a rebellion. To reinforce this point, he travelled with his immediate family and followers to Pietermaritzburg, and there made a demonstrative point of paying his taxes.

The government, in the meanwhile, indicated its intention to move against the rebels in Zululand, at which point Bambatha and his followers, a minority portion of the independent Zulu population, sought refuge in the Nkandla forest. Here, in a landscape of interlocking hills and valleys, its gorges thickly clad with forest, the rebels found an ideal refuge. They also, however, were easily quarantined, allowing a force of white volunteers and native levies to isolate them, and then flush them out at their leisure. The siege culminated in a climactic action fought on 10 June 1906, in which Bambatha was killed along with several hundred of his followers, with imperial causalities amounting to just three.

From that point on, and for the months that followed, small, protest-level disturbances flared up here and there, which occupied the authorities in a lengthy and rather ugly period of mopping-up. A large number of arrests were made, a great many civil trials and courts martial applied, with significant numbers of men executed, and others, including Dinizulu himself, exiled or imprisoned.

The Bambatha Rebellion was, of course, a hopeless quest, and in real terms not much more than the spontaneous reaction of a people by then at the end of their tether. And indeed, the Zulu were not alone, for similar millennial rebellions were taking place across the region, and, for that matter, continent-wide. Some higher profile examples of this were the Maji-maji rebellion in German East Africa, the Herero uprising in German South West Africa, the maShona and amaNdebele rebellions in Southern Rhodesia and the Bailundo revolt in Portuguese West Africa. Besides these, there were any number of similar, less conspicuous rebellions flaring up and dying down all over the continent, and affecting French, German, Belgian and Portuguese territories quite as they did British.

All of these were in one way or another provoked by the same conditions, and all to a greater or lesser extent were put down by European-led native battalions or constabularies. The rebels were in almost every case motivated by land alienation, coercion into labour, arbitrary taxation and the systematic dismantling of venerable social and political institutions. In each case too, the wider objective of the rebellion, if such existed at all, was to return to some utopian state of the past, prior to colonization and prior to slavery, and to re-establish indigenous rule over the country.

One can perhaps see these as the dying paroxysms of an indigenous society slipping irrevocably into history, with its more traditional elements confronting modernity with both fear and revulsion. It is significant also that in most instances hope lay in an eruption of violence under incendiary circumstances that would spark a more general uprising against colonial overlordship. This never happened, and as in the case of the Zulu, the rebellious elements were easily isolated and destroyed. A majority of the native population by then had come to accept the inevitability of white domination, at least in that generation, and was moving forward to whatever fate awaited the nation with an attitude of fatalism.

It is also worth pointing out that such rebellions were the last of their kind, and the last of what might be loosely termed the 'Native Wars'. The very next rebellion of any significance that took place in the region was one that erupted in Nyasaland in 1915, under the leadership of an American-trained cleric by the name of John Chilembwe.

John Chilembwe used his independent native church as a platform to launch an armed insurrection in Nyasaland – another British territory – which was, once again, relatively easily crushed. The difference on this occasion was the underlying ideology of the rebellion, which was not demonstrably revisionist, but which in fact pictured and espoused a modern, pan-African future configured along democratic, constitutional and parliamentary lines; but, of course, led by the black majority. Its heroes were the likes of Marcus Garvey, W. E. B. Du Bois, Frederick Douglass and Booker T. Washington. Although he did not attend any of its sessions, John Chilembwe was keenly interested in the pan-Africanist movement, and he was engaged with its architects, and the various black militant church leaders of the diaspora.

Indeed, it has often been observed that the John Chilembwe affair marked the beginning of the modern African liberation movement. Every significant rebellion from that point onward, armed or passive, with possible exception of the Mau Mau, was undertaken with a view to achieving similar conditions of modern government under independent black rule.

Another feature of such rebellions, including the Bambatha Rebellion, and indeed the John Chilembwe uprising was the opportunity that they offered to the colonial authorities to respond with disproportionate force and brutality. This was in order, one assumes, to drive home once and for all the message that the world had changed, and the old order was gone forever. The past would never return, the tribes would never rise again, and it would be to the native's ultimate benefit to understand that universal submission, to both tax, labour and colonial rule was now inevitable.

And this was certainly evident in the response of the Natal administration. Lord Elgin, British foreign secretary at the time, was in regular communication with the office of the territorial governor, Sir Henry McCallum. In response to a great deal of official and civic concern expressed in Britain over the sheer weight of executions, Elgin ordered a review of judicial procedure, to which Governor McCallum responded by urging the resignation of the entire Natal cabinet. The message projected to Whitehall was that the matter was in domestic hands, and the days of bleeding-heart interventions from the metropolitan capital were a thing of the past.

Lord Elgin dutifully retreated, and matters were thus concluded in Natal. By the beginning of 1907, the dust had largely settled, and besides a few holdouts here and there, the rebellion was over. Another point perhaps worth mentioning is that much of the imperial government's reluctance to forcefully intervene in Natal was because of the staunch support that the colonial authorities enjoyed elsewhere in the empire. This was heard mainly in

174

Australia, but also New Zealand and Canada, and even more so in Kenya, Rhodesia and Nyasaland, where vulnerable white minorities lived alongside huge native majorities, relying only on their perceived social and economic superiority to remain dominant. The slightest sign of weakness in the ranks would encourage even wider rebellions, and on a much larger scale. It might perhaps be worth noting too that, during the First World War, less than a decade in the future, there was strong initial resistance shown by the European minorities in Africa toward the recruitment of their native subjects for military service at home or in Europe. It was feared that if native troops killed white troops in battle in appreciable numbers, that myth of white superiority would be fatally eroded.

In the meanwhile, King Dinizulu was arrested and brought to Pietermaritzburg where he was tried for treason. His defence was mounted by Sir Harry Escombe, assisted by attorney and ex-prime minister of the Cape, William Phillip Schreiner, incidentally the younger brother of Olive Schreiner.

Schreiner's involvement gave the trial something of a political overtone, and although Dinizulu could not be indicted for any active engagement in the rebellion, he had clearly done nothing to supress it. He was found guilty, therefore, and sentenced to four years of imprisonment on Robben Island. Obviously his removal from Zululand was desirable in order that no powerful political figure around which resistance could coalesce remain, and his estrangement from his people signalled a final end to the rebellion.

When it was all over, it was calculated that between 3,000 and 4,000 Zulus had been killed, more than 7,000 imprisoned and 4,000 flogged. The response from all of the usual sources of protest in Britain was largely one of dismay, but in general the facts and terms of the rebellion were accepted in Whitehall, and the matter was buried at its earliest convenience.

There was, however, a curious postscript to this episode that involved the Natal Indians. Gandhi had by then become firmly established as leader of the combined South African Indian community, and bearing in mind the obvious congruence of the Indian and African struggles, it behoved him to at least comment. And as was his custom, this he did with enthusiasm, ventilating his opinions both freely and openly.

There was, of course, also a sharp similarity between Gandhi's conundrum on this occasion, and that which he faced during the Anglo-Boer War, and as before his initial verbiage tended to be ambiguous, and at times contradictory. Nowhere, however, in all of his written and verbal expressions surrounding this issue, is it possible to discern any overt and sincere expression of sympathy for the Zulu. In fact, in the end, Gandhi, on behalf of his community, simply embraced the crisis as a second opportunity to reinforce the pact of Indian loyalty to the imperial regime.

This position has always been regarded as seminal in Gandhi's civil rights career, and the moral question implicit in it defines in many ways the larger dilemma that he faced in South Africa. In this situation there could be no possible ambiguity, as there had been during the Anglo-Boer War, for the Zulu rebellion was a clear-cut *cri de coeur* from a nation on the very brink of destruction. Moreover, the Indian position in regards to the Zulu was substantially free of formal, discriminatory attitudes, and so Gandhi could hardly have held viable reason other than simple racism to eschew what should have been an obvious moral obligation. However, the lines of that obligation were confused, as history would more clearly define in the years to come, and what might on the surface have seemed an obvious equivalence of interests, was not in fact so obvious at all.

Between his return to South Africa in 1902, and the outbreak of the Bambatha Rebellion, some four years more or less, Gandhi had been hard at work building the foundation of his political career. First he sought entry to the Transvaal bar, which this time was granted without hindrance, after which he established himself in private practice in Johannesburg, balancing his time and energies between his public and professional obligations.

The latter were reasonably mundane, with routine briefs passing across his desk dealing with issues of immigration and licensing, property conveyance, the occasional complaint against one or other public ordinance and various other minor litigations and suits. This was his bread and butter work, but always his interest was more focused, and his efforts most prolific in his public and political work. This was where his heart lay, and his efforts were manifest in an almost unending torrent of correspondence by which hardly a civic department or cabinet desk in the colony was not in one way or another touched. At the same time, he built and maintained an organic personal and political correspondence, embracing a wide spectrum of individuals, nations, religions, disciplines and occupations. This outreach achieved a virtual crescendo when, in June 1903, he founded a newspaper entitled the *Indian Opinion*.

The establishment of the *Indian Opinion* was, in fact, a pivotal moment both for Gandhi and the wider movement, for it not only provided a platform for information and propaganda, but it also immediately internationalized Gandhi's presence. The newspaper was set and printed on a small commercial press working at the Phoenix settlement, an Indian commune north of

Durban, and at first it ran to just a few pages, featuring local news of interest to Indians, published in English and Gujarati, and served by a popular advertising section.[2] Soon enough, however, it began to evolve into a dedicated political platform, almost exclusively deployed by Gandhi himself, and carefully edited by him to build a propaganda base and articulate the aims and objectives of the struggle.

All of this gathering political energy, this girding of the movement, was reinforced by a rigorous and persistent spiritual education. Gandhi's religious platform was never doctrinaire for its own sake, but encouraging of belief in general, and a juxtaposition of that belief upon an obligation to community, shared responsibility and public service. He became obsessively controlling of his own appetites and weaknesses, and with a focus on naturalistic medicine, he promoted a carefully moderated diet, and a demonstrative distance from all carnal or temporal pleasures.

Towards the end of 1904, for example, his wife Kasturba returned to South Africa from India, joining him in Johannesburg. After being told that the sensual aspects of their relationship were now over, Gandhi put it to her that his work was now of such paramount importance to him that she would likely see very little of him.[3] Thereafter she was installed in his house on Rissik Street, where also lived a selection of Gandhi's friends, not one of whom was Indian.

At the time Gandhi shared a home in Johannesburg with a British Jewish couple, Henry and Millie Polak, the former of whom was a sometime legal partner. These were joined on occasions by a Lithuanian Jew of the name Hermann Kallenbach, and Gandhi's personal secretary, Sonja Schlesin, who also, incidentally, was a Jew, and who seemed to make no secret of the fact that she was in love with him. Into this confusing and non-traditional environment Kastruba Gandhi was thrust, suffering as a consequence a great deal of alienation and isolation. With a few exceptions, she appears to have been largely estranged from her husband, and she participated in the movement only very sporadically, and rarely obvious.

In the meanwhile, the *Indian Opinion* emerged as the crucible of Gandhi's thoughts, and the foundry of his evolving political and spiritual identity. In it he was free to publish his prolific outpourings on philosophy, politics, diet, lifestyle and religion. For example, in a series of three lectures delivered to the Transvaal Theosophical Society, published later in the *Indian Opinion*, he spoke first on Hinduism, then on Islam and finally on Christianity. Maintaining thus a determined universalism, he submerged himself ever deeper in a curious amalgam of politics, religion, lifestyle and asceticism,

177

cultivating his peculiar identity, and inviting upon himself in the process not infrequent accusations of being a quack or a crackpot.

In general, however, Gandhi possessed the ballast of character and force of personality to ride above such accusations, and on the whole his achievements spoke for themselves. However, although sure of himself, and of singularly decided opinions, it can hardly be doubted that the Bambatha Rebellion challenged him to in some way confront an element of the struggle that he had hitherto made, and would continue to make diligent efforts to avoid.

Modern perceptions of Gandhi range from his embrace by Christians as a new messiah, by Hindus as an avatar and by the global humanitarian and civil rights movement as a pathfinder. At the opposite extreme, however, he is often exposed as a self-possessed, sex-addicted, dictatorial and opinionated autocrat. Needless to say, somewhere in the middle will reside the truth, but the matter of the Bambatha Rebellion, and his response to it, has been continuously deployed by Gandhi's detractors as clear evidence that at heart he was a racist.

In 2004, American Sikh author, G. B. Singh, published a book entitled *Gandhi: Behind the Mask of Divinity*, which sought through various devices to expose Gandhi as something a great deal less than the Mahatma. The motivation behind this can only be guessed at, but in the matter of the Bambatha Rebellion, Singh unearthed a fruitful resource. Gandhi, he claimed, destroyed a significant portion of his personal archive immediately prior to leaving South Africa, in an effort, one can assume, to expunge his public position on this specific episode, and the Native Problem in South Africa in general.

What was destroyed was apparently a mountain of written material detailing Gandhi's early race perceptions, which, by the time he came to leave South Africa, he had come to realize were inappropriate. What he was unable to alter or destroy, however, was the archive of the *Indian Opinion*, and there is enough questionable race-orientated material in this to suggest at least the ghost of a possibility that the accusations made against him were true.

His early representations on behalf of the Indians of South Africa, as we have already heard, tended to be narrowly focused on ensuring that Indians were differentiated from blacks in local discriminatory legislation. He seemed often to adopt the same fundamental language and attitudes of the white settlers, and in fact he was responsible for more than one editorial submission that might have been lifted directly from some similar screed of the *Natal Mercury*. Consider, for example, this extract from a promotional speech delivered during his 1896 tour of India, the tone of which, again, is that Indians are not black, and please don't call us black:

> Ours is one continual struggle against a degradation sought to be inflicted upon us by the Europeans, who desire to degrade us to the level of the raw Kaffir whose occupation is hunting, and whose sole ambition is to collect a certain number of cattle to buy a wife with, and then, pass his life in indolence and nakedness.[4]

In the end, however, Gandhi settled on advising his followers once again to lodge their loyalty with the colonists, and to contribute matériel and manpower to the official police action against the Zulu. Possibly he saw the same merit as the whites in wrenching the raw kaffir free of the orthodoxy and limitations of his tribal existence, and breaking the shackles of social slavery to release the soul of the black man to redemption. Possibly he looked no further than the narrow needs of his own community, and possibly both. 'What is our duty during these calamitous times in the Colony?' he asked from the pages of the *Indian Opinion*. 'It is not for us to say whether the revolt of the Kaffir is justified or not. We are in Natal by virtue of British power. Our existence depends on it. It is therefore our duty to render whatever help we can.'

Soon afterwards, with his volunteers, armed with stretchers and medical satchels, he set off for the frontline. Many years later, with the benefit of hindsight, and no doubt seeing the wisdom of a recant, he wrote thus of the matter in his autobiography: 'I bore no grudge against the Zulus, they had harmed no Indian. I had doubts about the rebellion itself. My heart was with the Zulus.'

About this there can hardly be anything other than a hollow ring, although the episode does not end precisely here, for although history does not widely acknowledge it, some good did come of the Bambatha Rebellion.

A cordiality was established between whites and Indians on and about the battlefield, but wounded white colonial troops would rarely allow themselves to be administered to by Indian nurses. Wounded blacks, on the other hand, be they the battlefield wounded or those maimed by brutal floggings, were left out in the open, often without medical care at all. Few of these were reluctant to accept care from an Indian hand, and perhaps, as an unintended consequence of the whole regrettable episode, Gandhi threw across the first thin traverse of understanding between black and brown in South Africa.

This, of course, did not prompt him on behalf of the Indian movement in

South Africa to ally himself with the black political movement; far from it, that would not occur until the advent of the anti-apartheid movement of the post-Second World War era when South African Indians began to identify themselves primarily as South African. Perhaps, therefore, as the raw Kaffir was being broken on the wheel of British justice, his most honest reflection was that he simply did not know what to think. If anything, it would seem that the experience brought home to him the fact that the Indian struggle in Africa was not an African struggle, but an Indian struggle, and as such it belonged in India, and not in the emerging dogma of African liberation history. The two enterprises, he concluded, were fundamentally separate.

Chapter 21

The African Man

'No class of subject with any degree of intelligence and ambition to raise its standard of living, and to enjoy its rightful share in civilization, has ever obtained justice from a ruling class, over whom they have no control by share in representation; and no such class will ever be content to remain in such subjection.'
—Professor H. J. Wolstenholme (Smuts's Cambridge tutor)

The first, and perhaps the only substantial encounter between Mohandas K. Gandhi and a significant black political figure in Natal, a Zulu educator by the name of John Dube, took place a year before the Bambatha Rebellion, in August 1905. The occasion was a meeting of the British Association for the Advancement of Science (BAAS), held that year at a private home in Mount Edgecombe, a stone's throw from both Phoenix and John Dube's industrial school at Inanda.

Gandhi founded the Phoenix settlement in 1904, two years after his return from India, which he intended as a kind of collective headquarters for him and his small corps of activists and acolytes. It became home to a number of important members of the movement, as well as, of course, the presses of the *Indian Opinion*, and has since become something of a shrine to Gandhi and the civil rights movement in South Africa.

The settlement was located within a few miles of the small North Coast town of Inanda, which was home to John Dube's Zulu Christian Industrial School, and although, on an ideological level, both institutions shared a common objective, they existed and functioned without even a minimum of cooperation.

At the meeting of the BAAS, Dube took the opportunity to speak out against taxation, land seizures, poverty and social alienation, which was perhaps the first time that Gandhi had the opportunity to hear the black political agenda spoken by an educated black man, and he was impressed.

John Langalibalele Dube was born in 1871 at the Inanda station of the American Zulu Mission, his father an ordained priest and his mother a Christian convert. His primary education was received at the hands of the mission, which, in common with allied missions across the territory, sought to educate Zulu youth in basic literacy for the purpose of conversion and 'civilization'. His secondary education, however, was received at the nearby Adams College, founded in 1853, also by American missionaries, but somewhat more secular in tone and technical in its instruction.

From there Dube followed his mentor, the Reverend William Cullen Wilcox, back to the United States where he was enrolled at the Oberlin College in Ohio. During this period, he fell very much under the influence of the black American educationalist Booker T. Washington. Dube was enamoured particularly of Washington's concept of industrial education, and his 'learn-to-walk-before-you-can-run' approach to black emancipation and postbellum reconstruction.

Dube brought this concept home with him, and broke ground in the establishment of the first fully indigenous educational institute, the Zulu Christian Industrial School, also known as Ohlange High School. Modelled closely on Booker T. Washington's Tuskegee Institute, Dube sought to replicate the same principle of educating Zulu youth in industrial and trade disciplines for the sake of practical engagement in the modern economy.

In general, however, black political activity in Natal was muted, as it was in the Orange River Colony, and for broadly similar reasons. Black political organization was discouraged, and at times suppressed, and certainly no avenues of formal political expression were available to the wider spectrum of blacks. The Transvaal, however, differed somewhat, for here there existed a mass movement of migrant labour that resulted in the free exchange of social and political ideas, and a breakdown of the traditional barriers of tribe and language. Through the medium of religious and social organizations, vigilance associations and a vibrant cultural interchange, black political activity on the Rand was vigorous.

It was in the Eastern Cape, however, where the crucible of black political consciousness burned most brightly. Here, though the traditionalists clung with no less tenacity to their cultural memory, they yielded in increments their children to formal education. This education was provided by European, often American, missionary churches and outreach organizations, and was initially focused on literacy for the sake of conversion, and the creation of indigenous preachers and catechists. This was often, although not universally, accompanied by stringent efforts to westernize youth, to strip them of their tribal identity and to suppress indigenous social practices.

As early as 1854, government support and funding began to be channelled, first towards supporting mission schools, but later in the development of native schools that offered a more diverse and secular education. This opened the way for a handful of 'gifted' blacks to thereafter find their way to overseas universities, which in turn kindled a desire, and perhaps even an expectation that they would soon progress toward middle class, and in due course, with wealth and professional standing, and under equal political circumstances, they might lay claim to a congruent share in local and central government.

It was also under the shelter and direction of the church that the first native language newspapers and periodicals were established, maintaining, of course, a safe distance from politics by dwelling almost exclusively on social, religious and parish affairs. In 1876, *Isigidimi Sama Xhosa* (*The Xhosa Messenger*), the first authentic, Xhosa-run newspaper, was founded.

Isigidimi was established at the Lovedale Missionary Institute, an organization founded in 1824 by the Glasgow Missionary Society, which soon after became a focus of black education, and the seedbed for early black political propagation. Many among the first and second generations of black South African political luminaries were past pupils of Lovedale, and although the institution became a pariah to later generations of right-wing Afrikaner nationalists, in the early days of the Cape it proved to be a powerful force in the advancement of black consciousness.

Much of the impetus emerging from Lovedale, and the growing number of independent newspapers and publications, were to encourage and establish a bedrock of black voters as a mainspring to black political expression. The success of this was evidenced by the number of prospective white parliamentarians contesting seats in the frontier districts who were forced to modify and tailor their platforms to appeal to a mixed audience of blacks and whites. Although no authentic black political parties would emerge in the colony until the new century, social clubs and interest groups were forming all the time. Some of these had distinct political overtones, and an increasing number of militant and separatist independent churches developed, inspired by an emerging movement known as 'Ethiopianism'.

Here we enter the very genesis of modern African liberation politics. The Ethiopianist movement was inspired by the biblical psalm 68:31: 'Ethiopia shall soon stretch forth its hands unto God.' The English translation of this psalm varies in many contexts, and does not in every one offer the same interpretation. However, the implication of the psalm was taken to mean that Africa, and the people of Africa, including the African diaspora, would soon link hands with God in the common purpose of liberating themselves and all of the enslaved masses of the world.

Christianity found fertile ground in Africa, and among the many individuals and communities cast adrift by the collapse of their societies, and perhaps absorbed into culturally heterogeneous workforces, early missionaries reaped a bonanza. Africans willingly embraced the faith, finding within its precepts something so deeply appealing that even when the break came, and independent movements began to form, the rebels could not bring themselves to separate entirely from the core ideology. Instead, independent churches radicalized, and indigenized, and became proto-political organizations tending towards nationalism, cultural autonomy and disinterested in political unity or cooperation with the whites.

Their ideal was to cast off white domination, and to achieve as high a degree of independence as possible, while at the same time not abandoning the best elements of European civilization. The first formal separation along these lines came in 1882, with the formation of the Thembu Church under the leadership of a native Wesleyan minister by the name of Nehemiah Tile.

Nehemiah Tile clashed with his white superiors over the political flavour of his ministry, and, once released from white control and censure, his independent movement did indeed begin to express itself in noticeably political language. The organization was structured along the lines of the Church of England, but Victoria Regina was exchanged as titular head of the church with the Thembu paramount leader, Chief Dalindyebo. Traditional leadership within the community was revived somewhat thanks to this alternative hierarchy, and through the structure of an independent church the Thembu community discovered new avenues of protest and a new source of strength in organization.

However, as Nehemiah Tile began to advocate for the non-payment of taxes, and non-cooperation with the government, he came under the scrutiny of the authorities. Upon the first application of official pressure, Chief Dalindyebo abandoned the notion of rebellion and returned with little persuasion to the safety and respectability of the mainstream church. Soon afterwards the Thembu Church collapsed, but not before it had cast its spores, and before too long, similarly configured independent churches were rising and falling all over the colony.

The more radical Ethiopianist tradition, however, found its most fruitful expression where the internal diaspora was most concentrated, in the seething human heterogeneity of the labour compounds, the townships and city slums of the Witwatersrand. Here men from all over the region gathered, hybridizing their languages and merging their multiple traditions of lifestyle, culture and religion. Where societies thus mingled, the established churches provided both community and commonality, and where political activity had no home, nationalism found voice, and for the first time there existed the potential for a mass movement on a national level.

The Ethiopian Church was founded in Pretoria in 1882 by a progressive, if not entirely radicalized, black nationalist Wesleyan minister by the name of Mangena Mokone. It was he who identified Psalm 68:31 as the rallying cry of the movement that struck a match to the tinder, and soon enough a movement flared into existence. Mokone then lobbied tirelessly among the diffuse body of secessionist churches in the Transvaal, creating something akin to a franchise, seeking affiliation thereafter with the African Methodist Episcopal Church, a powerful black ministry in the United States. A certain James Mata Dwane, firebrand secessionist Methodist, travelled to the United States and negotiated the merger, returning sometime between 1896 and 1900 as the bishop of the new AME church in South Africa. The AME then established itself as the umbrella organization of secessionist, independent churches throughout the region.

This was a powerful, spontaneous and aggressive expression of black political ambition, and it was greeted, initially at least, with benign interest by the white establishment, and some small efforts at encouragement and support. Cecil Rhodes, for example, offered land and support to the church to establish itself in the Rhodesias, and provided funds for James Dwane to travel to Ethiopia in order to establish a chapter there, with others proposed in various colonies of east and central Africa.

The fate of the independent churches in South Africa, however, was in the short term to fracture, merge, refract and coalesce, until only a handful of dissociated independent churches remained in the shadow of the AME. The AME itself, however, stayed loosely affiliated with its sister organization in the United States, and would remain strong, to emerge in due course as the largest black church in South Africa. It is interesting in this context to note that the AME achieved official recognition in the Transvaal, but was banned in Natal, and gained no significant foothold in the Cape at that early stage.

In the meanwhile, as independent black churches were radicalizing, the native press was also separating itself from its orthodox church roots. John Tembo Jabavu, a Xhosa political activist and editor of *Isigidimi Sama-Xosa*, grew jaundiced at the interference of missionaries, and went on to found the innovative, but somewhat conservative *Imvo Zabantsundu* (*Black Opinion*). This was followed by the more radical *Izwi Labantu* (*Voice of the People*), founded by activist Walter B. Rubusana, and partially funded by Cecil John Rhodes in pursuit of an authentic African support base for his political platform. Rhodes, however, made it a policy to grant full editorial freedom to the black staff of *Izwi Labantu*, included among which were some of the most progressive and forward-thinking black African political figures of the age. A number of these would go on to found the South African Native National Congress, forerunner of the iconic African National Congress.

This utopian moment in the race history of South Africa formed part of the preamble to the Anglo-Boer War. As Milner, Chamberlain and others beat their chests and demanded that the Boer republics elevate their social and political standards to emulate those of the British, promises were widely circulated that upon victory in a future war, the British would force the equalization of race policy throughout South Africa. In much the same way as the Indians were inspired to believe that this would bring about universal race equality in South Africa, so did the blacks.

As a consequence, black, like Indian support for the British war effort, was comprehensive, and although the conventions of war forbade the large-scale arming and mobilization of blacks for combat, multiple supporting roles were filled by blacks. Black newspapers mobilized readily to the British cause, swearing loyalty to Her Majesty and welcoming imperial intervention.

And thus the war was fought, but at its conclusion, the British where confronted with a negotiated peace, and the deferral of any grant of comprehensive black political liberty went ahead under only the vaguest provisions that, while no progress could be immediately expected, no reversals would be tolerated.

From that moment onwards, black political and social aspiration became a phenomenon to be managed, and in general it came to be defined as the 'Native Problem'. The essence of the Native Problem was the speed with which blacks embraced and adapted to modern life and politics. Those in the era of Christianity and Commerce who had predicted generations, perhaps even centuries of cultural evolution before a black man could hold a pen, engineer a sprocket, compose an editorial or manage an electoral campaign, were, quite naturally, both surprised and unnerved.

The first serious effort to articulate the Native Problem, and thus define a solution, was an inquiry commissioned by Alfred Milner, the report of which was published in 1905. The substantive document begins by introducing the *dramatis personae* of the Native Problem, specifically the

Fingo, Basutho, Zulu, Hottentot and Bushman, or alternatively, any individual generally referred to as a 'Kaffir'.[1]

In the opening discussion, the question of land was introduced, and, with surprising candour, it was construed as desirable for there to be separate areas of black and white land ownership. Likewise, it was suggested that there be restrictions imposed against black squatters on white land, and limitations on land made available to black employees on white land, and, indeed, for black missionary staff resident in the native reserves. The suggestion that the areas of race overlap be corrected by the removal of blacks to native reserves was justified somewhat by the spurious advantages to be anticipated from this. The report concluded by acknowledging the right of those blacks chafing under communal tenure to buy land in areas of freehold if they could afford it, and to farm thereafter alongside white freehold farmers.

In its entirety, the document was detailed and thoughtful, but at the same time pragmatic in recognizing that there was no place in South Africa for a race utopia, and that certain accommodations were required to keep the peace. At some ill-defined point in the future, extensions would be added to the native reserves, and some sort of entry into the formal franchise devised, but such could wait, and it did.

The document then touched on native customary law, tribal administration, family life, habits, Christianity and morals, before alighting for a moment on the church separatist movement. The movement was acknowledged, but quickly ascribed to indiscipline on the part of the native clergy, accusations of low moral thresholds and an admission that the commission had little sympathy for the movement. However, in the interests of avoiding anything interpretable as religious persecution, and so long as the movements dissociated themselves from mischievous political tendencies, they should be recognized and held to a certain standard, but otherwise left well alone.

The native press, the commission likewise acknowledged, but dismissed somewhat as immature and not necessarily reflective of the opinions of the more staid and experienced men who were in closer touch with the masses – in other words, the traditional leadership.

In general, however, the report was prepared to acknowledge the emergence of the first saplings of civilization among the natives of South Africa, but was apt to reflect on the quaint and harmless aspects of native life as being its most attractive features. In controlled terms, the tendencies to political mischief and the waywardness of certain elements running far ahead of themselves were deplored. The tone was benign and the content sweeping, and the conclusion simply to maintain, and entrench here and there, the status quo.

This view that the black man was to linger indefinitely in a social hinterland did not account for the absorption by industry and mining of large numbers of blacks into the urban areas, in particular Johannesburg, and the imposition of hut taxes, or land taxes as was often preferred, which sat very heavy on the list of growing black grievances. There were many within the British administration who did not directly subscribe to this over-simplistic raft of solutions, and who argued variously that the Cape system of qualified franchise should be applied to all of the colonies, that it should be abolished altogether, that all native mobility in urban and white farming areas should be limited by pass laws, that no mobility restrictions should apply at all, and that mixed-race people should be granted the opportunity to express their European heritage rather than be forced to make common cause with the blacks, ultimately against the whites.

It is interesting to note Gandhi's view of all of this. His observations over the many books and theses written in later years vary, and at times he appeared capable of language that echoed the pomposity and insensitivity of the white establishment, and at others he reflected ruefully over the loss of innocence, and the evils of a too-ready embrace of the worst elements of civilization.

However, from his memoir of passive resistance in South Africa, one can draw arguably the most succinct definition of white attitudes to blacks in the new century. Even though written by a non-white – Gandhi himself – it was a view, ironically, which few whites would ever have dared to so openly express. What follows, therefore, is a definition of the 'Sacred Trust' in language both clear and innocent:

> Civilization is gradually making headway among the Negroes. Pious missionaries deliver to them the message of Christ as they have understood it, open schools for them, and teach them how to read and write, but many whom, being illiterate and therefore strangers to civilization, were so far free from many vices, have now become corrupt. Hardly any Negro who has come in contact with civilization has escaped the evil of drink. And when his powerful physique is under the influence of liquor, he becomes perfectly insane and commits all manner of crimes. That civilization must lead to the multiplication of wants is as certain as that two and two make four. In order to increase the Negro's wants or to teach him the value of labour, a poll-tax and a hut tax have been imposed upon him. If these imposts were not levied, this race of agriculturists living on their farms would not enter mines hundreds of feet deep in order to extract

gold or diamonds, and if their labour were not available for the mines, gold as well as diamonds would remain in the bowels of the earth.

And where upon this complex landscape of race politics did Jan Smuts stand? Upon his return to South Africa from England, replete in the afterglow of a fruitful political tour de force, he proudly circulated his memorandum to a number of interested parties throughout South Africa. One such copy arrived on the desk of Cape parliamentarian John X. Merriman, a clear-sighted, centre-left liberal whose position on the colour question in South Africa reflected a considerable core of his peers. These were men and women who were, on the one hand, unreconciled to absolute black inclusion, but on the other, cognizant that a point of inevitable accommodation was approaching, and sooner rather than later.

Merriman replied to Smuts by the very next post, noting that, notwithstanding the beauty of its liberal principles, Smuts's memorandum reminded him uncomfortably of the American declaration of independence, insofar as it ignored three-quarters of the population because they were coloured. He then went on to observe: 'I do not like the natives at all, and I wish that we had no black man in South Africa. But there they are, and our lot is cast with them by an overruling providence and the only question is how to shape our course so as to maintain the supremacy of our race and at the same time do our duty.'[2]

Merriman, as a Capetonian of the old school, and although wary of its potential to flood the electorate with non-white voters, advocated the Cape electoral system as a safety-valve. Although noisy and evil-smelling, he said, it was nonetheless the safest contingency against an explosion. To perpetuate the exclusion of blacks, Merriman suggested, it would be necessary only to keep the property and income qualifications high enough to limit their access to the voters' roll.

To this, however, Smuts replied, somewhat sardonically, that the war and the rinderpest had created such a class of poor whites that they too would be excluded if a colour bar were not somehow in place.[3] Although he sympathized with the native races of South Africa, whose land it had been long before the present policies of dispossession, he admitted that he did not believe in politics for the native, in fact he did not believe in politics at all as an avenue to the attainment of higher values. Indeed, the question in his mind was less the ability of the black man to adapt, but whether it was in his best interests to do so. He would not, he said, under any circumstances, make available the franchise to the wider native population of South Africa.

Chapter 22

The Black Act

'It is better to be violent, if there is violence in our hearts, than
to put on the cloak of nonviolence to cover impotence.'
—Mahatma Gandhi

The willingness of British prime minister Henry Campbell-Bannerman to
grant Smuts his request for responsible government was hailed by both sides
as a triumph of diplomacy, and evidence of the pragmatism and political
genius of both men. The decision, however, hid a number of small
expediencies, one of which was the Chinese labour crisis, and the other the
perennial Indian question in the Transvaal.

It had, at least in significant part, been upon the back of the Chinese labour
crisis that Campbell-Bannerman's Labour–Liberal coalition had toppled the
Conservative government. Now that the Liberals were in power, however,
the crisis became their own, and in the best traditions of a Chinese puzzle,
the multiple paradoxes of the situation continued to defy solution.

Smuts's and Botha's Het Volk party campaigned on the Chinese question
with the same passion as had the British liberals, but upon their platform the
Chinese were represented not as the innocent victims of an impersonal
empire, but as heathens, murderers and thieves. Both British and Afrikaner
labour in the Transvaal were united in their opposition to the continued
importation of Chinese, a fact brilliantly harnessed by Smuts as perhaps the
only unifying feature of the entire campaign. At the same time, however, the
British could hardly risk the collapse of an industry by bringing the practice
to an end, and nor, at least for the time being, could Smuts.

It was with some relief, then, that the British government handed the issue
over to the incoming government in the Transvaal, hiding behind the same
argument that Chamberlain had when approached by Gandhi five years
earlier. His Majesty's government sought, and was granted limited influence
over the self-governing colonies of the empire, and frankly, thank God for

that. The matter was therefore inherited by Smuts, who played it with consummate gamesmanship, and at the end of the Transvaal electoral campaign, sent it back across the net to the British.

In December 1906, the British government issued the letters patent of the new Transvaal constitution, within which a moratorium on both the further importation of Chinese labour and the renewal of existing contracts was stated. Provisions were also made for a repeal of the Labour Importation Ordinance, which could potentially have offered the opportunity for large numbers of Chinese to remain in the Transvaal as free immigrants. To seal this loophole, the Indentured Labour Laws (Temporary Continuance) Act of 1907 was passed to allow sufficient time for contracts to run their courses, but to phase out Chinese labour on the Rand over a period of some two and a half years.[1] This offered Smuts and the new government of the Transvaal a buffer to deal with the matter while at the same time granting the British the opportunity to wash their hands of it altogether.

The conclusion, therefore, of the Transvaal Chinese labour crisis bore upon it a stamp of both political expedience and the pathos of human propaganda. After 1906, for a variety of reasons, the tide turned in the matter of local and regional black labour, and increasingly the need for alternative sources of labour diminished. The political unpalatability of a large Chinese presence in the colony was now matched by their practical redundancy, and while the opportunity existed to get rid of them, the government of the Transvaal sought to do so. From 1907 until 1910, as batches of contracts expired, so the individual contract holders were repatriated back to China. This process continued until February 1910, marking the end of a labour experiment that had seen the arrival in the colony of some 63,000 individuals, and the removal of a similar number.

The procedure, however, was not without some trauma and resistance. Mine owners, who had underwritten the process at significant cost, protested the waste of money, and the waste of a labour resource that had finally reached a marketable point of proficiency. And, of course, few among individual Chinese saw any advantage in returning to an environment of continued poverty with the possibility before them of remaining in the economically vibrant Transvaal. Multiple petitions were drafted, one on a length of gold silk, and mine owners in many instances were seconded to petition on their behalf, but the authorities remained unmoved, and by the boatload the Chinese were sent home.

So much for the Transvaal Chinese question, but that did not answer the Transvaal Indian question. Upon the desk of the secretary of state for the colonies, none other than Lord Elgin, sat the draft bill of a new immigration law intended to supersede and rationalize the old republican rules of immigration. Royal assent was required, now something of a formality, since in Pretoria sat a popularly elected government acting under the terms of responsible government. This, however, did nothing to deflect the protests and petitions that began arriving on the same desk soon afterwards, for Gandhi was once again in a ferment, pointing out every permutation of disadvantage to Indians in the proposed new law, and appealing for it to be disallowed.

At last, it would seem, Gandhi had alighted on a powerful and emotive cause. The law under review was Transvaal Asiatic Registration Act, Ordinance No. 29, better known as the Black Act, and although its requirements were wide ranging, its intended purpose was quite clearly to close the door of the Transvaal to fresh Indian immigration, to clear out of the territory all of those illegally resident and to rigorously control the lives and liberties of those that remained.

What is interesting, however, is that this new legal statute was a British creation. Alfred Milner, of course, had by then left the shores of South Africa, taking with him his dream, but leaving behind an administration and civil service still dominated by his old Kindergarteners. The interests of these men were quite varied, and no longer, for the most part, focused exclusively on South Africa. Thanks to the free flow of administrative personnel between the various colonies of the empire, most of the Kindergarteners had by then some experience of government in other parts of the world, and had begun to form a picture of the empire as a whole in a more modern and structured context.

Among these was a 34-year-old bureaucrat and professional colonial civil servant by the name of Lionel George Curtis. Curtis was a contemporary of both Smuts and Gandhi, inasmuch as he was a British-trained lawyer and a subject of the same empire, but there the consanguinity of the three ended. Curtis was of the English middle classes, educated at Haileybury and Imperial Service College, an institution intended to groom future colonial administrators, after which he read law at New College, Oxford. He had served in the Anglo-Boer War as a member of the City of London Imperial Volunteers, seeing no action to speak of, but finding himself enamoured of South Africa, and keen to enlist when Milner cast about for young men of calibre and ability to staff the new British administration.

For a time, Curtis served as Milner's private secretary, and the two men shared the common objective of promoting British interests in South Africa,

Milner from an imperial perspective, but Curtis more as a means of ensuring that South Africa remained within the British sphere of influence as a pillar of the future federated British empire.

This marked a moment of ideological transition on many fronts. The new generation of British imperialists, defined very much by the likes of Curtis and Milner's other Kindergarteners, saw the empire in a very different setting to the older generation, those such as Milner himself. The question now was how to formulate a future structure that would accommodate, not only the divergent interests and aspirations of the various colonies, but to do so in a way that was compatible with the vast racial and ethnic variety that the empire contained. No better test case of this was there than South Africa, a theatre of extraordinary racial and ethnic diversity that, if all of its elements could be reconciled, would be a template for future world government.

At about this time, the concept of Social Darwinism as a means of quantifying racial diversity was gaining in popularity. Every year, more detailed anthropological and sociological studies of the human species in its many variants were adding to the overall picture. As that picture expanded, so the question of hierarchies began to occupy the minds of those imperial strategists attempting to create some sort of practical emulsion from the immiscible properties of the human race.

The 1859 publication of Charles Darwin's ground-breaking *On the Origin of Species*, notwithstanding the conservative backlash that it prompted, unleashed also an entire field of thought and study over the question of human evolution, replacing past tendencies to dehumanize the various aboriginal races of the world, in particular those subject to institutionalized slavery, with the more thoughtful concept of evolutionary progression. In the age of abolition, and the great global expansion that followed, the European races, in particular the British, felt a moral responsibility to promote aboriginal humanity, and to uplift those unfortunates to a status at least somewhat recognizable as civilized.

By the turn of the century, however, in particular in Africa, the movement towards African emancipation was too advanced to be arrested, and too robust to be ignored. The founding social ideal of the French empire, for example, to create black Frenchmen out of the elites of the African colonies, became subsumed by the sheer weight of expansion, and the impracticality of creating upwards of 60 million black Frenchman out of the bewildering cultural diversity of the new French empire. The question of 'association' superseded that of 'assimilation', which had always been an ideal rather than a practical policy, but association, in practical terms, could only be conceptualized with the European remaining the senior partner into perpetuity.[2]

This question, with all of its corollaries, absorbed the British administrative and academic elite in South Africa in a series of intellectual forums and discussion groups that centred on the question of race, race compatibility and future strategies for race management in a rapidly comingling world. Lionel Curtis, for example, was one of the founding members of the Fortnightly Club, an informal debating society comprising a clique of surviving Kindergarteners, members of government and various local academics and professionals. It was a free-ranging body dedicated to exploring a variety of issues of contemporary interest, with the subject of race enjoying a conspicuous priority. In 1903, for example, Lionel Curtis himself delivered a lecture entitled 'The Place of the Subject Races in the Empire' while another senior member posed the question 'Can the White Race Continue to Dominate South Africa?' Both of these titles hint equally at the conundrum and anxiety at the root of early twentieth-century white perceptions of race. Central to the fortnightly debates, however, and central also to informal discussion both within government and without, was the Indian question.

The Indian situation in the Transvaal at that time was fluid. A great many had abandoned the colony at the outbreak of war, and had remained outside of the borders of the Transvaal as the various post-war adjustments were taking place, but within a few years the mines had reopened and the economy was revitalized, offering Indians the opportunity to prosper once again. A steady stream of fresh arrivals repopulated the old Indian locations, while a number of Indian concerns long established in Natal sought to infiltrate agents and family members into the Transvaal. In consequence, a steady and noticeable increase in the number of Indians living and trading in the colony attracted the attention of the Asiatic Department, which was unable to equate a steadily bourgeoning Indian community in Johannesburg and Pretoria with a moratorium on the grant of new entry permits to Indians. Clearly something was afoot.

At about this time, an English native administrator by the name of Lawrence Elwin Neame gave voice to mounting white concern by writing and publishing what became an influential and widely appreciated critique on the threat of unregulated Indian and Chinese immigration. *The Asiatic Danger in the Colonies*, despite the eugenic tone of its title, was in fact no more than a thoughtful analysis of the likely long-term effect of unregulated migration through the many social and geographic gates unlocked by the advent of empire. In the context of the times, the book is refreshingly free of pejorative, and in many instances defined the risk as simply the diligence and productivity of the Indians and Chinese, and the threat this posed to European privilege and *laissez-faire*.

In a nutshell, however, as one reads between the lines, it is clear that *The Asiatic Danger in the Colonies* remarks most clearly on the intuitive anxiety felt by a relatively small white population contemplating the almost infinite potential for Indian and Chinese immigration. From the point of view of the administration, which by then certainly regarded itself as temporary, the question was less visceral, and centred more on how to prevent an Asiatic takeover of South Africa for reasons of global strategy. The net result was the same, however, and a great deal of forthright public discussion preceded the eventual tabling of the Black Act.

The act was drafted primarily by Lionel Curtis who, as the head of the Asiatic Department, was behind much of the heavy-handed enforcement of current regulations against the Indians. Under the new law, every Indian resident in the colony of the Transvaal, 8 years old or above, would be required to register his or her name with the Registrar of Asiatics, and to take out a fresh certificate of registration. Applicants were to surrender their old certificates and submit to full finger-printing, photo-identification and a declaration of any identifying marks. The document then issued was to be produced upon demand by any police officer or government official.

When Gandhi became aware of the existence of this bill, and digested its implications, he was naturally dismayed. He recalled the earnest protestations made by various British agencies in the Transvaal Republic that the unequal treatment of Her Majesty's subjects anywhere in the world simply would not stand. This had been much of the stated reason for declaring war a decade earlier, and how ironic it was now, after that war, that the British should be found sharpening those very weapons of discrimination so crudely forged by the Dutch.

The question, however, was how to take issue with it, because even to Gandhi it was quite obvious that the Indians were not playing by the rules, at least according to the law, and that he would be hard-pressed to argue against this. Instead, he settled on the *terms* of re-registration. Indians already registered as residents of the Transvaal Colony should be permitted to re-enter the colony under their pre-existing documentation, while fresh immigration should be controlled on the basis of a system of registration unchanged. In other words, no additional requirements such as photographic identification, or a full set of fingerprints, the latter of which, rather nebulously, he declared was an affront to Indian dignity.[3]

On the basis of this, Gandhi set about drafting petitions, and gathering support in a rather frenzied campaign of propaganda that initially seemed a little out of proportion to the issue at hand. As a lawyer, he could hardly have been insensible to the necessity of revaluating and updating legislation in the aftermath of a total regime change, and that a certain imbalance of attention applied to different races in such a racially charged social environment could also hardly have been unexpected. He would also have been fully aware of the difficulties confronting the colonial administration in the Transvaal over the matter of Anglo–Boer reconciliation, and what pragmatic concessions would be necessary for a smooth transition towards territorial union and self-government. This was not just a question of perceptions of superiority or inferiority, but a necessary phase of ending a war.

Gandhi, however, was at that point building a career, and while he would have furiously denied any suggestion of personal ambition, it would be stretching the imagination to conclude that there was none. By then his political philosophy had begun to transform parallel to his emerging spiritual/religious persona. He had founded the egalitarian Phoenix community, established the *Indian Opinion* and imposed upon himself the moral and practical disciplines that would see the gradual emergence of the Mahatma. The celibate, abstemious and barefoot ascetic was gradually eclipsing the urbane and self-possessed barrister. He had begun to develop a philosophy of selfless public service as a religious expression and a hybrid, Tolstoyesque ideal of non-resistance and non-cooperation.

On 1 September 1906, he led a delegation to Pretoria and there met Sir Patrick Duncan, another of Milner's Kindergarteners, and the last British colonial secretary of the Transvaal colony. To Duncan, Gandhi wasted no time in making plain popular Indian opposition to the new law, stating for the first time in terms both clear and unequivocal that the Indian community of the Transvaal would not abide by its terms. In his turn, Duncan remained steadfast, refusing to agree to any changes, and refusing moreover to consider withdrawing the application for royal assent. To this Gandhi simply reiterated that the Indian community of the Transvaal would not under any circumstances submit to re-registration. If gaol was the alternative, then he stood ready to be the first to step through those gates.

Gandhi, however, sought legal advice on the matter before plunging into a confrontation of this nature. He consulted a well-known Jewish barrister, Reinhold Gregorowski, who warned him that the moment was premature to roll out a programme of passive resistance, and that in the correct order of things, it would be necessary for the Indian community first to assemble a delegation to travel to London and petition the Colonial Office to disallow the new law.[4]

A few days later, a meeting was held in the Empire Theatre, Johannesburg, that hosted a capacity audience of local Indians, and during this meeting a general refusal to accept the terms of the new law was articulated and reinforced by a number of prominent men from the community. Gandhi was both surprised and gratified at the passion of this response, and speaking only late in the proceedings, he limited himself to laying out the practical and legal ramifications of resistance to the new law. A commitment to non-compliance was easy enough to make, he warned, but it would be less easy to carry through.

So, while a majority of speakers fulminated and hammered the table, Gandhi sat for most of the meeting in thoughtful silence. In a way he had been usurped, and scholars have since debated whether it was he who brought the concept of passive resistance to the table, or whether he simply took it up, and from it created the necessary political ideology. Either way, it was not he, at that formative moment, that drove the popular embrace of passive resistance, and one is left with the feeling that it was only afterwards that he claimed ownership of it.

However, quite naturally, it was he who was selected to lead a small delegation to London in order to plead the Indian case before the colonial secretary, the weary and much-burdened Lord Elgin. And thus it was, as preparations in Pretoria were underway for responsible government, and the presumption of local control, Lord Elgin found himself assaulted by the furious energies of Mohandas K. Gandhi. During his first few weeks in London, Gandhi was reported to have consumed as many as 5,000 penny stamps, firing off correspondence at a blistering pace, supported by an active and growing phalanx of British Indians. The latter, of course, was led by the ageing Dadabhai Naoroji, and buttressed by the more avuncular, but no less energetic Sir Mancherjee Bhownagree, both of whom kept the issue live on the floor of the House of Commons.

What the new law represented, Gandhi claimed, was a clear case of double standards. Everything that the British empire claimed to stand for was made a mockery of by this act of a subordinate colonial parliament. Of this obvious truth Lord Elgin was not insensible, but he was as clear as he was fair-minded, and more able perhaps than Gandhi to appreciate the situation for what it was. He submitted a request to the administration of the Transvaal to water down the worst language in the bill, but beyond that offered no commitment to advise His Majesty's government against approving the law.

The simple truth of the matter was that larger things were at stake than the sensibilities of a handful of Indians and, indeed, South Africa was not the only British overseas territory where expatriate settlers were on the defensive. The same was playing out in the two Rhodesias, Nyasaland and indeed Kenya. In the pending European war, Britain would survive only upon the loyalty of her colonies, and while India was of significant importance, the survival of India as a colony was dependent on British control of the major global shipping lanes, and that depended on the solid commitment of the British colonies of South Africa.

'I suppose there could be found,' Lord Elgin remarked in his summing up of the meeting,

> if not in the records of this office, at any rate, in the records of the India Office, despatches with my signature attached to them, protesting in as strong language as has been used here, against the restrictions on British citizens, and I do not go back from one single word. But we have to recognize the fact that all over the world there are difficulties arising on the part of white communities, and we have to reckon with them. I do not say that they ought always to succeed: they certainly ought not to succeed in points of detail which would, in any way, involve oppression. But the fact of there being that sentiment has to be borne in mind when we have to deal with matters of this description.[5]

Within a week Gandhi was en route back to South Africa. There he immediately embarked on a tour of Natal and the Transvaal, addressing large gatherings of Indians, urging them to get their houses in order, to avoid spitting, hawking or breaking wind in public, and to keep their homes, yards and shops scrupulously clean in an effort to provide no ammunition to the whites of the colony. He had not yet quite settled on a course of action, but while the Transvaal reconfigured itself as a self-governing British colony, he made ready to introduce himself to the next generation of colonial administration in the colony.

Chapter 23

A Meeting of Minds

'Smuts received me coldly, if not with mistrust. The lean, unsmiling visage, the piercing blue-grey eyes, the quick impatient speech, the frigid bearing of the new State Attorney – all were disconcerting. This was no man to suffer fools gladly or at all.'

—Sir Roderick Jones, London director, Reuters

And when that day came, Gandhi and his five companions purchased first-class train tickets in Durban, and began the slow journey up the escarpment to Pretoria. There, in due course, they presented themselves at the Ou Raadsaal, the old Council Chamber, and then allowed themselves to be ushered into the book-lined offices of the new colonial secretary, the 37-year-old General Jan Christiaan Smuts.

Although very little has been written or spoken about this first meeting between Smuts and Gandhi, the events that followed have tended to suggest that the two men were immediately drawn to one another. Their similarities in many ways outweighed their differences, and should the barriers of race and circumstance ever have been removed, one can imagine that each would have found much in the other to impress and entertain him.

However, despite a lengthy and pleasant prelude, both men were under pressure to keep matters businesslike, and so the embrace of two like minds untangled. As was typical for both men, Gandhi spoke and Smuts listened, and after an hour or so, Smuts finally leaned back in his chair, glanced at the clock, nodded at Lane hovering in the doorway and guided the meeting to its conclusion. He admitted that much of what he had heard was new to him, and although it was all food for thought, and notwithstanding his commitment to consider the matter and respond, he was forced to concede that on the main questions his mind remained unchanged.

Gandhi, however, had not yet finished. He offered the unexpected proposition that the Indians of the Transvaal would *voluntarily* submit to registration, if either the application for royal assent to the law was withdrawn, or the law itself not enforced. It was the *inequality* of the law, its direct targeting of Indians and its implied compulsion that wounded the Indians, not so much the sting of a flash bulb or the impression of a digit or two on a registration form.

In reply, Smuts acknowledged the difficulties that the law imposed on the Indian community, but confirmed that he would consider no relaxation of its general terms. There was simply too obvious and widespread a misuse of the current methods of registration, resulting in an extensive and quite blatant traffic in illegal immigration.

Smuts was reminded by Gandhi that the terms of re-registration were unacceptable to the Indian population of the Transvaal, in reply to which Smuts expressed his regret, but remarked that simply because a criminal might find the enforcement of the law odious to his profession, he cannot be held exempt from it. There was every reason to suppose that the act would be granted royal assent, after which the Indian community would be held accountable under the law in common with all other residents of the colony. If the law offended the Indian community based on laws and conventions applicable in India, then let the Indians return to India to be subject to those laws. So long as they wished to reside in the Transvaal, the Indian community would be required to submit to the laws of the Transvaal.

The two men then shook hands and parted company, immediately after which the Transvaal prime minister, General Louis Botha, who had been listening on the other side of a door, entered Smuts's office and asked his friend and colleague how serious he thought Gandhi was. As he left the building, Gandhi no doubt asked himself that same question: Where to from here?

The fact that he had made the suggestion to Smuts that Indians voluntarily re-register suggests that Gandhi either fundamentally misunderstood the intent of the law, or that he expected Smuts to immediately understand the lateral extent of his thinking. Smuts was not concerned with the inconvenience of those forced to endure renewed bureaucratic procedure under a revised law, but with the large numbers of Indians illegally resident in the colony, and the many others waiting to enter illegally. Voluntary registration hardly answered to that question. To Smuts, as to any practising technocrat, voluntary compliance was no principle upon which to base a law. Laws are by definition mandatory, and enforcement exists as a necessary factor of compliance.

A MEETING OF MINDS

In later years, in particular in regards to the parting of the ways between Hindu and Muslim in India, Gandhi would make numerous similar, and extraordinarily quixotic proposals that caused his more orthodox colleagues to scratch their heads and wonder at times if he had gone mad. In fact, Gandhi remained throughout his life committed to the idea that given the chance, an individual or a constituency would veer always toward the right thing. This would become a pillar of his later passive resistance movement, and it is not altogether surprising that he left the meeting in an optimistic frame of mind. Smuts was a man of obvious intelligence and integrity, and so he would quite naturally come around to the obvious moral conclusion. It was simply a matter of time and persuasion. He was wrong, Gandhi was right, and as such the matter would in due course be resolved.

What Gandhi could never have entirely appreciated, however, although he made great efforts to do so, was the elemental fear that Indian immigration generated in the Transvaal. Quite as Natal had evidenced Mauritius a generation earlier as an example of how things could end up, so the Transvaal needed now only to point to Natal. Though Gandhi could argue all day long that the intentions and objectives of the Indians in the Transvaal were innocent, it would make no difference at all. Indian immigration was seen as potentially infinite, and all that held back the flood was a dam wall of flimsy legislation, and with the very last ounce of his resolve, Smuts would ensure that that law remained in place.

Gandhi, in the meanwhile, set to work. Within days of the meeting, letters and petitions began to fly off in all directions, and the pace of cable traffic between London, Calcutta and Pretoria quickened. As he laid the foundations of the struggle, however, Gandhi was at the same time groping for some philosophical validation for what he was feeling, and what he was acting upon. He was already acquainted with Tolstoy, and was enamoured of Tolstoy's essential sentiment of outrage against unjust authority, but in Tolstoy something was lacking. What that deficit might be is perhaps best articulated by Tolstoy himself, in an open letter written to the Indian independence movement in December 1908: 'This phenomenon seems particularly strange in India, for there more than two hundred million people, highly gifted both physically and mentally, find themselves in the power of a small group of people quite alien to them in thought, and immeasurably inferior to them in religious morality.'[1]

It was this identification of religious inferiority that struck an immediate chord with Gandhi, who valued his moral/religious superiority no less than Smuts his intellectual. However, more importantly, the concept segued naturally into an ideal expressed by Henry David Thoreau, another great influence on Gandhi, who, in his seminal essay, *Civil Disobedience*, might have been speaking almost exclusively to him: 'I think that we should be men first, and subjects afterward. It is not desirable to cultivate a respect for the law, so much as for the right. The only obligation which I have a right to assume is to do at any time what I think right.'[2]

So it was that Gandhi chose to classify himself as a man first and a subject later. It was not enough, however, for him to adhere to the pattern of civil disobedience defined by Tolstoy and Thoreau, for they were theorists, never to be granted an opportunity to influence an authentic revolution.[3] Gandhi would create a pattern of civil disobedience that was specific to his own needs, and congruent with the religious ideology of his constituency.

A few days later, the *Indian Opinion* announced a competition to be held by the British Indian Association to find a name for the new movement. Gandhi's son Maganlal suggested the word *sadagraha*, an idiomatic Hindi term meaning firmness in virtue. This Gandhi tampered with slightly to create the even more ambiguous composite, *satyagraha*, taken from the Sanskrit word *satya*, implying love, and *agraha*, meaning firmness. Upon this he meditated for some time before announcing to the community that the programme of passive resistance would henceforth be known as *satyagraha*.[4]

At that point, other than in its basic precepts of non-compliance with the law, and the style of analogies that Gandhi used to explain it, the concept was vague. Its specific Indian, or perhaps even Hindu, identity came about at that point only because a vast majority of its adherents were Indian Hindus. Many weeks and months seated on a cold concrete bench in a variety of South African prisons would transpire before Gandhi could coherently express the deeper subtleties of the movement. For the time being, however, a war was afoot, and it would be this fight that would define the nature of the wider revolution to follow.

The opening shots of the war were typically rhetorical, and while Gandhi fired off letters and editorials, the community met in an ongoing series of public assemblies where the majority swore absolute non-compliance with the new law. The gathering pace of the movement was buttressed by expressions of sympathy and support from India, and encouraged by unmistakable signs of wavering in Whitehall. Not since the Sepoy mutiny of 1857 had such a fervour of nationalist sentiment gripped the Indian public. During that uprising, rebellious Indian troops had rallied around the name of the last surviving Mughal emperor, but this time popular support solidified around a religious zealot with authentic, revolutionary ideals. Nothing here

202

could be 'put down'. Troops could not be rushed from here or there to meet resistance with oppression. It was a popular movement based on non-violence, and subject peoples the world over were watching very closely. The British empire was on trial, and under the terms of its own charter, the case was unanswerable.

In the meanwhile, the fury of all this preparatory work did not go unnoticed in the white community. A fortnight or so later, a letter appeared on Smuts's desk from the governor-general, Lord Selborne, now something of a ceremonial figure, but a thoughtful man nonetheless, and a valued friend of Smuts. Selborne was undertaking his own diplomatic offensive, meeting liberal whites and uncommitted Indians, and generally attempting to build bridges. His letter appealed to Smuts to find some way to head off a crisis. Could not voluntary registration be implemented as a compromise? Creating Indian martyrs would be an unwise strategy bearing in mind the state of things in India and Kenya, and surely a compromise was possible?

To this Smuts replied in his customary style. He had enjoyed his meeting with Gandhi, he admitted, and would be willing again to meet him in the spirit of friendliness, but the fact remained that there was simply no support among his constituents to consider any softening of his position.

Chapter 24

Satyagraha

'The spirit of Satyagraha rightly understood should make the
people fear none and nothing but God.'

—M. K. Gandhi

On 1 July 1907, the Black Act was granted royal assent, and came
immediately into effect. Within a week an Office of Asiatic Registration
opened its doors in Pretoria, and there, officials of the Asiatic Department
sat in readiness.[1] Indian and a handful of Chinese pickets were posted outside
the office by the Satyagraha committee, to intercept any Asians attempting
to enter and to hand out anti-compliance literature to those turned away. Some
small amount of molestation was recorded, and perhaps a little over-vigilance
on the part of the police, but in general each side went about its business
peacefully, and with due courtesy to the other.

Gandhi, in the meanwhile, divided his time evenly between Natal and
Transvaal, following a routine of frenetic work, organizing, publicizing and
building the organization from the ground up. He made free use of the *Indian
Opinion* to counter a furious barrage of hostile European press, deflecting
reams of scurrilous pejorative and spiteful accusations that were freely traded
in all four of the colonies.

The British press, for the most part, maintained a more circumspect tone,
treating the matter in a thoughtful and restrained manner, and on the whole
taking sides with the Indians. The Indian press, needless to say, fulminated
in fitful, and sometimes even hysterical support for the Transvaal Indians.
Bearing in mind the mercantile character of the Transvaal community, this
overseas support, although encouraging, did not comfort those fearing local
reprisals, a boycott of Indian shops or the arbitrary cancellation of licences.

Gandhi toured the districts of Pretoria and Johannesburg, soothing fears
and fortifying resolve, offering such thoughtful advice to the wealthy that
they might avoid carrying cash on their persons, lest they be tempted to reach

into their pockets when the hand of the law came to rest upon them. In general, however, the community held firm. The genius of *satyagraha* seemed to be that it framed itself in religious and spiritual terms, which placed it where a majority of Indians could not easily ignore it. Gandhi himself was assuming the aspects of a religious figure, his asceticism increasingly manifest in his appearance and manner of dress, which, of course, added a certain amount of force to his message. *Satyagraha* did not seek simply to impose the will of the masses through non-compliance, but it sought to convert the enemy to a complete acknowledgment and embrace of the *truth*.

And what was this truth? Gandhi at that point was not entirely sure, but the language and mood of *satyagraha* was such that it appealed mainly to young men with some education who found in the tenets of pacifism, and passive aggression, a very satisfying model of resistance. Behind these were the women, a constituency within which Gandhi always enjoyed conspicuous success, and it was they who quite often influenced the wealthier and less educated men who had more to lose than most. These were in some respects the Randlords of the Indian community, wealthy men thriving under a discriminatory system that compensated for its exclusivity by the free distribution of money and opportunity.

One such was a Gujarati Muslim shopkeeper, unnamed in Gandhi's memoir, who made a significant point of registering according to the law, and then acting to persuade his family, employees and customers to do the same. This individual was approached by the Satyagrahis, and an unsuccessful attempt was made to return him to the fold. The effort must have been forceful, however, for the police were summoned, and Gandhi was warned to speak and act only within the law. He then resorted to the *Indian Opinion*, naming and shaming individual dissenters whom he reprimanded for taking out a 'title deed to slavery'.

The Muslim–Hindu divide proved to be perhaps the most challenging problem. Both sides in the Transvaal claimed favouritism against the other, and accusations of bribery and partiality were freely exchanged, with Muslims claiming that Hindus had orchestrated their victimization by government, and vice versa. The majority of Indians in the Transvaal, as elsewhere, were Hindu, and since *satyagraha* was largely a Hindu concept, no small amount of Gandhi's energy was applied in assuring Muslims that the weight of the struggle was to be evenly borne.

Despite all of the problems, incongruities and contradictions, Gandhi seemed nonetheless to have set the match to an authentic popular movement, and Indians from Johannesburg and the Rand willingly joined in solidarity with those in Pretoria. Public meetings, protests, speeches and social gatherings went on, and were generally well attended. The government was urged, even at that late hour, to accept the compromise of voluntary registration.

Then, in October 1907, after having registered no more than a handful of Asiatics, the Pretoria office closed its doors and the process moved to Johannesburg. Here the largest and wealthiest Indian community resided, and here too it was felt that matters would somehow come to a head. So far a generally watertight compliance with the movement had been achieved, with no violence, no obvious coercion and no evident breaking of the ranks. Both sides held their respective positions, and a breathless sense of anticipation hung over the colony and, indeed, over the empire.

On the government side, not an inch had so far been yielded. No police action had been mounted, no public order arrests made and no overt public propaganda disseminated. Unlike Gandhi, Smuts uttered not one press pronouncement, keeping his cards close to his chest.[2] He was, however, under considerable pressure behind the scenes. Winston Churchill, with whom he was now friends, consoled him with an acknowledgement that it was indeed unfortunate that an advance force of Indians had established a beachhead in the Transvaal, but did it really make any sense at such a delicate time to harass them, or to bind them up with vexatious regulations when the same result could be achieved voluntarily?

The Transvaal agent-general in London, Sir Richard Solomon, likewise warned Smuts to tread with caution. Why, he asked, could Smuts not simply have softened some of the harder edges of Lionel Curtis's original draft, bearing in mind that Curtis, a competent man to be sure, had never heard his common touch complimented. To make martyrs out of the Indians at this moment would serve no useful purpose.

Most impactful, however, was a short tract in a much longer letter written to Smuts by his old Cambridge mentor, an atheistic and at times anarchic old academic by the name of H. J. Wolstenholme. Wolstenholme was a man of singular views, and from his vantage of almost total hermitage in a cottage on the outskirts of Cambridge, he enjoyed a remarkably well-informed perspective:

You look at home and are content to hope that the agitation with you is 'dying out', but its reverberations in India and its embarrassing effect on the English government of India, its effect on the relations of East and West will not readily die out. You forget that these 'poor devils' belong to a race, or complex of races, with an ancient civilization behind them, and a mental capacity not inferior to that of the highest Western peoples, who are developing rapidly a feeling of nationality and a capacity for the more active and practical life of the more materialized west.

These were powerful words, and considering the source, they could hardly have been read without discomfort. The elderly tutor went on to add that, while the Indians of the subcontinent might look down on their own labouring classes, and deny them a great many social gifts and advantages, yet mishandle those lower classes in a foreign country and watch the Indians throw up their arms and protest. 'And it would surely be wise statesmanship,' Wolstenholme sagely concluded, 'as well as good Human fellowship, to concede in time and with good grace what is sure eventually to be won by struggle.'

While the opinions of a man like Wolstenholme did not by any means reflect the views of the average Englishman, such things were indeed already under discussion in British liberal and intellectual circles. It was becoming increasingly clear to the salient political elite that India was lost to the empire, and what remained was simply to establish a process of disengagement. It could be as easy or as difficult as Britain chose to make it, but in the end, what happened in the Transvaal would happen on a much larger scale in India, and what happened in India would without doubt inform the future of Africa.

Of none of this advice was Smuts enamoured, but he could hardly fail to see the truth in it. It was easy enough, however, to wax liberal in Cambridge without a hint of opposing opinion to consider. On his left Smuts could hear the clamour of those British liberals to whom he owed so much, but on his right the Transvaal electorate, to whom he owed no less, was clamouring with equal determination to be heard. In the end he made it clear to all that he would demonstrate the mercy of the law only after he had stamped on the protest the mark of its authority.

And so it continued. Having extended the deadline once or twice, Smuts established 30 November 1907 as the date by which all Indians were to be registered. Figures vary on how many complied, but certainly it was very few.[3] While a handful of illegally domiciled Indians fled the colony, most remained, with many crossing back and forth between the two colonies in open defiance of the law. Smuts, however, refrained from arresting for the time being, and as the deadline approached, a great deal of pre-emptory hue and cry rose in the community, and telegraph traffic between Calcutta, London and Pretoria grew frenzied.

And then, in a sudden move, Gandhi was arrested in a sweep that netted over a hundred key Satyagrahis. A few days later, the entire haul was brought before a magistrate and asked to show cause why all should not be deported for non-compliance with local immigration requirements. Each man declined to do so, after which the hammer came down on a mass deportation order, with periods of grace ranging from seven days to two weeks.

Thus began Gandhi's *satyagraha*, one of the great and iconic episodes of modern imperial history. It is a story that has been often repeated, and each time, more often than not, with a greater emphasis on the violent racism of the white government confronting virtuous Indian forbearance. In a generally civil age, however, matters were dealt with throughout the crisis with resolute courtesy, and absolute regard for the dignity of those subject to British law. When Gandhi finally found himself standing in the dock, having ignored his deportation order, he was forced to beg the presiding magistrate for the harshest sentence applicable, fearing that the sting of his campaign would be muted by the reserved application of law.

In the end, he was sentenced to two months' simple imprisonment without hard labour, part of which he served in a general prison known as the Old Fort. The Old Fort, located on Constitution Hill, close to the centre of Johannesburg, was a mixed facility, and to their displeasure, Gandhi and the 150 or so imprisoned Satyagrahis were detained in the native wing.

Before too long, however, and under loud protest, the Indians were relocated to an exclusive wing where they were granted such privileges as writing and reading material. They were also provided with specific religious facilities, and the standard prison diet of corn meal and vegetables was waived in favour of rice. Certain Satyagrahis complained in letter to the *Indian Opinion* of being forced to share prison facilities with blacks, adding that if Indians were not permitted to use the white entrances to public buildings, then a third entrance should be provided.

And so passed an uneventful two months during which Gandhi found the time to meditate and reflect on what he had started. Either during this, or a later term of imprisonment, he chanced to read Henry David Thoreau's lengthy essay, 'Civil Disobedience', a moment that has been claimed by many historians to be his road to Damascus.

All of his legal training, and his years of practice could not but have left him with an appreciation and respect for the law, but his reading of Thoreau triggered the epiphany that revolution cannot be achieved under the law. The legitimacy of government, ratified only by the vote of a majority, cannot in itself be regarded as a divine validation. The challenge of *satyagraha* was, therefore, to determine at what point the majority transgressed, after which it was the responsibility of individual Satyagrahis to ensure a spirit sufficiently translucent to make that determination. According to Thoreau, it is impossible for a human being to define and oppose all evil in the world, but all men must contribute to the whole by refusing to participate in any evil. Nonparticipation can perpetuate no violence, as violence perpetuates violence, and if a cause has merit, it must inevitably succeed.

Sitting at a wooden desk in a common cell, jotting down his thoughts, perhaps preparing an editorial for publication in the *Indian Opinion*, Gandhi slowly began to define the theory of *satyagraha*, and as a consequence to understand it. This first prison experience, although only lasting a few weeks, proved nonetheless to be formative. It gave him a captive audience, and his irrepressible optimism and the simple amiability of his character endeared him to all. He developed then the beginning of a cult following, and it might perhaps not be overstating the matter to suggest that the Mahatma was born precisely then and there.

Smuts, in the meanwhile, left Gandhi to stew, until one day, in casual conversation with the political editor of the *Transvaal Leader*, a certain Albert Cartwright, he mentioned that he might consider opening negotiations with Gandhi if the latter was of a mind to compromise. Cartwright was a liberal pressman, one of very few in the Transvaal, and perhaps sensing a scoop he volunteered to serve as an intermediary, an offer that Smuts accepted.

From Pretoria Cartwright travelled directly to Johannesburg, calling on Gandhi in the Old Fort with a proposal. Gandhi listened, and replied promptly, reiterating to Smuts that it was the compulsion of the law that outraged the Indians, and that if voluntary registration could be agreed upon, the Indians might see their way clear to calling off the protest.

So it was that on the stroke of noon, on 30 January 1908, a black Model-T Ford left the gates of the Old Fort prison and drove along Empire Road towards Johannesburg's Park station. In the back seat sat Gandhi, dwarfed by a burley constable on his right and the Johannesburg superintendent of police on his left. It was the latter who escorted him through the front gates of the railway station, across the concourse and into a second-class carriage travelling north. Two and a half hours later, walking the short distance between Pretoria station and Church Square, the two men arrived at the Ou Raadsaal, where they were admitted into the building through the trade entrance.

This time, the curtains of Smuts's office were halfway open, and a warm summer sunshine flooded the room. Smuts rose from his desk to greet his visitor, shaking his hand with genuine pleasure, and offering one of two seats that had been arranged around the Turkish rug. Lane entered, greeting Gandhi with the civility due any visitor, before setting down a tray of tea. Gandhi did not drink tea, but took a thimble-full of milk and a glass of water.

This time the introductions were brief, and the conversation steered to the point with a minimum of formality. As far as Gandhi was concerned, the situation remained unchanged. The Transvaal Indians were prepared to press on with their protest until every member was imprisoned, and they would remain under terms of incarceration until there had been acceptable changes to the law.

No minutes to this meeting were taken, and Smuts himself neither spoke nor wrote anything about it, so the question of what precisely was agreed to after this lies between the two men themselves. However, in his book, *Satyagraha in South Africa*, written two decades after the fact, Gandhi had this to say: 'The substance of the proposed agreement was that Indians should register voluntarily, and not under any law … and that if a majority of Indians underwent voluntary registration, government would repeal the Black Act, and take steps with a view to legalize the voluntary registration.'

This was according to Gandhi, but the likelihood is far greater that Smuts simply deliberated aloud the possibility of standardizing procedure by merging the Asiatic Registration Act with the general immigration laws of the colony. By doing so, the Black Act would naturally fall away. If there was any ambiguity in this, and there certainly was, Smuts made no effort to clarify it. In the meanwhile, he advised, a programme of voluntary registration would be acceptable to the government, so long as full compliance was guaranteed by Gandhi himself.

This Gandhi accepted immediately – Smuts had done the 'right thing' – and a deal was struck on a simple shake of the hand. Smuts then put a telephone call through to the office of the attorney-general and ordered the release of all Indians held in the Transvaal on public order offences. Gandhi, now a free man, confessed that he did not have three shillings for the train, which Smuts immediately dipped into his pocket and lent him, and the two men thus parted in a mood of good humour and mutual triumph.

Back in Johannesburg, Gandhi immediately set to work, summoning the Satyagraha committee as a matter of priority to ensure that the difference between voluntary and mandatory registration was understood before the newspapers reported the fact the following morning. This was no easy task, and writing some years later he paraphrased what must have been a very difficult speech: 'Our struggle [is] aimed not at the abrogation of this principle but at removing the stigma which the Black Act sought to attach to the community.'

A more vague and unsound position it is hard to imagine a lawyer adopting, for even though the law was unequal and discriminatory, it nonetheless existed as a law, and therefore mandatory submission to its statutes was surely inevitable. It is also true that Gandhi had in the first instance demanded a complete repeal of the law, based on its obvious discriminatory elements, and his insistence now on voluntary rather than mandatory compliance can be seen as nothing less than a compromise to himself, rationalized only later by the creation of supporting rules of *satyagraha*.

None of this was well received in the community, and while some members slapped him on the back and congratulated him for a job well done, others grumbled behind the scenes that he had sold out. When asked what guarantees he had been given, Gandhi lapsed into hazy doctrine, portraying the Satyagrahi as one fearless of betrayal, stalwart in his own righteousness and impervious to infidelity. Smuts might do what he would, but nothing could dilute or diminish the divine purpose of *satyagraha*: 'And such is precisely our position regarding registration, which cannot be affected by any breach of faith, however flagrant, on the part of the government. We are the creators of this position of ours, and we alone can change it.'

In the end he produced a carefully crafted editorial in the *Indian Opinion* that in essence expressed the difference between the honour of voluntarily washing a man's feet and the humiliation of being forced.

The very next day, he set off on foot from his home on Rissik Street in order to be the first to present himself at the registration office. He was, however, intercepted by a small party of Pathans and Punjabis who accused him of selling out, and then set upon him with clubs and sticks in an attack so unexpected and ferocious that Gandhi was felled immediately. Thereafter he was kicked and beaten, and a duel ensued between a lone supporter wielding an umbrella and a knot of armed attackers, until a detachment of police arrived on the scene. Gandhi and his companions were escorted to the office of a nearby attorney, and there, in a state of shock, Gandhi issued a short statement, asking afterwards that a registration official be summoned in order that he might not be diverted from submitting his registration. The matter was played down in the *Indian Opinion*, and only reported in any detail by the European press.

In the meanwhile, in a generally friendly and peaceful atmosphere, the programme of voluntary registration went ahead. The community submitted without protest, and perhaps with some relief, and in general it appeared that the matter had been amicably resolved. Then, entirely without warning, an announcement was made by the Office of the Colonial Secretary that the window of opportunity for voluntary registration in the Transvaal would close after three months, after which the standard application of law would apply. When news of this reached Gandhi he could scarcely believe his ears. By then a majority of Indians in Pretoria and Johannesburg had registered, and immediately the naysayers and malcontents began to point fingers at him. His supporters, of course, closed ranks, but it was quite clear that he had been duped. Slim Jannie had played a masterful opening manoeuvre, and no doubt Gandhi could see it quite clearly then.

For a while he floundered, firing off waves of correspondence, and heating the bearings of the *Indian Opinion* in ream upon ream of bitter protest. Within a few weeks, however, he collected himself, and proposed in the absence of any better strategy to burn all registration documents. Several letters of protest were sent directly to Smuts, who ignored them, but summoned Gandhi once again to Pretoria for a third face-to-face meeting.

Here Smuts was pointedly accused by a humiliated Gandhi of a breach of faith. This he rejected entirely, reminding his legal colleague that this law, as with all laws, was an act of parliament, and was therefore beyond the power of any individual cabinet minister to advance or repeal. He could do no more than table a bill, and even this he had given no commitment to do. Gandhi, as a lawyer, should surely appreciate that no law could stand on the basis of voluntary compliance alone.

All of this Smuts was disposed to say in simple and plain language. His professional forbearance did not falter, but his position remained unyielding. Gandhi was made to understand that the wider constituency of whites in the colony did not like him or his compatriots, and with very few exceptions would be overjoyed to see his entire race depart the colony. This was the basis of immigration restrictions in the Transvaal, and Smuts wondered aloud how much better off the Indians might have been had Gandhi remained in India.

Gandhi then took his cap in hand and approached his own people. He requested a meeting of the Indian leadership, and there attempted to explained the situation. It was a difficult story to tell, and clearly it was not universally accepted, for ten years later, when he committed it to paper, one can still feel the stinging mortification of the moment: 'You know the stuff we Indians are made off, men whose momentary enthusiasms must be taken at the flood. If you neglect the temporary tide, you are done for.'

It is also quite clear that he did not blame himself. He was guilty not of incredulity, he argued, but of trust, and of that he could never be ashamed. The Satyagrahis, he insisted, must enter the struggle with an even temperament and accept the inevitable reverses with divine forbearance.

And yet, he was angry, and disappointed, and his responses reflect that fact. His treatment of Smuts was peevish, and his accusations petulant and childlike. He had been made to look a fool, and he did not like that. He reported to Smuts that he had been assaulted in the street because of it, and that in the present mood of the population, many more similar assaults would follow. To this Smuts's private secretary, the long-suffering Ernest Lane, expressed his sympathy, but confirmed that no voluntary registration would be acknowledged beyond the date published, adding for effect that if Gandhi himself, or any member of the community, felt under threat of violence, they need only seek the protection of the police.

For the time being, therefore, the question of the Black Act was laid to rest, leaving the local and British press to pick over the bones of what had for a while been quite a feast. Gandhi returned to the routine work of law and organization, bruised but undefeated, and now at least appraised of precisely what to expect. For the time being the attention of the political establishment shifted to the question of unification as preparations to take the next logical political step after responsible government were made. It was now the responsibility of the leaders and elders of all four colonies to meet and determine if such common cause existed among them to create a federation.

Chapter 25

A House Divided

'It is undoubtedly a fact that the [Black] Act has met with an organized resistance from the Asiatics, the possibility of which was never contemplated, and the grounds for which are still difficult to understand.'

—Jan Christiaan Smuts

'As one studies the unfolding conflict from 1908 until 1914, one has the feeling that Gandhi could see in advance what course it would follow, whereas Smuts, time and time again, was taken by surprise.' This was the view of William Hancock, author of a sweeping, two-volume biography of Jan Smuts that remains the definitive chronicle of his life. It is the opinion of this author, however, that both men at that moment were improvising under an extremely fluid set of circumstances. Smuts had on his plate an emerging labour unrest on the mines, the gradually spreading spectre of far-right Afrikaner nationalism and the complex political obligations thrown up by South Africa's imperial relationship. Both men were entering uncharted territory, and neither really had a clear sense of where all of this was going. As the dust settled on this first round, however, Smuts was relieved for the time being to put the matter behind him, and to turn his attention to the question of South African unity, and preparations for a national conference due shortly to open in Durban. Here the various self-governing colonies of the future union would discuss a federal relationship, inter-white relations and, perhaps most emotively, the question of the native franchise.

The conference, although an inter-territorial affair, would nonetheless attract international attention, simply because the resolution of South Africa's complex issues of division and unity held ramifications for the entire world. Smuts was the international face of South Africa, and it gave him no pleasure to approach such a monumental moment in South African and British history while at the same time dealing with a high-profile Indian protest.

For his part, Gandhi allowed the dust to settle in order that he might meditate and reflect on what had taken place. He was quite aware that he had triggered the onset of a mass movement, but he realized also that for it to flower and grow it would require firm direction and leadership. His reputation had been damaged, and Smuts had emerged with the satisfaction of that at least, but he was determined now that nothing like it would happen again. Although the failure of the first act of *satyagraha* had been in large part due to his own naivety, he also identified a lack of detailed coordination and effective politicization.

He had not, for example, fully appreciated the risks and uncertainties felt by those of wealth and influence who would quite naturally be reluctant to join the movement on the level of grassroots activism. Those men could better serve the revolution through financial and political support. The foot soldiers of *satyagraha* could only be those who could realistically spend long months in prison, and in so doing could rely on the practical and financial support of the community. It would be necessary therefore to build a core of activists whose sole function was to undertake the tasks of *satyagraha*.

For the time being, therefore, he ordered no renewal of the protest, but encouraged its continuation as a low level community action. Unlicensed hawkers, for example, continued to openly trade in the suburbs of Johannesburg and Pretoria, shopkeepers were encouraged to allow their trading licences to lapse and of course Satyagrahis continued to enter and leave the colony without documentation. Gandhi dutifully defended as many of these as he could, but shortly before noon on 10 August 1908, he was stopped and asked by a policeman to present his certificate of registration, which, of course, he refused to do, at which point he was arrested, arraigned and once again given leave of deportation.

In the interim, he and other Indian leaders, including the Chinese leadership, attached their signatures to a letter to the director of Asiatics, a certain Montford Chamney, demanding the return of all documentation pertaining to the voluntary registration of Asiatics, claiming that registration had taken place under false pretences. This went unanswered, and was followed by an appeal to the Supreme Court within which Gandhi submitted as evidence an exchange of letters between him and Smuts after the fact, which the court threw out, stating that none could stand the construction of a breach of faith.

In the meanwhile, a parliamentary bill to legitimize the voluntary registration of Asiatics, as Smuts insisted had been agreed between the two men, came under debate in parliament. To coincide with this, a meeting of some 2,000 Indians was held at the Hamidia Masjid mosque in the southern suburbs of Johannesburg. There the community waited, ostensibly for news that the parliament of the Transvaal had voted to repeal the Black Act, as Gandhi continued to maintain had been promised, although obviously neither he nor anyone else expected this to happen.

During this debate, Smuts spoke at length, airing his views on the entire crisis, and expressing at the same time considerable personal confusion. He pointed at the Black Act itself, noting that, according to statistics available to him, some 7,000 Indian heads of households were currently resident in the Transvaal, an increase of perhaps 5,000 on those legally registered under pre-existing laws. This suggested at the very least a massive influx of illegal immigration in the period since British rule, justifying in totality the imposition of extra laws and statutes.

He noted also an expectation held, and articulated by the Indians that His Majesty's government would disallow the law in question, to which he expressed amazement. Such laws were commonplace, and normal, and it was the sovereign right of any government to control its boundaries, and moreover, should the Indians desire their legal treatment to merge with that of the white population, then ought they not to treat the law with due respect, and cease to engage in such blatant abuse of it?

Such was his position, obviously, and on the surface it was not entirely without merit. He felt that Gandhi was chasing political martyrdom for a greater purpose, and imposing martyrdom on his credulous followers for the same reason. His efforts to embarrass the government of the Transvaal were solely to achieve a repeal of the act, and his efforts to repeal that act contained political overtones that were as yet not obvious, although they could reasonably be surmised.

In the meanwhile, an Indian messenger waited at the telegraph office in Johannesburg for the official result of the parliamentary ballot, after which he jumped on a bicycle and sped down Jeppe Street, arriving a few minutes later at the Hamidia Masjid mosque where the telegraph was handed to Gandhi. The news was greeted by the crowd with applause, after which a fire was solemnly lit in a large three-legged pot smeared on the inside with kerosene wax, and there several thousand registration documents were gravely discarded, and burned.[1]

The following day Gandhi was summoned once again to Smuts's offices, but this time he was introduced by Ernest Lane into a conference room filled with stern-faced worthies of the white Transvaal establishment, most notably Prime Minister Louis Botha. Discussions were again cordial and restrained, but considerably less friendly, and although the government yielded some minor concessions – to permit the return and registration of pre-war Indian residents, to exempt children under sixteen and to accept a thumbprint or signature instead of a full set of prints – upon the substantive issues, it remained firm: the law would stand, and both immigrants and residents would register according to the law, and thereafter remain subject to its terms.

Gandhi then lowered the bar somewhat, accepting a moratorium on lower-class Indian immigration, but arguing that 'educated Indians' be permitted to enter the territory under standard restriction.[2] To this each white man set his jaw and shook his head, and the meeting ended with the same cordiality, but without concession. A few days later the facts were confirmed by a bill tabled in parliament containing the promised amendments to the act, but without any concession on Indian immigration, educated or not.

The expedited bill passed through the Transvaal parliament in just twenty-four hours, after which it was dispatched to Whitehall alongside an appeal for quick approval. Gandhi wrote a heartfelt letter to Smuts, appealing for a statesmanlike solution, to which Smuts disdained to reply. Gandhi then crossed from Natal into the Transvaal with a group of colleagues, and was there once again arrested, arraigned and duly sentenced to a prison term of two months with hard labour.

This time, however, the sentence attracted international attention. Protest meetings were held in India and Britain, and the matter came under discussion in clubs, parlours and parliaments across the British empire. Smuts might have held the advantage in the political war, but Gandhi was gathering strength in the moral war.

Two months later, Gandhi was released having served his full sentence, and at the moment that the iron gates of the Old Fort closed behind him, he returned to the business of defending the many Satyagrahis still being processed by the courts. Indians left prison, and returned, some as many as half a dozen times.

At the end of February 1909, Gandhi was once again arrested for illegally crossing from Natal into the Transvaal, receiving this time the maximum sentence of three months with hard labour. To the presiding magistrate he commented: 'I will continue to incur the penalties so long as justice, as I conceive it, has not been rendered by the state to a portion of its citizens.'

Upon this the hammer came down, and Gandhi returned dutifully to a cell in Volksrust prison (Volksrust in the Transvaal, on the Natal and Orange River colony borders). Smuts, however, although seeing no point this time in ordering an early release, nonetheless arranged certain privileges for Gandhi, including books and writing paper, and he waived any obligation to hard labour. From his own library he sent Gandhi two books, one on philosophy and the other religion, the former, according to some sources, was *Walden; or, Life in the Woods* by Henry David Thoreau, which, if true, would have been a coded admission that he wished to understand his opponent.

To this Gandhi responded by ordering a pair of leather sandals to be made in the workshops of the Phoenix settlement, and these he sent to Smuts as a gift. This immediately struck a chord with Smuts, and touched, he kept them, and wore them for many years as slippers.

Chapter 26

The New South Africa

'Providence has drawn the line between black and white and we must make that clear to the natives, not instil into their minds false ideas of equality.'
—Christiaan de Wet, the last state president of
the Orange Free State

On 12 October 1908, prime ministers and plenipotentiaries from all four colonies met in Durban in what was styled a National Convention. The dominant issue on the table was the federal structure of a future union, but the native franchise proved arguably to be the most emotive and challenging question. The two major parties to this discussion were the Transvaal and the Cape Colony, each representing opposing and perhaps irreconcilable traditions. The Cape argued for the qualified franchise as a standard rule for the union, which the other three colonies opposed.

At the conference, Smuts understudied for General Botha, and in almost every respect occupied the chair. He did not pioneer the concept of union, and nor did he devise its practical blueprint, but it was he who dealt with the more delicate fraternal matters of reconciling English and Dutch, plastering over the cracks, merging differences and brokering agreements.

On 2 August 1908, with he and Gandhi still at one another's throats, Smuts received a letter from William Philip Schreiner, ex-prime minister of the Cape, and a leading Cape liberal. Readers might recall his legal defence of King Dinizulu a year earlier in the aftermath of the Bambatha Rebellion. The essence of the letter was a plea for Smuts's support in the formulation of a fair and equal constitution for the republic under creation.

Before touching on the content of this letter, it might perhaps be profitable to introduce Schreiner more fully. William Schreiner was, of course, known best for being the younger brother of the ferocious South African liberal/feminist Olive Schreiner. Olive Schreiner occupied a position at the very centre of the club of Cape liberals, and was untiring in her advocacy of a free and equal society, and her brother William, or 'WP' as he was better known, having inherited the same principles, led the ultra-liberal Cape fringe. He had been an unsuccessful prime minister, proving himself just too liberal, and in 1900, he was forced to resign. His parliamentary seat – Queenstown in the Eastern Cape – was secured and held thanks to his passionate pro-Bantu policy, and he positioned himself very much as the informal voice of the black majority of South Africa.

In the opening paragraph of the letter, Schreiner confesses his anxiety at this, perhaps the most pivotal crossroads in the history of South Africa. Decisions made here, he wrote, 'must have enormous and far-reaching consequences on our destiny as a people'. The colour question, he went on – he would not use the word 'native', for that too narrowly implicated blacks – would be the most pivotal, and far-reaching to be answered by the convention. An ethnocentric constitution, ratified now, would achieve nothing more than to procreate future generations of discriminatory legislature, such that South Africa's destiny would ultimately be one of separation and institutionalized, statutory racism. Could the liberal Cape tradition alone be robust enough to stand up to the interests of three territorial partners that were hostile to it?

'The freedom to which all men are born in a free land is as true as their alleged equality is false ... But,' he argued, 'their freedom cannot be real if they do not have full opportunity to achieve equality.'

Schreiner was then 51 and Smuts 38. The two had been acquainted for many years, and the familiar tone of the letter suggests that they were on friendly terms. No reply to the letter was ever archived, however, but it can be assumed that if Smuts replied, his reply would have been non-committal. How easy to point out the problem without offering a solution. The South African colour problem had to do with a popular view in the colonies that the 'kaffir' was incapable of civilization, and how does one legislate fairly with that in mind?

Such was the mood as the doors of the conference opened. A small contingent of establishment blacks had been invited to observe, and to offer such opinions as were requested, but of the fifty or so delegates and invited guests, no Indian or coloured person was present. Smuts, representing the Transvaal, occupied a seat alongside prime ministers Abraham Fischer of the Orange River Colony, Frederick Robert Moor of Natal and John Merriman of the Cape. It is interesting to note, however, that most of the substantive correspondence and communication that emerged from the conference was that between Smuts and Merriman.

Merriman is an interesting character. He bore upon him the mark of an unadulterated Englishman who wished for the new country, and its future race policy, to exist on entirely 'Whiggish' terms, and according to the middle ground of race dogma.[1] Until his death in 1926, he and Smuts maintained a cordial if somewhat stiff friendship that acted often as an ideological bridge between the liberal south and the traditionalist north. Merriman had much to say at this conference, as, indeed, did Smuts, and the tenor of both is best defined by the first motion to be introduced by Merriman, and the conference's reaction to it.

Merriman proposed limited but universal suffrage throughout the union, based on a qualification that would deny the vote to poor and uneducated whites, but allow it for non-whites who had attained a respectable standard of prosperity and education. This motion was voted on and comprehensively defeated. A qualified franchise as a general, territory-wide policy would never be acceptable, and nor would any suggestion that non-whites be granted representation on a separate electoral roll, or at a reduced ballot value.

Merriman accepted this rejection, but in doing so he made it clear that the Cape Colony, although a partner in the union, would tolerate no removal of its qualified franchise. And while the Cape remained thus wedded to its liberal race policies, Natal, in the aftermath of the Bambatha Rebellion, took up the opposing corner, arguing for absolutely no political rights for non-whites whatsoever.

However, even Merriman was in agreement over the question of federal representation for blacks. While they could be represented on a local, committee level in the Cape, no facility would be made available for them to sit in any federal parliament, no matter how much practical or theoretical access they were granted to the franchise. One or more black men might sit in the House as part of an appointed committee, to speak on behalf of black interests and present black opinion, but unelected and without voting power.

This provision was sacrosanct, and those imperial observers present were forced to admit that if Britain wanted peace in South Africa, this would have to be the minimum position. Whites in the country, in general, would step no further into the unknown than that.

All of this happened to conform precisely to Smuts's own position. His entire dialogue on the 'Native Problem', recorded mainly in his copious correspondence, tends to confirm that he was entirely opposed to black political representation as a matter of principle, and this would remain the case for the remainder of his life. For all of his brilliance, and his passion for art, beauty and the humanities, he simply could not resolve in his mind what he saw as the fundamental incompatibility of black and white in South Africa. Some of this, of course, had to do with the demands of his constituency, but one is also left with the feeling that even if he was free to pursue his own policies, the result would not be much different.

In a letter written to the British economist and social scientist John A. Hobson, Smuts shed some light on the workings of his mind in this regard:

> My impression is that the only sound policy at this stage is to avoid any attempt at a comprehensive solution of the various questions surrounding the political status and rights of the native. With the chaotic state in which public opinion on this subject is at present, any solution … would be a poor compromise which might probably prejudice a fairer and more statesmanlike settlement later on.

In the Treaty of Vereeniging he had inserted the clause that only upon responsible government would the question of the native franchise be considered, and it was his and the majority opinion that the matter should now be further deferred for consideration by a federal or union parliament. It was enough that the convention found a suitable formula for the equality of rights and language between the two white races. To expect a settlement of the colour issue would perhaps have been a bridge too far.

In the meanwhile, a steady, albeit distant clamour of condemnation for all and every aspect of union drifted in on an occasional breeze from the *Indian Opinion*. Gandhi was building up a head of steam, and although he would have much to say about it in the months and years to follow, for time being the Indian question was not under discussion, and nor did Gandhi attempt to force it on to the agenda.

The black population of the colonies, however, and those blacks present at the conference, in general supported closer union as a positive development. The Bambatha Rebellion had confirmed the futility of violence, and at that moment in history, there appeared to be no particular cause for anxiety. The British repudiation of her pre-war promise to equalize race policy throughout the four territories had not affected the black population to quite the extent that it had the Indian. British guarantees were accepted – technically the black franchise had not been denied, but deferred – and it was felt that when an open avenue of inclusion in national politics was made available, it was the duty of the 'civilized' black community of South Africa to ensure that it was ready.[2]

The agreement, when finally it was made public, tilted noticeably to the right. The liberal wing accepted that if the views of the hardliners, who were in the majority, were not accommodated, then there would be no union of South Africa at all. However, although it fell far short of the minimum hopes of the Cape, the draft document also did not go as far as the right wing of the Natal legislature would have preferred. The document was debated in all four houses separately, and amended slightly here and there, but on the whole it passed muster without major modification.

To put the matter in context, Abraham Fischer, premier of the Orange River Colony, who was not by any means a dyed-in-wool hardliner, and was never either unfriendly or unaccommodating of Gandhi, nonetheless was utterly unable to embrace the ideal of equal political rights, or indeed any political rights at all for blacks. The argument that many civilized blacks were reaching a state of maturity that justified some entry-level inclusion in the social charter was rejected out of hand. Simply because some Africans had achieved a veneer of civilization, it could not be claimed that Africans on the whole were ripe for equality. The law of self-preservation, Fischer concluded, was ultimately stronger than any other.[3]

In the Cape, in the meanwhile, although the residual breezes of liberalism continued to stir, as blacks grew more politically active, white attitudes hardened. Merriman and his inner circle claimed some regret that the Cape system had not been extended to the rest of the proposed union, but expressed also a sense of optimism that a proposed two-thirds majority would protect the limited political rights of Cape natives into the future.[4]

In the end, it was Schreiner who was the lonely little white boy pointing out the nakedness of the king. As the document passed through the Cape parliament, it was obstructed on almost every point, indeed, on some sixty-two occasions, as Schreiner bitterly argued against this proposal or that. Although pointless to detail all of these here, the essence of his argument was that the compromise of rights and freedoms in pursuit of a political goal was a betrayal of all that was good and noble in British tradition. Union with honour, he cried, for was it to be only a white nation? Did only white people live in this land, and was it only they who would enjoy the fruits of nationhood?

Schreiner organized a shadow conference, the South African Native Convention, that met in Bloemfontein to consider a unified black response to the findings of the National Convention. Thirty-eight delegates gathered in a school hall in the Waaihoek township, and there the discussion was dominated, and perhaps overshadowed by a comprehensive address given by the member for native affairs in the Orange River parliament.

The Reverend Dewdney Drew, noted for his pro-African sympathies, had been invited by Schreiner to speak, and he did so quite freely and candidly, in an effort, no doubt, to portray matters as they were. Although recognizing that the union bill fell short of 'equal rights for all civilized men', Drew was also inclined to adopt a cautionary tone. He advised acceptance of the broad terms of the document in the belief that any agitation would simply stir the embers of white paranoia, inviting an even deeper erosion into the rights and liberties of blacks.

It was, he said, deeply regrettable that the northern colonies had succeeded in banning blacks in a future federal legislature, in which, in his opinion, a great many were now qualified to sit. It was also a tragedy that the only overlap between the races in South Africa was on the level of labour, where the lowest castes of each could be relied upon to despise one another. If more white leaders were willing to meet black leaders, they would no doubt be astonished at what had occurred in a brief half-century. The perception that a majority of whites held of blacks in South Africa was unfortunately informed entirely by the standard of sophistication general to the servants that tended their homes.

But so it was, and nothing could now be done to alter the fact. It would be better to cast the fate of the South African natives to the evolutionary process, and to accept what rights and liberties were granted. The wise among them could use those rights and liberties to prove that they were to be trusted with greater political responsibility in the future.

Drew then attempted to highlight the advantages of the draft act, most notably the fact that a standardized and territory-wide native policy would ease many of the difficulties created by ill-defined laws and procedures. Blacks, of course, would be better represented than hitherto by the inclusion of members sitting in the central legislature specifically to represent their interests, and that Cape parliamentarians who depended on the black vote could be relied upon to fight on their behalf.

The latter themes, of course, were optimistic, and would be proven by history to be as insubstantial as Smuts's frequently uttered plea that the matter best be left for wiser brains of the future. It would soon become clear that the wiser brains were those of the past. Union lit a small fire under the pot of right-wing Afrikaner nationalism, and before too long it began to ominously simmer.

However, much of this remained in the future, and the various delegates to the National Convention obediently attached their signatures to the full text of a draft constitution. Ultimately, no amendments other than those of a technical nature were required, and the bill passed through the British House of Commons easily. A royal proclamation set 31 May 1910 as the day upon which the new constitution would come into effect. The Union of South Africa was born, and in the words of Jan Smuts:

[A]nd when the darkness of night has passed at last and the light of a new national consciousness dawns, the scales fall from man's eyes, they perceive that they have been led, that they have been borne forward in the darkness by deeper forces than they ever apprehended to a larger goal than they ever imagined, and they stand silent in the presence of that greatest mystery in the world, the birth of the soul of a new nation.[5]

Chapter 27

The Mahatma

'These people who have offered such a threat to the government have no idea of its power.'

—Jan Smuts

It was at about this time that Gandhi's correspondence and journalism became less littered with the pejorative term 'kaffir', and as he began increasingly to make use of the more neutral 'African'. This, in the view of many historians, marks the moment that he acknowledged, or was at least made aware of the existence of an organized black political movement. This need not imply that he embraced it, for as we have heard, he did not, but simply that he began now to see it more clearly in the context of the wider struggle.

Gandhi could offer no common cause to blacks, with whom he had almost nothing in common. If whites in the colony had, upon which to base their impressions of blacks, the relationship of master and servant, Gandhi was denied even this. He did not keep black servants. His friendship with John Dube was cordial but distant, and it seems that he was nervous and uncomfortable in the company of educated blacks.

What he did have, however, was a weapon. Its conception was not original, of course, but he was the first to deploy it. He took the opportunity offered by the National Convention to enter a period of self-examination, the progression and results of which he communicated freely to his followers through the pages of the *Indian Opinion*. This laid the doctrinal foundation of *satyagraha*, what he now saw as a tool of universal emancipation, something more than the sum total of its parts, perhaps even a religion.

He also arrived at the conclusion that an amalgamation of the colonies in South Africa would only strengthen white control, pushing deeper into the future any hope of a final victory. This brought into focus the ultimate objective of the Indian struggle, and he realized that the limits that he had set himself were impractical in the long term. Quarantining the Indian struggle simply ignored its future complexion. Quite as the future of India lay in the hands of Indians, so the future of Africa lay in the hands of Africans.

The most rational way forward, therefore, was to clearly identify an objective, and in achieving that object, leave South Africa on a high note. Black Africans certainly had no use for celibacy, vegetarianism, quack-medicine and faith as weapons of war, and if in African hands lay the future of the African struggle then there would be the best place to leave it.

In the meanwhile, the National Convention drew to a close, and with a draft act ready for imperial perusal, the various prime ministers and senior ministers prepared to travel to London to witness its adoption into law. To this Gandhi had no choice but to respond, and it was agreed that he would lead a delegation to London to argue the Indian position, which was simply that an amalgamation of the four colonies into a single British dominion would disadvantage Indians, and should therefore be disallowed.

About this, however, there was an air of formality. Gandhi and the Indian question were not seen then as much of a threat to the current political process, and his machinations at that point could be safely ignored. Of far greater concern to the white prime ministers gathering in London was a delegation organized by William Schreiner purported to represent black and coloured opinion. Schreiner had failed to influence policy at the convention, and this was seen as something of a last-ditch attempt to head off a total defeat. His message was framed against the same exhausted principle that Gandhi was trying to refurbish, simply that a unified South Africa should not be achieved at the cost the essential principles of empire. Schreiner, however, added the additional warning that should this act be allowed to pass, it would simply open the door to a future regime of institutionalized racism that would eventually overwhelm the union, and the region.

One is left with the feeling however, that for all of its magnificent intent, Schreiner's petition amounted to no more than the dying kick of the Cape liberal donkey. Of its twenty-two signatories, a majority were white, among them churchmen of all denominations, politicians and society figures. Clearly it was a white effort, and perhaps the last of its kind, for although the delegation comprised a number of blacks, there was a sense in the wider black community that whites speaking on behalf of blacks no longer had any effect, or held any relevance.

Gandhi, in the meanwhile, accompanied by a largely disinterested Muslim companion by the name of Haji Habib, left South Africa a few weeks ahead of Schreiner, travelling by rail to Cape Town, and there boarding the *Kenilworth Castle* for Southampton. To his astonishment, however, as he happened to be leaning on the rail observing the crowd below, he noticed a short, stocky and bareheaded woman in a plain frock rush the gangplank before it was raised, and jostling through the crowd, she eventually found him and embraced him, making a great display for the sake of those down below. Wishing him bon voyage, the woman kissed his cheek and escaped the ship just as the plank came up.

This was William Schreiner's sister, the 54-year-old Olive Schreiner who, alongside her sister, Helena Stakesby-Lewis, were the doyennes of the Cape liberal movement.[1] Gandhi was at the same time surprised and delighted. The symbolism of this unexpected encounter established him in an inner circle to which Smuts also belonged, and if nothing else, it was an early sign that he was transcending.

On board the *Kenilworth*, he found himself sharing the first-class deck with the Cape prime minister, John Merriman, also en route to London, and for want of alternative company, the two men took to strolling the decks together. It did not take long for Merriman, a tall and rather morose-looking man, to warm to Gandhi, and from Merriman, Gandhi was granted his first unabridged insight into the white view of the common landscape. He heard the back story of the qualified franchise, of the negotiations that had led to the peace and the intricate and immeasurably complex psyche of the Afrikaner.

Of William Schreiner, Merriman was scathing, notwithstanding the fact that the two men were house colleagues. The best that could be said of it, Merriman complained, was that Schreiner failed to understand the wider implications of what he was doing. If he were to succeed in persuading the imperial government to disallow the South Africa Act based on the non-white franchise provisions, it would achieve nothing more than alienate and polarize the white population of the colony at a crucial time. He regarded Schreiner as ill-informed and irresponsible, and to the limits of ethics and authority, he sought to disrupt his preparations.

Thanks to this encounter, however, Gandhi arrived in London somewhat predisposed to Merriman's position, and certainly less disposed to Schreiner's. Obviously he believed what he wanted to believe, but the net result appears to have been a marked coolness towards Schreiner when the latter arrived in London, and attempted to forge a practical and ideological alliance with Gandhi.

A cornerstone of Gandhi's position was to make no overtly political demands on behalf of the Indians. He was aware that what white colonists feared most was an Indian with a vote, and he therefore made no overtures for such. Schreiner, on the other hand, made central to his platform a belief that all qualified men, regardless of race or religion, were deserving of access to the vote. The question of the franchise, therefore, was a hot potato that Gandhi had no interest in skinning, and ultimately, whatever the wider moral question, at that moment Schreiner's deputation offered him no advantage at all.

In the meanwhile, carried along entirely on its own momentum, the South Africa Act was debated in the House of Commons on 20 September 1909, and passed with a minimum of amendment. A few days later, King Edward VII issued the proclamation that the Union of South Africa would be established on 31 May 1910, at which point Schreiner, utterly defeated, threw in the towel, and soon afterwards returned to South Africa.

Before his departure, however, a rather melancholy farewell breakfast was held by the Aboriginal Protection Society, the Anti-Slavery Society, the London Missionary Society and a handful of liberal peers and parliamentarians. The gathering was poignantly addressed by Tengo Jabavu, who expressed his regret at the turn of events, noting that less than a decade earlier he had been invited by the Afrikaner Bond to stand for parliament in the Cape, something that would now be utterly unimaginable. How things had changed, he reflected sadly, adding that a parting of the ways had finally been reached between the white and black races of South Africa.[2]

Gandhi, in the meanwhile, gave the passage of the draft act scant attention. His first call in London was to the home of Dadabhai Naoroji, where he was warmly welcomed by the elderly nationalist as a colleague. By then a vibrant community of Indians was established in Britain, within which Gandhi's name was now well known. He established himself at the Westminster Palace Hotel on Victoria Street, and there engaged in meetings and discussions, and held court with a great many prominent Indians over the matter of Indian independence.

Local Indian attention in London was focused at that time not on the issue of South African union, and nor, for that matter, Indian home rule, but on a 26-year-old Indian student, Madan Lal Dhingra, who stood in the dock at the Old Bailey accused in the assassination of an obscure ex-Indian government official by the name of Sir William Hutt Curzon Wyllie. The latter had been gunned down in London on the evening of 1 July, as he and his wife attended an event organized by the National Indian Association. Killed also was a certain Dr Cawas Lalcaca, a Parsee physician from Shanghai who attempted to come to Sir Curzon Wyllie's aid.

This assassination has since come to be regarded as the first revolutionary act in the Indian independence movement, and that which set the clock ticking on the British Raj. Its symbolism perhaps most acutely portrayed the passing of the baton from the older generation of moderates to the young radicals. The trial polarized the diaspora, and ended, predictably, with a guilty verdict and a sentence of death. When asked if he had anything to say before sentence, Dhingra delivered a short but condemnatory polemic, denying that the court before which he stood enjoyed any jurisdiction over him at all: 'In case this country is occupied by Germans, and the Englishman, not bearing to see the Germans walking with the insolence of conquerors in the streets of London, goes and kills one or two Germans, and that Englishman is held as a patriot by the people of this country, then certainly I am prepared to work for the emancipation of my Motherland.'

To Gandhi, this episode crystallized in his mind the fact that South Africa was now only relevant as a tripwire for something far greater. For the first time, he was inspired to write to Leo Tolstoy, now 81 years old, and fading into a distant era. The content of his letter was suitably humble, and the reply suitably perfunctory, but the all-important contact had been made. He had read and studied Tolstoy since his student days, and yet now, quite suddenly, he felt qualified to contact the master directly, and to address him, if not as an equal, then at least as a journeyman colleague.

Against all of this, the official purpose of Gandhi's mission was obscured somewhat, and he tended towards the end to lose interest in it. Utilizing the local offices of a liberal peer by the name of Lord Ampthill, Gandhi went through the motions, but when Lord Ampthill returned wearily from his consultations with Smuts and Botha to plead with Gandhi to accept what was on offer, Gandhi was not aggrieved to decline.

Botha conceded the acceptance of six educated Indians per annum into the Transvaal solely as an administrative discretion, but no relief from the articles of the law was offered, and certainly no commitment to repeal it was made.

Writing to the Colonial Office, Gandhi then reported formally on the failure of his mission, announcing that he would meet and address various interested bodies in and around London before returning to South Africa to continue the struggle. Then, on a purely political leg of his visit, he toured the British capital, speaking widely, and sharing with a great many up-and-coming young revolutionaries his views and philosophies on the pending struggle.

Among these was a 19-year-old youth, urbane and cultivated, who was studying law at Trinity College, Cambridge, and who had graduated from Harrow as a fine example of modern Indian youth. Jawaharlal Nehru, the son of a wealthy Indian lawyer, was captivated by what he heard, and he would remember, and be influenced by that encounter throughout a long and illustrious political career. From it would flower a friendship, and a degree of political comradeship that would survive radically divergent views, and bitter disagreements, until Gandhi's death in 1948.

On 13 November 1909, meanwhile, Gandhi boarded the *Kildonan Castle* at Southampton, and set sail for South Africa, landing in Cape Town a fortnight or so later. During that time, he wrote his first book, *Hind Swaraj*, or *Home Rule*, pitching his claim to a place around the table of Indian revolutionary leadership, and at the same time articulating with considerable confidence his vision of non-violent revolution. In the preamble to *Hind Swaraj,* Gandhi noted:

> I have written some chapters on the subject of Indian Home Rule which I venture to place before the readers of Indian Opinion. I have written because I could not restrain myself. I have read much, I have pondered much, during the stay, for four months in London of the Transvaal Indian deputation. I discussed things with as many of my countrymen as I could. I met, too, as many Englishmen as it was possible for me to meet. I consider it my duty now to place before the readers of Indian Opinion the conclusions, which appear to me to be final.

The core of his argument was that it would not be enough for India to simply inherit and operate the same institutions of government vacated by the British, altering nothing that they created, but that the Indians should redefine their nation in their own image. Indian independence, he maintained, was only possible through *satyagraha*. As a pillar of *satyagraha*, *swadeshi*, or self-reliance, would see the Indian reject all and every British innovation, product, institution or trade, culminating in a rejection of western values in their entirety. Equally critical of Britain and India, Gandhi advocated a fresh start under conditions of spiritual submission, public service and self-sacrifice.

Again, the significance of the book is less in its essences or thesis than in its implications. It was produced and printed in Phoenix – in English and Gujarati editions – and distributed at a pace that the presses of the *Indian Opinion* could scarcely maintain. It was widely circulated and widely read, and although critical appraisal was not always positive, it was generally accepted and understood that a great presence had arrived.

Chapter 28

Labour Imperium

'The wages system forever – provided ours are high and yours are low; an injury to one is an injury to all – unless he is black. Down with capitalist exploitation – of Europeans only.'

—Anon

The Union of South Africa came officially into being on 31 May 1910. General Louis Botha was confirmed as the first prime minister, a populist figure supported by the cold competence of his friend and minister of interior, mines and defence, Jan Christiaan Smuts. The subsequent formation of a pan-South African Afrikaner Party – the South Africa Party – did not entirely unify the Boer and, before too long, the plaster that had covered so many a deep crack began to crumble.

Beginning in 1887, the imperial government convened periodic empire conferences that brought together the various prime ministers of the self-governing colonies. The Empire Conference of 1911, the first at which the Union of South Africa was qualified to attend, had the additional significance of coinciding with the coronation of King George V, marking it as something of an epochal event on the British social calendar.

Of course, Prime Minister Botha represented the Union of South Africa, although doubtless he and Smuts would both have preferred Smuts to have done so. There was, however, the beginnings of a crisis in the Union, and Smuts was better equipped than Botha to deal with such things, as Botha was better equipped to deal with matters of diplomacy that required authentic charm and likability.

At the heart of the crisis lay the simple fact of an accommodation with the British. Concentrated in the Orange Free State, but represented in pockets all over the colony, were elements of Boers unreconciled to defeat, and scheming for a return of the republic. Within this caucus a great deal of bad blood circulated, much of it directed towards Botha and Smuts, two pedigreed Afrikaners seen now to be in bed with the British.

232

Smuts's brokerage of the peace settlement, his overtures to the British and his advocacy of South African engagement were all seen as a traitorous *volte face*. Now, his overarching power in government engendered deep suspicion. And that Botha was regularly reported in the news to be junketing freely with the British, meeting this one and that, visiting stately homes and shooting grouse with the peerage, even accepting a privy councillorship and the honorary rank of general in the British army, bridled this section of the white community unbearably.

The matter under discussion during this particular Empire Conference was the federation of the empire, and the statutory rights and responsibilities of the dominions, in particular in regard to common defence. The idea that the fighting men of South Africa, so recently decimated by the British, and their women and children starved and killed, should now be called upon to fight for the British was more than the hardliners could bear. It was intolerable, and soon it might be expected that Botha and Smuts would be asking for coolies in government, and giving the kaffir the vote.

The chief voice of this loathing was, of course, James Barry Herzog, who kept warm the embers of resentment, and identified enemies of the people with the passion and moral flexibility of Robespierre. In his arsenal he wielded the blunt instrument of race and labour, the twin bellwethers of the great Afrikaner grievance.

Right-wing labour is something of a South African, or perhaps a colonial phenomenon. Labour at the time typically implied a workers' alliance under a communist or socialist flag. In the African colonies, however, this transmogrified into a vociferous and fanatically racist ideology protecting the interests of white workers against black. The South African left wing can therefore be divided between the liberal intellectuals who advocated the integration of the races without much risk to themselves, and the white labour movements for whom integration implied direct competition with blacks in schools, residential neighbourhoods, clubs and institutions, but most importantly in the workplace.

By the end of 1912, the Witwatersrand employed a round figure of about 200,000 blacks and some 25,000 whites, a majority of the latter originating from Britain. In the absence of organized or syndicated labour unions, an unregulated system favoured a peripatetic white working class moving between mines and colonies in a constant search for easier and better working conditions. The government had no mechanisms to deal with sophisticated labour issues, nor to identify unrest, resolve conflicts or generally to regulate an unruly sector.

As the Chinese began to disappear, black labour began to fill the void, and mine owners and shop floor mangers were naturally tempted to employ semi-skilled blacks in favour of higher paid, semi-skilled whites. This was a practice widely disapproved of, and extremely deleterious to the future prospects of white labour. Although Indian labour did not appear in the Transvaal in any numbers, across the border in Natal, the home of South Africa's coal mining industry, they were employed in significant numbers.

This was the beginning of Smuts's duel with Transvaal labour, fuelled by the militant right, which would culminate in 1922 in a wholesale insurrection, almost a coup d'état. Johannesburg was fundamentally hostile to Smuts, and seldom did he feel disposed to visit it. In 1910, it was a wild and boisterous city, a gold-rush town, with a racy and undisciplined vigour that saw haphazard development and unregulated economic activity everywhere. The mine owners and sundry capitalists – the Randlords as they were known – built large, elegant and spacious homes, and contributed to an urban architecture that was imperial on the outside, but utilitarian throughout. Corrugated iron was the material of choice, and its deployment was ubiquitous. On the fringes of the city, and even sometimes within, ochre-coloured mine dumps grew and evolved, punctuating the empty acres and undulating grassland with a gritty and industrial malevolence.

In the heart of the city, a small law office still bore the legend 'M. K. Gandhi Attorney', even though the proprietor was now engaged in a minimum of legal work. The *Hind Swaraj*, now in its umpteenth edition, had included law among those professions best removed from the face of the earth, and the lawyer himself was ever more deeply engaged in his political work.

From London Gandhi had travelled directly to Phoenix, where for several months he sat in relatively quiet meditation, reflecting on what the trip had taught him. As he did, he watched and listened carefully to the squabbles underway in Pretoria, and the ever more factional and acerbic parliamentary debates. He noted too the increase in labour unrest on the Rand, and the rude language traded between workers and mine owners. All was not well in the camp of the white man, he surmised, and he wondered to himself what opportunities this might offer to him.

In the meanwhile, on the larger stage, he saw quite clearly what many others were beginning to see: that British India was a spent force, and that Congress was now a party of revolution. The responsibility of Indians was to prepare themselves for change, and be ready. There was little now that could practically be achieved in South Africa that could not be better achieved in India. South Africa would not be emancipated in isolation, but only as part of a much larger defeat of European imperialism, and the army leading that fight would be Indian, not African.

Gandhi then looked at his own army of Satyagrahis, and was rather disheartened by what he saw. His permanent corps of Satyagrahis had dwindled to a handful, while the larger community was tired and wary, and no longer altogether trustful of Gandhi. He had not thought very deeply at the onset, never imagining that the struggle might have phases, and now the movement required reorganization, and a bedrock of ideology. It needed a cause.

In the absence of such a cause, however, Gandhi attended to the housekeeping, organizing his small band of loyalists and refining the ideals of *satyagraha*. This he did on an evolutionary scale, freely sharing his doctrinal journey in the pages of the *Indian Opinion*. The concept was defined by a great many principles, and no fewer codes, and as the sole archivist, his word on the matter tended to be law.

Satyagraha was organic, but at the same time limited. It was against the code of *satyagraha*, for example, to extend an action beyond the limits of its definition. One can assume that this meant that *satyagraha* was not an ongoing programme, but a specific response to a specific matter. This gave it a beginning and an end, which suited Gandhi's needs at that time, but proved rather inconvenient in the larger picture.

'Satyagraha' he wrote, '[if] offered on every occasion, seasonable or otherwise, would be corrupted into Duragraha.'[1]

It was now necessary to identify a new focus of the struggle, and to begin the movement afresh. Gandhi, therefore, studied the general immigration statutes of the Transvaal, and identified one particular clause as potentially actionable. This was the requirement that all new applications for entry into the Transvaal submit to a literacy test. This did not differ much from the Australian literacy test upon which it was modelled, and in both cases, the opportunity existed for any individual interior department official to filter out undesirables based on a simple criterion of written and spoken English. The obvious imbalance in this was the absence of any right of appeal, and the disadvantage this created for those whose first language was not European.

A few days later, as Smuts was handed his mail, the ever solicitous Lane rolled his eyes and pointed at one particular letter addressed in that most familiar scrawl. Smuts opened it and read it, and then returned it to its envelope with his brow knitted in an angry frown. In his elaborately courteous language, Gandhi had pointed out the likely imbalance of this clause of the law, detailing exhaustively the potential for discrimination and abuse, and concluding with the polite suggestion that the law be amended. With a virtual civil war underway in parliament, and threats of labour unrest on the Rand, the very last thing that Smuts was interested in was another tryst with Gandhi.

For the time being, therefore, Gandhi's correspondence remained unrequited. As the latter sat meditating on a straw mat in the sunshine of Natal, Smuts was engaged in the exhausting business of formulating a defence policy, creating an army, consolidating the Union, pre-empting labour action, controlling capital and dousing factional fires left, right and centre. He had absolutely no time to deal with the petty issues that occupied the vacancy of Gandhi's mind, and he was apt to tell him so with silence.

Gandhi then turned his attention elsewhere. He returned to Johannesburg from Natal, and retreated to the sanctuary of Tolstoy Farm, situated on a tract of land close to the town of Lawley, on the line of rail some twenty miles southeast of Johannesburg. The property had been donated to the Satyagraha movement by the architect and businessman, and fervent Gandhi admirer, Herman Kallenbach.

Here Gandhi founded a collectivized community intended to provide a base of support for his inner corps of Satyagrahis. Although the Satyagraha committee was well funded, it was actively supporting several hundred Satyagrahis rotating in and out of prison, and there was no telling now how long this war of elephants and ants would last. As Gandhi himself put it: 'There was only one solution for this difficulty, namely that all of the families should be kept at one place and should become members of a sort of cooperative commonwealth.'

The movement owed a great deal to Kallenbach, who had for a long time numbered himself among Gandhi's closest friends. Of Lithuanian origin, he emigrated from East Prussia to the Transvaal in about 1896, just as the mining boom offered a builder and architect the opportunity to make a fortune, which he did.

He and Gandhi could hardly have been more different, for Kallenbach was a swarthy man of substantial appetites, and of a robust and sporting temperament. His physique had been sculpted by many hours in the gymnasium, and his complexion darkened by a joyous embrace of the South African outdoors. He rode, he hunted, he climbed mountains, he skied and he fished. His offices were located close to Gandhi's on Commissioner Street, and in 1904, or thereabouts, the two men met and formed a loose but friendly liaison that grew more complex and intimate as the years passed.

Kallenbach was something of a theosophist, and was attracted to Gandhi's idiosyncratic ideas on diet and lifestyle. Sometime after their first meeting, Gandhi wrote to Kallenbach while the latter was on a visit in Europe, informing him thus: 'My diet yesterday was four bananas, three oranges, one lemon, half a pound of tomatoes, dates, two and a half ounces of peanuts, twelve almonds and a paw-paw. Two motions in a day.'

Such intimate details fascinated Gandhi, and Smuts was apt on occasions to sit in wonderment as the little Indian, in a prelude to some difficult discussion or another, would suddenly query his opponent's diet, the colour of his stool and the frequency of his motions. This he would follow with advice on diet, a suggestion of rationed sexual intercourse and instructions for a strictly regulated pattern of sleep and meal times.

While Smuts might have found this harmless and amusing, Kallenbach was spellbound. Their loose acquaintance matured quickly into mutual admiration and fondness, and at least in the opinion of some historians, further still into a warm friendship that might at some point have crossed over into intimacy.[2] It was Kallenbach who made available the land upon which Tolstoy Farm was founded, and there he designed and built a house that the two men shared.

Kallenbach, it might perhaps be profitable to note, was not by any means Gandhi's only European friend. He was rich in friends, of all kinds, many of whom were white, but most conspicuously, a disproportionate number were European Jews, and a great many women.

Gandhi met Henry Polak, for example, a radical Jew, at a vegetarian restaurant in Johannesburg, and claimed a lifelong disciple in both him and his Christian feminist wife, Millie. Millie Polak was an earnest and devoted friend to Gandhi, and quite possibly in love with him. Her husband was Gandhi's first legal partner, and although he was initially wary of Gandhi's unrefined qualities, his wife was wholly incautious, and submitted to Gandhi's simple charm with almost complete abandon.

There were others too, of course, and future friendships of a somewhat more strategic nature developed over time between him and Emily Hobhouse, Florence Nightingale, Olive Schreiner and the future Vicereine of India, Edwina Mountbatten.[3]

Among Indians, however, although he had thousands, and by the end millions, of followers, he appeared to have very few friends. His relationship with his wife, for example, once its carnal element had ceased, became prickly and formal, and affectionate only in consequence of the institution that they shared. With his sons he was even less forgiving, and an open breach with his older son Harilal was never entirely healed.

Harilal converted to Islam, and in the midst of the religious tensions of the time, he took to calling himself Abdulla Gandhi. His early death was attributable to alcohol, and it can only be assumed that his relationship with his father somehow contributed to the failure of his life.

Among Indians, however, none sat higher in Gandhi's estimation than Gopal Krishna Gokhale, the ex-president of the Indian Congress, and the man who had offered him sanctuary during the arid years. Gokhale was a heavyset, corpulent and soft-spoken man, a fine and persuasive speaker and, despite his unprepossessing appearance, a charismatic personality.

Just a few years older than Gandhi, Gokhale's early entry into the Indian political leadership was based on an impressive education and a steady journey up through what administrative doors the British left open. Likewise, he climbed the ranks of Congress, and elected president in 1905, he advocated the spiritualization of politics, religious tolerance and a moderate, negotiated increase in Indian self-government

When, early in 1912, Congress authorized a deputation to visit South Africa, Gokhale was naturally chosen to lead it. This was a moment of profound importance to Gandhi, for it not only validated his position, but it offered an opportunity to rally and motivate his followers. The movement was moribund, and as Gandhi put it: 'Stray Satyagrahis now and then went to jail. But when there was no occasion for going to jail, anyone who observed the external activities of the farm could hardly believe that the Satyagrahis were living there or that they were preparing for the struggle.'

Matters were not helped by Smuts's own experiments with passive resistance. Police and government officials ignored the routine transgressions of the Satyagrahis, issuing arrest warrants only when unavoidable. Agitation over the literacy test did not excite the mass mobilization that Gandhi had hoped, and so clearly a higher order of grievance was needed. Gokhale would excite popular interest, and when put into the ring with Smuts, the issue had to be something of resounding popular interest.

About this Gandhi thought deeply, and in the end he settled on the £3 tax, still on the Natal statute, and levied against indentured workers opting to remain in the colony. Gandhi decided that Gokhale would champion this issue when his visit transpired, and word of the fact was duly disseminated to Gokhale himself, and the various organising committees.[4]

When news of this new point of grievance reach him, Smuts was at last moved to protest. The £3 tax, he pointed out, was a requirement of the contracts signed by Indian indentured workers at recruitment, and under current regulations, recruits were so exhaustively tutored in the implications of their contracts that they could hardly be unaware of any single point or clause. The literacy test was a legitimate issue, but this was fraud.

Nonetheless, the matter was now on the table, and there it sat. With Gokhale already on the high seas, Slim Jannie realized that the fight was on again, and to it he began reluctantly to apply his mind.

A few weeks later, as the RMS *Saxon* steamed into view in Table Bay, and then settled in her moorings, thousands of people stood on the quay side to greet it. Cape Town delivered up all of its Indians, and a great many Coloureds too, while others had travelled down by train from Johannesburg and Durban to greet the great Indian nationalist. The Indian reception committee, however, was usurped, for before disembarkation an official government delegation was admitted on board ship, and there Gokhale was formally welcomed to South Africa by the minister of the interior and the people of Cape Town.

Then, after a brief moment granted to acknowledge the Indian reception committee, Gokhale was whisked off and installed at the table of honour at a private reception at City Hall. There to celebrate him was the mayor of Cape Town, various members of parliament and local officials, including among them William Schreiner, Mary Elizabeth Molteno, Olive Schreiner, the leader of the Cape Coloured community, Dr Abdullah Abdurahman and various members of the local Indian community. Gandhi, of course, had been invited, but not numbered among the honoured guests, and nor was he invited to speak.

The following day, Gokhale attended an informal meeting with justices Sir Rose Innes and Richard Solomon, with another on the sidelines with William Schreiner and former mayor Sir Frederick Smith. Next he was introduced to the former prime minister of the Cape, John X. Merriman, with whom the first open discussion of Indian grievances was held. The meeting was pronounced satisfactory, and a summary of concerns was forwarded thereafter to the government.

And this, indeed, proved more or less to be the pattern throughout Gokhale's four-week tour, with one public reception following another, and banquets and galas and high-profile meetings exhausting the frail health of the distinguished visitor. It can hardly, therefore, be said that Gokhale was snubbed, and behind it Gandhi could see exactly what Smuts was up to, and it irritated him.[5] In his memoir, he admitted to only the meetings and briefings that Gokhale held with Indian associations and individuals, refusing to acknowledge the many venerable Europeans that he was also introduced to, and the steady profusion of official banquets and receptions that entertained him.

Only one full day was allotted for Gokhale to visit Tolstoy Farm, and it was there that Gandhi and Kallenbach at last had him to themselves, and there that the weary and rather overwhelmed diplomat was coached for his pivotal meeting with Smuts. It was there too that for the first time he was given a brief of what to expect, and one can almost picture the colour draining from his face.

At Pretoria station, Gokhale, closely chaperoned by Gandhi, was met by a deputation of local Indians numbering some 400, and formally greeted by the deputy mayor and a cohort of supporting municipal dignitaries. The by-then established routine of galas and banquets followed before Gokhale finally found himself on the stone steps of the Ou Raadsaal. There he was welcomed into the cool interior, and shown into a conference room where waiting for him was the prime minister, General Louis Botha, supported by General Jan Smuts and Abraham Fischer, current interior secretary. For the entire meeting Smuts was polite and pleasant, but largely disengaged, for on this occasion the avuncular charm of Botha was found to be of greater value than the cold steel of Smuts's intellect.

As soon as the meeting broke up, however, Smuts issued a press statement indicating that the government was favourably disposed to consider the question of amending the immigration policies of the Union and repealing the £3 tax. According to Gandhi, when Gokhale left the meeting he was in high spirits, remarking to Gandhi that he might just as well return to India then and there, for the entire matter had been settled.

This for Gandhi was probably the worst possible outcome. Although he was inclined to disbelieve it, the press reporting that followed the meeting forced him to clap politely along with the rest. The whole episode painted Gokhale as the man who arrived in South Africa and cut through the Gordian Knot like butter, diminishing the reputation of Gandhi who had laboured then for almost two decades to achieve nothing comparable.

Easy it is to imagine Smuts smiling to himself as he read the newspapers the following morning. Krishna Gopal Gokhale, the Honourable CIE, the bespectacled, ailing and credulous Gokhale, had been duped, and Gandhi, poor Gandhi, had been outmanoeuvred once again.[6]

Chapter 29

Women and Children First

'That terrible Judgement!'
—Mohandas K. Gandhi

For the time being, Gandhi could do nothing but join in the celebration, dust Gokhale down and accompany him on the express train to Lourenço Marques. There he was rapturously received by the small Indian community, and to general appreciation and applause he repeated the rather self-congratulatory proclamation that matters in the Transvaal had been resolved. The same was true in Zanzibar, where he changed ships, and from where Gandhi would return alone to South Africa. Even the Germans joined in the fanfare by welcoming the venerable Indian on board the SS *President*, a German East Africa Line ship, rendering him all possible service and sparing no effort to assure his comfort.

Back at Tolstoy Farm, Gandhi awaited news of the repeal, and was rewarded with silence. Eventually he inquired, to which Smuts, on behalf of the government, replied that, although insignificant from a revenue point of view, the £3 tax was considered a relevant instrument, and would not be repealed. With regards to the Black Act itself, repeal could only take place upon a favourable vote in parliament, and no such debate was scheduled.

When news of this reached Gokhale he poured a little cold water on expectations, remarking that assurances had never been absolute, and apologizing if more than that had been expected. He nonetheless found himself with more than a little egg on his face, which Gandhi did nothing to clean, but went ahead, not unhappily, in planning of a new phase of *satyagraha*.

Then, somewhat out of the blue, the Cape judiciary delivered a judgement that offered Gandhi an open goal. On 14 March 1913, Justice Searle for the Cape Supreme Court effectively invalidated all marriages in the Union not celebrated according to Christian rites, and/or not registered by the registrar of marriages. The judgement came about consequent to an application for

241

entry into the Cape of the wife of a Muslim trader under the qualification of marriage in India.[1] According to the judgement, and having regard to the terms of the Cape Colony Marriage Order in Council, the marriage had been celebrated in a mosque under Islamic rites, and could not therefore be deemed monogamous, and so was invalid. Entry for the woman into South Africa was denied.[2]

It is quite likely that by the very next post, Justice Searle received a letter from Jan Smuts demanding an explanation for such crass idiocy, but by then, unfortunately, the damage had been done. Gandhi seized on the matter, interpreting it to mean that henceforth all Muslim and Hindu marriages in South Africa were invalid, all Indian wives concubines and all Indian children bastards. A barrage of correspondence followed, supported by the usual flurry of editorials in the *Indian Opinion*, and before too long, ripples of the affair were washing up on the shores of India and Britain.

In respect of the predominance in native society of customary marriage and polygamy, the Searle judgement also made provision for marriages not conducted according to Christian rites to be registered as an alternative with the registrar of marriages. This implied that legal provision could quite easily have been made for Indians in general upon appeal, if such had really been at the root of the problem.[3] Instead, a mass meeting was held in Johannesburg to protest the judgment, accompanied by all of the usual histrionics, and recapitulated the following morning in a hundred newspapers.

Then, two months later, parliament produced a revised Immigration Bill which represented for the first time a common, national immigration policy, and one can assume that its reading offered government the opportunity to smooth out and soften some of the harsher edges of previous laws. This, however, after a deceptively friendly debate, proved to be impossible.

Smuts was at that time under enormous pressure. Industrial unrest on the mines had begun to spread to other key sectors, taking on an ugly Briton–Boer complexion, with underlying antagonism directed towards black and other non-white labour. Smuts himself was under attack for his pro-British policies, and while the British and Indian governments were demanding meaningful immigration reform, the right wing of parliament was agitating for the opposite. Herzog was thumping the table and demanding even greater entry restrictions for non-whites, more stringent controls on those already resident in the provinces and calling for South African neutrality over the matter of imperial defence.

Throughout the immigration debate, therefore, Smuts was forced to trim his sails and ride hard against a reactionary wind, with needless to say the key elements of the new law offering very little relief to the Indians. The criteria for entry was left more or less unchanged. Any person or class of persons deemed by the minister, either on economic grounds, or on account of standards or habits of life judged to be unsuited to the requirements of the Union, could be precluded upon the discretion of individual immigration officials at any port of entry.

The theoretical criterion remained the ability of an individual to read and write in a European language, but the practical criterion remained race. Since Indians were the only non-Europeans seeking entry into the Union in any numbers, the racial bias of the act affected none but they. Such exemptions as were offered applied only to illiterate or unskilled Europeans, and again, this was entirely upon the discretion of individual immigration officers.

On the whole, the provisions of the act in relation to Indians reflected the attitudes and prejudices of both wings of the House, but provisions as they applied to blacks began to reveal quite clearly the growing influence of the right. Pre-existing restrictions on the free movement of blacks remained unchanged, and so by implication blacks were regarded, and treated under the law, as non-citizens, if not entirely aliens.

All of this, nonetheless, played very neatly into Gandhi's hands, and a correspondence was maintained between him and Gokhale, keeping the latter informed, and priming the Indian establishment to expect a renewal of protest in South Africa. Smuts was also granted the same privilege, as one after another Gandhi's letters journeyed across his desk, each unfailingly polite and formal, but warning him no less of pending action.

For the time being, however, Smuts was less concerned with the Indians than his own constituency. He now held the portfolios of defence, finance and justice, and in the former capacity he was engaged in containing South African labour while at the same time building the structures and institutions of an army. In both instances, the fault lines were white on white. White labour was split along language lines, as indeed were white attitudes towards the pending war.

A few months earlier, some 20,000 white mineworkers had downed tools and provoked an ugly series of confrontations with the government that had pitched the colony to the very brink of anarchy. Twenty-five deaths were recorded in a series of clashes and security actions that saw Smuts appealing to the governor-general for the deployment of imperial troops. In the face of all of this, a handful of threadbare Satyagrahis explaining their illegal entry into the Transvaal in a non-European language, and refusing to impart their particulars, could hardly have been of immeasurable concern.

243

Smuts was, however, aware also that the world was watching. Twice-daily reminders of this fact arrived on his desk with the morning and evening post. The British governments in London and Calcutta were deeply concerned at the recent turn of events, in particular the invalidation of Indian marriages, and the disenfranchising of Indian children. The Searle judgement had left open the possibility of women joining the protest in large numbers, and if the imprisonment of male Satyagrahis caused the world to shake its head in wonder, the mass incarceration of women would do a great deal more. Had Smuts himself, just over a decade earlier, not pointed the finger at the British for penalizing Boer women and children, and was he prepared now to do the same to the Indians?

Chapter 30

Dénouement

'It is easy to get into prison by committing a crime but it is difficult to get in by being innocent.'
—Mohandas K. Gandhi, *Satyagraha in South Africa*

Towards the end of 1913, small groups of Satyagrahis, representing for the most part the permanent population of the Phoenix settlement, among them Gandhi's wife, Kasturba, began to appear on the Transvaal border, attempting to illegally cross from Natal.[1] All were duly detained, brought before a magistrate and sentenced to three months' simple imprisonment, first in Volksrust, and later in Pietermaritzburg. Gandhi was stirred by his wife's imprisonment, and although he had orchestrated it, the tenor of his correspondence and contributions to the *Indian Opinion* grew condemnatory. He referred to the £3 tax as a 'blood tax', directed at the most vulnerable, and indefensible as a consequence. It was the duty of all Indians to rise up against this outrage, and to support and defend the sisters of the movement in their hour of testing.

From Phoenix he set off to Johannesburg, determined to be arrested as he crossed into the Transvaal, but he was not. In Johannesburg he held meetings, and worked feverishly to generate support for a renewal of *satyagraha*. He was at once tormented by doubt and anxiety, but he was confident too, vigorous and persuasive. Early in October, the first Muslim women joined the protest, and sensing what was afoot, Smuts ordered that unless the Indians resorted to egregious methods, all were to be allowed to proceed back and forth across the frontiers as they cared, and to undertake what unlicensed trade they wished, without fear of arrest and as far as possible left alone.

Some ten or twelve women were then mobilized in Johannesburg and sent east with the intention of crossing illegally into Natal, where an effort was made to take down their particulars, but when this failed they were allowed to continue on their journey. Gandhi then ordered them to proceed deeper into Natal, and to seek refuge in the coal-mining town of Newcastle where a great many indentured and free Indians served as labour. While there they were to openly incite the Indian workers to strike over the question of the £3 tax, which would be an arrestable offence not easily ignored.

For a strategy conceived rather on the back foot, Gandhi was pleasantly surprised to learn a day or two later that Indian indentured workers on a handful of the Natal coalfields had indeed downed tools and come out on strike. Smuts, when he was informed, was completely broadsided, finding to his dismay that Gandhi had fled back to Natal on the first available train before an order could be given for his arrest. Soon enough, the figure of the Mahatma appeared among the striking coalminers, now dressed in the costume of the common labourer, his hair close-cropped and his feet in sandals. Within a week the strike had spread across the mining sector and had begun to affect the sugar estates.

For Gandhi, the Natal labour action, although entirely unplanned, proved to be an immediate game-changer. With upward of 3,000 pliable, working-class Indians ready to respond to his direction, he had to think fast. Indentured Indian labourers on the Natal coal mines worked under the same basic conditions as blacks, and were, as a consequence, housed in compounds and entirely dependent on the mine for the basics of their survival. This obviously rendered them vulnerable to intimation and threats, and Gandhi was anxious, therefore, to move as many as possible off their respective colliery complexes.

This, however, immediately made them his responsibility, and as sugar production ground to a standstill, the trickle of sugar estate workers joining the strike turned to a flood. As he struggled to cope with the sheer numbers, it might have gratified him to learn that in Pretoria Smuts was fielding urgent appeals from just about every sector of industry, but in particular the Natal Chamber of Mines, all urging him to reconsider the £3 tax. Was this petty sum so vital to the treasury that it was worth the collapse of the mining industry in South Africa?

The gold mines of the Rand were dependent on coal, as was the transport sector, and almost every other branch of industry to some degree. With half of the mining industry on strike and the other half threatening, with letters of interest and concern flooding into his office, and with the press beginning to question his policies, Smuts began to feel himself painted into a corner.

In the meanwhile, converging on the town centres of Dundee and Newcastle, thousands of striking miners mingled in conditions that might quickly turn to a crisis of sanitation and hunger. The various city burghers and mine owners remained in a position to threaten and coerce, forcing Gandhi to the conclusion that the best course of action in the short term would be to transport them all, in some way, to Tolstoy Farm, where a more coordinated response could be devised. However, without the means to transport such a large and growing mass of people, he decided to simply walk. Thus he led his new army of Satyagrahis, tentatively numbered then at about 2,500 individuals, but growing daily, west along the main trunk road towards Charlestown, positioning them away from the influence of the mine owners, and closer to the Transvaal border.

At what point this improvised movement of industrial refugees transformed into a pilgrimage it is hard to say. However, at some point Gandhi turned his rabble of strikers into freedom marchers, establishing inadvertently the last substantial pillar of *satyagraha*, and founding a strategy that would stamp his name eternally into the global revolutionary consciousness.

The concept was brilliantly simple. He would march his Satyagrahis towards Tolstoy Farm, and if they were not arrested en route, which, of course, was his first hope, then the conversion of the farm into a centre of the struggle would provide additional, perhaps unstoppable momentum. He knew that he now held a strong hand of cards – not an unassailable hand, for he knew Smuts well by then – but a strong hand nonetheless. The publicity from what was taking place, if carefully managed by the likes of Polak and Kallenbach, and his growing army of well-wishers and admirers all over the world, would be explosive to say the least.

And indeed, the implications of what he had begun captured the imagination of the Indian public, and news of it reverberated throughout the diaspora with a satisfying immediacy. Indian traders and merchants turned out at every stop along the dusty road to Volksrust, cheering their progress, with many joining, and others offering sustenance and succour wherever possible. Gandhi constantly exhorted his pilgrims to follow at all times the rules of virtue and godliness, of cleanliness, courtesy and sexual probity, and to respect wherever possible those whose lands and settlements the march passed through.[2]

Behind him, across the vast reaches of the Natal sugar plantations, and even in the works departments and petty industries of many towns and cities, Indian indentured and free labourers spontaneously responded to the march. Wildcat strikes broke out across the region, crippling large sections of industry overnight. Figures have always been speculative, but certainly the number of Indians responding directly or indirectly to Gandhi's call to action ran into the tens of thousands, and from the government's point of view, the situation began to spiral rapidly out of control.

Smuts, however, kept a cool head. He was aware that white labour was watching, waiting only for some convenient spark to touch their own keg of powder. To this could be added an army of black labour and, indeed, an entire black nation. On Monday, 3 November Smuts was summoned to the offices of the governor-general, Herbert Gladstone, where the two men held a frank discussion, and Smuts was again urged to find a solution to the crisis before matters in India followed suit.

Smuts, however, counselled caution. Gandhi, he suggested, had bitten off rather more than he could chew. It was all very well to stand in the back of the bus and shout 'fire', but when everyone stood up and rushed out, a degree of practical political acumen would be required to manage them. And for all of his charisma, Smuts suspected that Gandhi was not that man.

Two days later, however, Smuts blinked and authorized Gandhi's arrest as the marchers crossed into the territorial limits of the Transvaal. The following morning, Gandhi appeared before a magistrate in Volksrust, charged with public order offences, and was granted bail upon request. He immediately returned to the head of his march and continued onwards. Thirty miles farther on, he was arrested again, brought before a magistrate and granted bail for a second time.

It is difficult to determine the hidden dynamics at work during that crucial week, but Smuts's unwillingness to imprison, or detain Gandhi on remand, suggest at the very least a case of the jitters, but also perhaps an attempt to balance the contradictory demands and pressures that he was under. At some point, however, decisive action would be required, for despite the arrests, and no doubt a great deal of implied threat, Gandhi and his followers held firm, and as Gandhi himself alternated between freedom and incarceration, the march continued steadily onward. When he was arrested for the third time he was held in custody until trial, and finally sentenced to a total of a year with hard labour.

This was the end of the march, but not the end of the protest. The marchers were mollified by earnest assurances from government agents that their grievances would now be dealt with, and in somewhat more compliant mood, they boarded trains for dispersal back to their various places of employment.

No repercussions were recorded, but strike action continued, and the situation remained on a knife's edge. By the middle of November, upward of 15,000 combined mining, sugar estate and general Indian labourers were on strike in Natal. As Gandhi sat in prison, the momentum of the movement continued to build, until a turbulent 1913 ended with the spectacle of imperial troops deployed into rural Natal to help control the ever-widening effects of the strike. As the clock struck midnight on 1 January 1914, upwards of a thousand Satyagrahis remained incarcerated in various prisons, and in his New Year address, the Viceroy of India issued a public call for a commission of inquiry into events in South Africa.

In the midst of all of this, Gandhi was precisely where he needed to be. His most potent work for the time being could be done under the anonymity of imprisonment, and with some breathing space at last, his organization could finally get to work consolidating the enormous advances that his few days on foot on the highways of Natal had accrued.

It is perhaps worth noting that Polak and Kallenbach, two of Gandhi's closest friends and associates, were also arrested and briefly imprisoned for their various roles in the protest. Polak, in a lengthy but restrained speech delivered upon sentencing, declared that, as a Jew, and in the light of global persecution of his co-religionists, he found it was impossible to stand back and observe the courageous efforts of a victimized people to gain what was rightfully theirs. It was a grave and poignant moment.

Gandhi, in the meanwhile, was quickly removed from Volksrust to Bloemfontein gaol, separated from his friends and left in isolation. He was spared the rigours of hard labour, but not, on this occasion, the continued application of his sentence. One can easily imagine that Smuts was conflicted about this, but also angry and frustrated. Snippets of reflection recorded then, and over succeeding years, suggest that he was more affected by the episode than he was ever inclined to admit. At that point, with the bruises still fresh on his conscience, he was forced to swallow, for the second time in his life, the sensation of losing a war after winning every battle.

Inevitably, however, the matter would have to be brought to a conclusion, for the Indian issue, notwithstanding all of its theatrics and exaggerated profile, was of secondary importance in the face of white labour. The strikes of a year earlier had been concluded only after a humiliating climb-down by him and Botha, and Smuts was determined that this would not happen again. As minister of defence, it was his responsibility to create the institutions and structures of a territorial armed force that would inherit responsibility for internal security and external defence. Should the ongoing disturbances on the mines, and elsewhere, flare again into violence, he would now be better prepared to deal with it.

And then, abruptly, his mind was torn away from this myriad of concerns by the return to his mind of a sombre memory. In Bloemfontein, a monument had been conceived and constructed to commemorate the thousands of Boer women and children who had died in British concentration camps, and Smuts, quite naturally, was invited to attend and to speak at the unveiling ceremony.

The monument was built around a concept sketched out by a woman who was associated with that phase of South African history perhaps more than any other. That 'bloody woman', Emily Hobhouse, one of the first of the great British reformers, had made it her mission to publicize and administer to the awful fate of many Boer women and children in these camps. She and Smuts met soon afterwards, and in that strange and barbed era of two races reuniting, it was helpful to Smuts to be befriended by an Englishwoman who immediately admired him.

Emily Hobhouse was a dear friend of Olive Schreiner, and of Smuts's wife Isabella, and all three women corresponded with one another for so long as each lived. Both Emily Hobhouse and Olive Schreiner had been enamoured of Smuts as a young man of such Platonian radiance, but they had become more critical of him as he entered politics and found himself forced to mould with the clay of circumstance an imperfect replica of ideas he had once held with such certainty.

Nonetheless, all remained friends, even after a fourth presence appeared on the fringe of their circle. The Mahatma, whose more steady intellect was embellished by such a wondrous beauty of spirit, and a mischievous charm of which Smuts could but dream, was borne aloft by his virtue, and loved for it. On the other hand, the women, and others besides, tended often to chide, and take Smuts to task in a friendly way for the methods he employed against Gandhi, and the unpleasantness of it all.

Naturally, Emily Hobhouse would be present at the unveiling of the monument, and she travelled from Britain to Cape Town, frail in health, but determined to be present. As the train from Cape Town approached De Aar in the northern Cape, however, she collapsed, and was removed to convalesce at the home of a local well-wisher. There she wrote a long and plaintive letter to Smuts, enclosing the speech that she had intended to deliver, but also appealing to him to find it within himself to heal the wound of race and colour in South Africa.

It was, she wrote, fundamentally a moral issue, and never could governmental power prevail over a great moral and spiritual upheaval. To this she added the more sombre point that, upon this issue, Smuts could never have right on his side: 'You see the gravity of the situation is that India keeps it [the British empire] going with her money and will until all handle for

250

doing so is withdrawn, because she is using you or rather the position here as a whip to beat the old horse with.'

And so it was. Ms Hobhouse excused her interference upon the plea that she had been asked by Gandhi to facilitate a break in the ice. This was almost certainly untrue, and one can justly conclude that Gandhi received a similar letter from Ms Hobhouse urging him to soften his position, excusing her interference with the admission that Smuts had asked her to do it.

On 18 December, two days after the unveiling ceremony in Bloemfontein, Gandhi was released from the Grootvlei prison and driven to Bloemfontein where he was put on a train for Durban. There, after days of celebration, meetings, speeches and temperate junketing, he was informed through the Satyagraha committee that an official inquiry had been commissioned to look into the events of recent months, and the Indian question in general.

Chapter 31

An Omission of Inquiry

'Their grievance really is moral and not material and so, having all of the power of the spiritual behind him, he [Gandhi] and you are like Mrs Pankhurst and [Reginald] McKenna, and never, never, never will governmental physical force prevail against a great moral and spiritual upheaval.'

—Emily Hobhouse

The trigger for the authorization of a commission of inquiry, always the preferred option of a British government in a tight corner, was ostensibly a speech delivered in Madras by the Viceroy of India, Lord Hardinge, who was responding in turn to a petition submitted by the Madras Provincial Congress Committee. Congress, it seemed, saw in the Transvaal situation an opportunity to exert leverage over the British government, which it knew to be anxious over the question of Indian compliance in the British military calculation.

And Lord Hardinge responded robustly, condemning the flogging and killings of South African Indians (entirely anecdotal, for such was an aberration if it occurred at all), and that if the government of the Union of South Africa wished to justify itself in the eyes of India and the world, then it would have no choice but to grant a searching board of inquiry upon which Indian interests would be represented.

Representing Indian interests, of course, implied an Indian serving on the commission, which was more than Smuts at that moment was able to stomach. Instead, the commission comprised three European members, the highly respected jurist Sir William Solomon, and two laymen, Lieutenant-Colonel James Scott-Wylie of the Durban Light Infantry, and Edward Esselen, a businessman and politician, and close friend of Smuts.

Sir William, of course, could be relied upon to exercise absolute impartiality, but of the other two, Gandhi expressed reservations. His inclination was to reject the commission out of hand for its obviously monochromatic complexion, but instead he petitioned Smuts for a revision of its constitution. About this there was now something of a formulaic flavour, and apart from a mild exchange of demand and rejection, the commission was assembled and began taking evidence.

In the meanwhile, Indian strikers freed from prison were escorted back to their places of work, and there monitored very closely. Gandhi portrayed this as a simple transfer from a prison complex to a prison camp, but in fact mining compounds were fenced in and contained as a matter of standard security, and the presence of law enforcement officials and other monitors was probably a precaution to keep the Satyagrahis out rather than the miners in.

Nonetheless, it was a helpful piece of propaganda, and Gandhi made good use of it. Content with that, however, he abated the protest, and although boycotting the commission, allowed it to go about its work without picketing or any unnecessary outpourings of correspondence.

In fact, Gandhi could now see an end to the matter, and at such a delicate point it would have seemed irrational to complicate matters with additional protest. His correspondence with Gokhale and other Indian nationalists indicated very strongly that he had identified the moment as right to wrap up the South African issue, and move on towards India.

Perhaps desirous of a warm conclusion to the whole affair, Gandhi made a considerable effort to arrange a final meeting with Smuts, which after much prevarication was scheduled for 6 January 1914, on which day Gandhi appeared in the foyer of the Ou Raadsaal. His head was shaved, he wore a bleached calico shirt and trousers and was barefoot. Lane, of course, uttered no word of comment as he ran his eye sharply from toe to crown, but informed Gandhi with regret that the general was engaged in dealing with the ongoing action of white mine and industrial workers, and was unable to meet the appointment.

Ernest Lane perhaps did regret the inability of Smuts to meet his nemesis on this final occasion, for the spectacle of it would have amused him, although it is likely that Smuts himself regretted it for reasons sincerer. He might perhaps have looked forward to the opportunity to comment on events, and to see for himself what this man had become. Gandhi had forged his personality very carefully, and he knew precisely who his audience was.

The power of *satyagraha* lay in its appeal to the powerless. It was a weapon that even the weakest could wield, so long as cohesion and unity of purpose were maintained. Gandhi now knew that he had the power to inspire the masses, and to define and present the simple grievances of common people as matters of epoch-making significance. As Gandhi looked forward to the battles of the future, and Smuts grappled with the conflicts of the moment, the two men parted company with the briefest of farewells, snatched in the few minutes that Smuts later found to personally meet with, and shake the hand of, the Mahatma.

Matters thereafter played out in a predictable manner, and without obvious rancour. The working lives of South Africa's Indians returned to normal, and relief was offered in due course to the indentured workers by the removal of the £3 tax, and the dignity of Indian womanhood restored by the recognition of their marriages.[1] A bill to this effect, the Indian Relief Act, was published in the last week of May 1914, and piloted through a turbulent reading by the skilful hand of Jan Smuts, who was in no way less interested in a conclusion to the matter than Gandhi.

Gandhi, in the meanwhile, was advised by Gokhale and a number of other influential personalities in India to accept whatever was the conclusion of the matter, raise no fresh issues, publish no editorials and write no letters. The matter was over and he was needed in India. On 16 July 1914, Archduke Ferdinand was gunned down on the streets of Sarajevo by a radical Bosnian by the name of Gavrilo Princip, which snapped the final chains of restraint holding back of the two great European alliances, and within months they were at each other's throats.

Gandhi, his wife Kasturba and his friend Herman Kallenbach boarded the *Kinfaus Castle* in Cape Town on Saturday, 18 July 1914. After several weeks of celebration, his final departure, although emotional, was muted. A handful of friends and admirers escorted him to the gangplank and waved as he boarded, and then waited quayside as the elegant two-funnelled steamer slipped beyond Robben Island, and eventually out on to the open sea.

Smuts, informed immediately by telephone as the ropes were cast off the *Kinfaus Castle*, leaned back in his leather chair and gazed at the ceiling of his office for a long time. Presently he returned to a letter that he had been in the middle of composing to Sir Benjamin Robertson, an Indian government official visiting South Africa on a mission to investigate the condition of Indians in the colony. He had been detailing the facts of the compromise reached with the Indians, and with a mixture of relief and sarcasm, he ended the letter with the words: 'The saint has left our shores, and I sincerely hope forever.'

Epilogue

Soon after the Jameson Raid, and the collapse of his career, Cecil John Rhodes took refuge in his colony of Rhodesia, concerning himself for a year or more with only his legacy, and his monuments. He brokered a peace with the warlike amaNdebele, an ideological and blood relative of the Zulus, he acquired two large estates, and he began to work towards some sort of racial balance in the colony, perhaps having left it too late to really undo the damage he had done, but he tried nonetheless.

He lived long enough to see victory in the Anglo-Boer War, but not the amalgamation of the territories that he had tried so hard to achieve. His death in Muizenberg, Cape Town, when it came, was slow. He suffocated slowly as his lungs filled with fluid, until, after several days of diminishing breathing capacity, his heart failed. He was forty-eight. His body was transported to Rhodesia by special train, pausing often for thousands of admirers to pay their respects. He was interred in a tomb cut into the rock of the Matopos hills near Bulawayo, and there, for several years, a spontaneous amaNdebele guard of honour held vigil.

Gandhi's career after South Africa is the stuff of modern legend, and little here can or needs to be added to it. He lived to see the independence of India from Britain, but he was assassinated a year later, dying upon the altar of Hindu–Muslim separation. His legacy, of course, is firmly established, but it has not escaped occasional tarnish. It perhaps might not be overstating the matter to claim that he was deliberately excluded from the principal business of independence in the end, his idiosyncrasies proving too much of a challenge to his Congress colleagues, and not always compensated for by his massive popularity. His presence in the world, however, obviously transcends politics, and he was certainly never configured for formal political leadership, and certainly not some vague administrative appointment. He was an ambassador of peace, a religious leader at the core, and politics in the end was perhaps nothing more than a by-product of that.

In 1939, an anthology of impressions of Gandhi, his life and career was produced and published to celebrate the 70th birthday of the Mahatma, and to this Smuts was invited to contribute. One can imagine that this was not an easy task, but in the end what he offered up was a thoughtful essay entitled 'Gandhi's Political Method'. Here he attempted to analyze that difficult subject, but in the end the effort is probably better remembered for the few

255

autobiographical reflections that proved more valuable that two thousand words of superficial observation. In part he wrote:

It was my fate to be the antagonist of a man for whom even then I had the highest respect. In prison, he had prepared for me a very useful pair of sandals which he presented to me when he was set free. I had worn those sandals for many a summer since then, even though I feel I am not worthy to stand in the shoes of such a great man.

The sandals he returned as a gesture of belated friendship, and these Gandhi accepted. Smuts went on to remark that his encounters with Gandhi had been difficult, and timed unfortunately, but he conceded easily that a debt of gratitude was owed to the Mahatma, for the fact, if nothing else, that he revealed to the new nation of South Africa a skeleton in her cupboard. Smuts was unable to attend Gandhi's funeral, but he remarked in writing on the death of his curious antagonist that: 'A prince has passed away and we grieve with India in her irreparable loss.'

The Indian question in South Africa over-spilled eventually into that other great community of Indians in Africa, East Africa, where Indians had been introduced first as bonded labour in the construction of the Uganda Railway, and later as military personnel engaged in the German East Africa Campaign of the First World War. The dynamics of the growth and expansion of Kenya's Indians was not dissimilar to those of Natal, and although occurring a generation later, the political conclusions and the perceived remedy were largely the same.

Once again, the question of India itself, and the restive Indian political movement, persuaded His Majesty's government to tread very cautiously in dealing with another generation of prejudicial and obstinate white colonists outnumbered by Indians, and Indians making the same demands of full representation in exchange for taxation.

This time, however, a war had been fought, empires had fallen (Russian, German, Hapsburg and Ottoman) and the concept of empire had changed. In a 1923 Commons debate, the then colonial secretary, Lord Victor Cavendish, revealed the results of a great deal of British hand-wringing and introspection. The imperial government had a message that it wished to send to its colonists overseas, be they white or brown. In part, Lord Cavendish's speech read:

Primarily Kenya is an African territory, and His Majesty's Government think it necessary definitely to record their considered opinion that the interests of the African natives must be paramount, and that if, and when, those interests and the interests of the immigrant races should conflict, the former should prevail. Obviously, the interests of the other communities, European, Indian or Arab, must severally be safeguarded ... But in the administration of Kenya His Majesty's Government regard themselves as exercising a trust on behalf of the African population, and they are unable to delegate or share this trust, the object of which may be defined as the protection and advancement of the native races.

The empire had, in effect, run its course. The dominions had bonded to Britain under conditions of war, but in the many territories scattered across the globe, and in particular in Africa, it was increasingly clear that colonial rule was coming to an end.. Notice was served that these territories would not be governed by a white minority indefinitely.

As history would prove, that minority would not yield easily, and would in places dig in its heels, and a handful of wars were fought, but in the end the inevitable process continued. In South Africa, however, the British relationship could not be so easily resolved, and the dynamic that played out was in many respects entirely predictable. As blacks knocking on the door of the establishment grew louder, and more insistent, the establishment simply added new bolts to the door. In the end the door was so thoroughly locked that it could only be broken down.

However, the year of Gandhi's departure from South Africa was 1914, and as he returned to India, and was welcomed into the inner circle of Indian nationalists, Smuts returned to war. At the outbreak of hostilities in Europe, the British imperial government determined that the radio relay stations and deep-water ports of German South West Africa were a threat to Allied shipping in the south Atlantic, and that the territory must be brought under British control. At that early stage of the war, however, the British lacked the organization and manpower necessary to undertake such an operation themselves, and the government of the Union was asked to undertake it upon its own resources.

To this request, Botha and Smuts agreed. Both were eager to prove the viability of the Union and to confirm the loyalty of the dominion, but perhaps most importantly, to occupy the western seaboard through direct South African effort, which would enhance a South African claim to the territory at a later date.

The operation was commanded by General Louis Both himself, but it was substantively coordinated, planned and executed by the 45-year old General Jan Christiaan Smuts. The campaign was, as most military historians will agree, the first major operation in mobile, mechanized desert warfare ever staged, and to this day it remains the essential tactical template. In a war of manoeuvre and engineering, a large South African force eventually ran the German garrison to ground, extracting from it eventually an unconditional surrender.

Smuts was celebrated throughout the allied regions for this achievement, and indeed, it was a masterful opening performance, spoiled only by a rebellion in the ranks of the Union Defence Force that saw some 600 Union Defence Force troops attempting to cross the Orange River and declare for the Germans. The rebellion was thwarted, however, and mainly by Smuts who was minister of defence. This brought South Africa into the war on behalf of the British, which won Smuts very few friends among his own people, but a great many elsewhere.

The next major manoeuvre on the African battlefield was the occupation of German East Africa, and here Smuts impressed his mark as a first-tier military commander. German East Africa was a vast territory south of the equator, broadly corresponding with modern-day Tanzania, which was the flagship German African territory. A British and colonial force was incumbent in British East Africa, facing a German garrison of native Schutztruppe (Protection Force) under the command of a brilliant and mercurial German commander by the name of Colonel Paul Emile von Lettow-Vorbeck.

The Allied campaign to occupy German Territory had stalled under imperial command, and it was not until a large force of South Africans, commanded by the now *British* Lieutenant-General Jan Christiaan Smuts, that matters progressed. Smuts was placed in command of the entire campaign, commanding a British and Commonwealth force representing every nation under British domination. At 46, Smuts was the youngest man to date to hold such a rank in the British Army, an uncommon achievement for a man with no formal military training.

Under the punishing conditions of an East African wet season, he and von Lettow-Vorbeck played an intricate game of pursuit and evasion across the entirety of the southeast African interior, which, although Smuts secured effective occupation of the territory relatively easily, did not end until von Lettow-Vorbeck's formal surrender three days after the official armistice. The two men then remained friends and correspondents until Smuts's death in 1950.

EPILOGUE

At the practical conclusion of this campaign, Smuts was taken off the battlefield and summoned to London, ostensibly to represent the Union of South Africa at the Imperial Conference of that year, but more practically to contribute to the British high command, indeed the British supreme command, as an appointed member of the war cabinet of Prime Minister David Lloyd George. Here he was entrusted with issues of global political significance, from the question of Irish home rule to the campaign in Palestine, although for the most part he acted as adviser, and post-war strategist.

At the end of the war, Smuts remained in London assisting and advising the British government as the terms to be imposed on the defeated central powers were defined and quantified. He was party, and a reluctant signatory to, the proposals ultimately presented at the Paris Peace Conference of 1919.

During this period, and somewhat upon his own recognizance, he began to give thought to two concurrent issues. The first was how to manage the vast political vacuum that would inevitably accrue with an Allied victory in Europe, and the subsequent collapse of the German, Hapsburg, Ottoman and Russian empires. This would release from imperial control hundreds of individual territories without a tradition of independent rule, and the question would be how, and under what aegis were these to be integrated, managed and contained.

The second issue was how to draw an increasingly isolationist United States more deeply into world affairs, and in answer to both of these questions, Smuts gathered up US President Woodrow Wilson's rather vague blueprint for a league of nations, to which he added a raft of practical measures for its operation. The result was a ground-breaking booklet, something of a manifesto, entitled *The League of Nations: A Practical Suggestion*. This was submitted to the US presidency for consideration, and thereafter became the practical blueprint for the League of Nations, and indeed, the United Nations that would succeed it.

Central to Smuts's thinking in formulating the precepts of the League of Nations, and indeed the British Commonwealth, was his philosophy of holism, a concept that had been under construction in his mind since his first hearing Cecil John Rhodes speaking on collective unity at Victoria College.

Holism would in due course become a household word, but then it remained defined in Smuts's philosophical thinking as simply the fact that whole entities, as elemental components of reality, have an existence that exceeds the sum of their parts.

And so it must be true for nations, and societies. As an alternative to global empire, Smuts proposed world government, and although an imperfect representation of his vision, the League of Nations sought precisely that.

Then, in 1939, embarking on his second term as prime minister of South Africa, an ageing Jan Smuts was called upon once again, this time to contribute to the charter of the United Nations, as the organization that was to succeed the League of Nations in a post-war world. For the first time, however, Smuts began to reveal himself as a man out of step with his age, and the leader of a nation increasingly at variance with the tide of world history.

He was challenged considerably by an obvious conflict between the ideals of the United Nations, in particular the Declaration of Human Rights, and the reality of South Africa's emerging race policies.

At a plenary session of the United Nations, held in San Francisco, Smuts came under direct censure from the Indian ambassador for the ongoing mistreatment of South African Indians, which served notice on him and his government that the old order had well and truly passed.

Smuts's views on race remained largely unchanged throughout his life, a fact that he aired quite candidly in a lecture delivered to the Oxford Students Union in 1929:

> It is doubtful if the old master–servant relationship will be tenable for many more years to come. The white man sees a grave danger for his children. The black man thinks he sees the days of emancipation approaching. Both are straining to further their ambitions. Trouble-mongers and agitators, mostly half-educated natives, some Indians and a few misguided whites, are at work among the native masses. They use persuasive words and draw illuminating, over-simplified comparisons. The gullible native is not proof against this insidious propaganda. He is growing restive and unhappy. It is idle to maintain that this phase of unrest is the result of poor housing conditions. It goes much deeper than that, for it is in fact a national madness, a surging phase of unrest.

In a world of fermenting nationalism, however, Smuts was apt as he aged to seek ever deeper refuge in intellectualism. He began to rationalize formal segregation as a solution to the fundamental incompatibilities of race, but he was never sufficiently committed to it to implement it as policy. Instead, he ruminated and meditated on palaeoanthropology and evolutionary divergence, reaching the conclusion that human rights were an earned concept, and dependent, at least in part, on the evolution of the personality, meaning that the basic rights of man, like personality, were conditioned, and thus conditional.

And what might be those conditions? Until death he remained a paternalist. He clung to the concept of the Sacred Trust, a term that he inserted into the covenant of the League of Nations, and which reinforced what he still believed was the obligation and burden of the civilized races. It remained the responsibility of the white man to guide the black man forward under firm but fair superintendentship, in preparation for that day in the deep future when he might arrive at a state of parity, and perhaps, later still, be granted a share in his own destiny.

Smuts retired from active politics in 1948 upon his electoral defeat by the right-wing Afrikaner National Party. This marked a turning point in the history of South Africa. The central theme of the general election of that year was race. Smuts had begun to acknowledge, and then argue that the stringent restrictions imposed on black lives and politics were impractical, and that a pragmatic revaluation of the South African race landscape had become essential to avoid a future disaster.

He was, however, swept away in the end by the rise of Afrikaner nationalism, and his old ideological enemies. The National Party, led by Daniel Malan, an un-reconstituted hardliner, argued for heavier restrictions, enforced separation and the complete political disempowerment of blacks. The National Party narrowly took the election, and formal apartheid was soon to follow.

Two years later, in 1950, Smuts died at the age of 80, and by so dying he avoided culpability for the evolution of apartheid. What he was guilty of was omission, not commission, and of failing the uncommon scope of his own intellect by his inability to recognize and acknowledge the obvious.

In the end Smuts has tended to be better appreciated abroad than at home, and the British, at the very least, are fair-minded in their willingness to acknowledge greatness. In Parliament Square in London, at the heart of the old British empire, there stands among the many figures represented, a high-browed and hawkish man in military boots and jodhpurs, a tunic and Sam Browne, with his hands behind his back, and facing Westminster Cathedral across the square. This is Jan Christiaan Smuts. Alongside him in this pantheon of modern heroes stand men such as Abraham Lincoln, Winston Churchill, Benjamin Disraeli, David Lloyd George and, yes, Mohandas K. Gandhi. In 2007, however, a newcomer was welcomed into that unique fold, a man by the name of Nelson Mandela.

Notes

Introduction
1. *Collected Works of Mahatma Gandhi*, Vol. I, pp. 105-6

Chapter 2 – Smuts's South Africa
1. The 'Khoikhoi', or 'people people' or 'real people' or 'Khoi', spelled Khoekhoe in standardized Khoekhoe/Nama orthography, are the native pastoralist people of southwestern Africa. They have lived in southern Africa since the fifth century AD. When European immigrants colonized the area after 1652, the Khoikhoi were practising extensive pastoral agriculture in the Cape region, with large herds of Nguni cattle. The Dutch settlers labelled them Hottentots in imitation of the sound of the Khoekhoe language, but this term is today considered derogatory.
2. Bantu: relating to or denoting a group of Niger–Congo languages spoken in central and southern Africa, including Swahili, Xhosa, and Zulu.
3. Xhosa: a member of a South African people traditionally living in the Eastern Cape Province. They form the second largest ethnic group in South Africa after the Zulus.
4. It remained legal to hunt and kill San, or Bushmen, until 1936, when the last permit was issued in Namibia by the South African government.
5. *Mfecane*, isiZulu, means 'the crushing', also known by the Sesotho name *Difaqane*, the scattering, forced dispersal or forced migration, or *Lifaqane*. This was a period of widespread chaos and warfare among indigenous ethnic communities in southern Africa during the period between 1815 and about 1840.
6. The various pygmy groups of central Africa are not generally regarded as belonging to Bantu language groups.
7. Campbell, Colin Turing. *British South Africa: A History of the Colony of the Cape of Good Hope from its Conquest 1795 to the Settlement of Albany by the British Emigration of 1819 [A.D. 1795—A.D. 1825]* (John Haddon & Co. Cape Town, 1897) p. 20.
8. The word kaffir is a South African ethnic slur referring to black people, formerly considered to be a neutral term. The word is borrowed from the East African slave trade, and derives from the Arabic term *kafir* meaning disbeliever or heretic, or one without religion.

NOTES

Chapter 3 – Gandhi's South Africa
1. The entrance to Durban harbour was obstructed by a sandbar that limited access to all but the smallest coastal traders. Dredging operations began in 1895, and it was not until 1898 that the water depth reached 18 feet, affording entry to larger ships.
2. For the purposes of this requirement, Yiddish was regarded as a European language.
3. In future years, the phenomenon of rickshaws would begin to reflect uncomfortably the class and race delineations of a discredited age, and they were consequently phased out of most colonial capitals. In Durban, however, the tradition proved resilient, remaining an almost exclusively Zulu preserve, and something of a canvas for the modern expression of traditional identity. Zulu rickshaw costume, although of questionable authenticity, nonetheless remains, even to this day, a feature of the cultural landscape of Durban.
4. Bulpin, T. V., *Natal and the Zulu Country* (Books of Africa, Cape Town, 1969) p. 333.
5. Between 1860 and 1911, a total of 152,184 registered indentured labourers arrived in Natal.
6. By the turn of the nineteenth century, the Indian population of Mauritius dominated the Afro-Creole and European populations combined.
7. 'Proclamation by the Queen in Council to the Princes. Chiefs and People of India', published by the Governor-General at Allahabad, 1 November 1858.
8. *Natal Mercury*, 9 September 1890.
9. Ibid, 7 August 1891; *Supplement to the Blue Book for the Colony of Natal, 1891–2*, p.B.57.
10. *Sheth* is an honorific applied to Indian elders and men of significant stature.

Chapter 4 – Equal Rights for all Civilized Men
1. He returns to his equals.
2. Sheepskin in this context implies a kaross, a simple cloak worn about the body, and comprising sheepskin with the fur still intact, or other animal skins of accentuated quality depending on the social rank of the individual.
3. Rousseau, Jean-Jacques. *A Discourse Upon the Origin and Foundation of the Inequality among Mankind*. (R. & J. Dodsley, London, 1761) p. 257.
4. *Report of the Parliamentary Select Committee on Aboriginal Tribes* (British Settlements) (William Ball, London, 1837) p. 1.
5. Responsible government in the context of the British empire was the grant of almost total autonomy over domestic affairs and the devolution of a great

deal of administrative authority to a local legislature, a local cabinet and a popular prime minister. The territory would be superintended by a governor, but under diminished powers. All important legislation, however, was required to be granted Royal Assent before signing into law.
6. William Porter, Cape Colony Legislative Council, 9 March 1852.

5. Chapter 5 – Influence
1. The greatest period of British imperial advancement occurred between 1870 and 1900. The period prior to this was what was known as the Age of Indifference, when Britain was satiated as an imperial power, but multiple factors, some strategic yet others economic, saw the empire rapidly expand during this period. Ruskin, with his many exhortations, no doubt contributed something to this.

Chapter 6 – A Changing World
1. Between transcendental and realist, and not transcendental realist, as in Emmanuel Kant.
2. Hancock, W. K., *Smuts, Volume 1: The Sanguine Years, 1870–1919* (Cambridge University Press, Cambridge, 1962) p. 49.
3. Hancock, W. K. and Van der Poel, Jean (eds.), *Selections from the Smuts Papers: Volume 1, June 1886–May 1902* (Cambridge University Press, 1966) p. 485.

Chapter 10 – The Imperial Factor in South Africa
1. In fact, the territory of Transvaal was annexed to the British in 1877 by none other than Sir Theophilus Shepstone, and returned to the Boers in 1881 under a carefully crafted, but ill-timed treaty. Just five years later gold was discovered in the ZAR, the South African Republic, which entirely changed the geopolitical map of the region.
2. A third regional power was Portugal, which claimed the territories of Portuguese West and East Africa, the future Angola and Mozambique. Portuguese allegiance was technically neutral. The French were not active in the southern African region.
3. India would ultimately contribute over a million men to allied defence, vast amounts of equipment and raw materials and cash loans, and it is arguable whether, without India, the Allies could have prevailed against the Central Power.
4. Canada and Australia were beginning to formulate policies and statutes aimed specifically at curbing Asiatic immigration.

5. Dadabhai Naoroji had failed to retain his parliamentary seat in the 1895 general election; however, Conservative Sir Mancherjee Merwanjee Bhownagree had won a seat representing the London constituency of Bethnal Green North East. As Naorji had gained the nickname Narrow Majority, Bhownagree, something of an establishment figure, became known as Bow and Agree.

Chapter 11 – The Colossus
1. In 1892, a cartoon of Cecil John Rhodes standing astride the continent was published in *Punch* magazine, following Rhodes's announcement of a telegraph and rail link from the Cape to Cairo. The cartoon was entitled 'The Colossus of Rhodes', after which this became the semi-affectionate nickname of Cecil John Rhodes.
2. Hancock, W. K. & Van der Poel, Jean (eds.), *Selections from the Smuts Papers: Volume 1, June 1886–May 1902* (Cambridge University Press, 1966) p. 72.
3. *uitlander*: Akrikaans for foreigner, or outsider, which was the name given to the expatriate, mainly British population of the Witwatersrand following the discovery of gold in 1886.
4. Some 25,000 ordinary shares in the British South Africa Company had been distributed among key Cape Dutch personalities prior to the forging of the alliance.

Chapter 12 – God's People
1. The Central Highlands, also known as the White Highlands, lie between Mount Kenya and the Aberdares range. Climatically this was a region suitable for white settlement, but it also happened to be the traditional homeland of the Kikuyu people, and as both populations grew, competition for land and pressure on labour sowed the seeds of the Mau Mau uprising that would erupt a generation later.
2. Gauntlett, Jeremy, 'James Rose Innes: the making of a constitutionalist' in *Consultus* (1988).
3. Fort Hare was a predominately black university founded in 1916.
4. Mashonaland is a province of modern-day Zimbabwe, home to the chiShona-speaking peoples of that country.

Chapter 13 – The Great Betrayal
1. The original occupation of what would later be Rhodesia took place in 1890, and was limited to the territory of Mashonaland. Matabeleland required a military conquest, which was provoked, and executed successfully in 1896, with Jameson at the head of BSACo. forces. Victory was premised primarily

on machine-gun and artillery engagement against set-piece spear and shield charges, which relatively easily obliterated the much-storied amaNdebele regiments.

2. The British high commissioner was Sir Hercules Robinson, an appointment engineered by Rhodes to facilitate covert imperial support for the scheme.

3. At its nearest point, the Bechuanaland Protectorate border lay only about fifty miles from Johannesburg. Rhodesia was some 400 miles to the north, and the Cape likewise to the south.

4. A *sjambok* is a leather whip used typically as a cattle whip, but often carried by gentlemen as an accoutrement.

5. The Jameson Raid has since become one of the most iconic episodes of the period, foreshadowing the Anglo-Boer War and typifying the British love of heroic and triumphant failure.

6. Mark Twain of Rhodes: 'When he stands on the Cape of Good Hope, his shadow falls to the Zambezi.'

7. 1881 saw the Boers defeat the British in what has come to be known as the first Anglo-Boer War, a series of skirmishes characterized by the astonishing Boer victory at Majuba Hill.

Chapter 14 – The Disposition of God

1. A *dhoolie* was, and is, an Indian version of the sedan chair or litter, used initially for human transport, but later as an organized ambulatory corps of the Indian Army.

2. *Natal Mercury*, 30 October 1899.

3. Canon Booth was, and remained, a friend and admirer of Gandhi, becoming involved in the later publication of the *Indian Opinion*, and described by Gandhi as a venerable gentleman very much loved by the Christian portion of the Indian community.

Chapter 15 – Of Passive and Violent Resistance

1. Kruger had been willing to then order a surrender, but President Steyn of the Orange Free State would not hear of it, and the war continued.

2. Individual Cape Dutch joined the war on the side of the Boers, and a handful on the side of the British, but the community as a whole remained neutral.

Chapter 17 – Transitions

1. *Sati* is the Hindu practice of self-immolation required of Indian wives upon the funeral pyre of their husbands.

2. Buffaloes, goats, sheep and even turtles are slaughtered in the tens of thousands.

3. The Asiatic Department came into being as a consequence of the Asiatic Act, or Law No. 3 of 188, passed in the Republic of Transvaal. This law was applied to persons belonging to any of the native races of Asia, including so-called Coolies, Arabs, Malays, and Mohammedan subjects of the Turkish empire.

Chapter 18 – Fear and Labour

1. Eight of the ten deepest mines in the world are located in the Witwatersrand.

2. Before 1899, for example, the Transvaal Chamber of Mines recorded a figure of 107,482 Africans at work in the mining sector, a figure that declined in May 1904 to 70,608. (Grant, Kevin. *A Civilized Savagery: Britain and the New Slaveries in Africa, 1884–1926* (Routledge, London & New York, 2005) p. 85.)

3. The Chinese Exclusion Act was a United States federal law signed by President Chester A. Arthur on 6 May 1882. The Chinese Immigration Act of 1885 was a Canadian act of parliament that placed a head tax of $50 on all Chinese immigrants coming to Canada. The Chinese Immigration Act, 1923, known today as the Chinese Exclusion Act, was an act passed by the Canadian parliament, banning most forms of Chinese immigration to Canada.

4. Many of the firearms used by the amaNdebele and Zulu in the wars of pacification that took place between 1879 and 1896 were acquired through this means. These were used in internal conflicts, for hunting and for further trade.

5. The Portuguese had a unique system of colonization that saw their overseas possessions characterized as official overseas provinces, governed as part of the body of the state.

6. The *prazo* system gradually gave way to chartered companies, and the two companies most complicit in this trade were the Portuguese Companhia do Niassa, with a concession covering the territorial expanse of the modern-day Niassa province of Mozambique, and the Companhia do Zambézia, likewise controlling what would become the Zambezia province.

7. Grant, Kevin. *A Civilized Savagery: Britain and the New Slaveries in Africa, 1884–1926* (Routledge, London & New York, 2005) p. 83.

Chapter 19 – A New Horizon

1. In the African context, only Liberia and Ethiopia did not fall under formal annexation or diplomatic protection, although Liberia was practically

controlled by an expatriate minority, and Ethiopia was occupied briefly by the Italians. Japan and China were the only significant global powers that escaped European control.

2. For the time being, India remained a Crown Colony under the rule of a Viceroy.

3. Hancock, W. K., *Smuts, Volume 1: The Sanguine Years, 1870–1919* (Cambridge University Press, Cambridge, 1962) p. 207

4. Ibid, p. 215.

5. Both Het Volk and Orangia Unie borrowed the key elements of their constitutions from the Afrikaner Bond, and all three formations shared most aims in common.

Chapter 20 – Teach the Natives a Lesson

1. The Rinderpest epidemic of the 1890s affected the entire continent. It is thought to have originated in the Horn of Africa with the introduction of Italian cattle, and from there it spread rapidly south. An estimated 5.2 million cattle died south of the Zambezi alone, and indigenous populations continent-wide suffered the consequences.

2. Phoenix was the site of Gandhi's collective settlement and Inanda where Dube had established his Zulu Christian Industrial School. These two establishments lay within five miles of one another.

3. In 1906, at the age of 38, Gandhi took a vow of *brahmacharya*, typically regarded as chastity, and a stepping stone towards a more refined spirituality.

4. On 19 December 1894, Gandhi made a similar comment: 'A general belief seems to prevail in the Colony that the Indians are little better, if at all, than savages or the Natives of Africa. Even the children are taught to believe in that manner, with the result that the Indian is being dragged down to the position of a raw Kaffir.'

Chapter 21 – The African Man

1. South African Native Affairs Commission 1903–1905.

2. Hancock, W. K., *Smuts, Volume 1: The Sanguine Years, 1870–1919* (Cambridge University Press, Cambridge, 1962) p. 220.

3. Rinderpest is a cattle disease that swept across the region immediately prior to the war, wiping out vast numbers of cattle.

Chapter 22 – The Black Act

1. Yap, Melanie & Leong, Man. *Colour, Confusion and Concessions: The History of Chinese in South Africa.* (Hong Kong University Press, Hong Kong, 1996) p. 130.

NOTES

2. In the context of the French African empire, 'assimilation' as an early ideal demanded the complete surrender of all indigenous cultural identity, and was available only to the elite, while 'association' pictured the selective absorption of French language and administrative traditions without the complete abandonment of traditional identity.
3. Indians in India were only subject to full fingerprinting if they were convicted of a criminal offence.
4. Reinhold Gregorowski would later be appointed Chief Justice of the Union of South Africa.
5. Cd. 3308, speech to the Transvaal Indian deputation, 8 November 1906.

Chapter 23 – A Meeting of Minds
1. Tolstoy, Leo, 'A Letter to a Hindoo', 14 December 1908.
2. Thoreau, Henry David, 'Resistance to Civil Government (Civil Disobedience)', 1849.
3. According to Vladimir Lenin, 'no Russian liberal believes in Tolstoy's God, or sympathizes with Tolstoy's criticism of the existing social order.'
4. Mohandas Gandhi in *Satyagraha in South Africa*: 'Truth (*satya*) implies love, and firmness (*agraha*) engenders and therefore serves as a synonym for force. I thus began to call the Indian movement Satyagraha, that is to say, the Force which is born of Truth and Love or non-violence, and gave up the use of the phrase "passive resistance", in connection with it, so much so that even in English writing we often avoided it and used instead the word "satyagraha" itself or some other equivalent English phrase.'

Chapter 24 – Satyagraha
1. It was decided to roll out the registration process on a district by district basis, in order to forestall the development of a colony-wide movement.
2. Smuts had sent a representative to speak, ostensibly on behalf of Botha, at a number of meetings of the Indian community, urging the community in a conciliatory manner to accept the fait accompli of law, and to comply with the law in a peaceful manner, but with no offer at all to entertain any changes to the law.
3. In a letter to Richard Solomon, Smuts quotes Howard Pim claiming that 700 out of a possible 7,000 Indians had registered.

Chapter 25 – A House Divided
1. This iconic three-legged pot still stands in the grounds of the Hamidia Masjid mosque today.
2. Gandhi suggested just six 'Educated Indians' a year be granted permits.

269

Chapter 26 – The New South Africa
1. 'Whig' in the British tradition implied an interest in the monarch acting under the direction of parliament. In this context it implied the management of the Union of South Africa without interference from the imperial government, and in the context of the 'native question' that blacks live under autonomous circumstances removed from the oversight and interest of whites: segregation in effect.
2. Address by the Reverend John Langalibalele Dube after his election as president of the South African Native National Congress, reported in the *Indian Opinion*, 10 February 1912: 'Although, as a race, we possess the unique distinction of being the first-born sons of this great and beautiful continent; although as a race we can claim an ancestry more ancient than almost any round about us, yet as citizens of the glorious British Empire, we are the last-born children, just awakening into political life, born on January 8, in this the year of grace 1912. Yes, politically, new-born babes, we are still very young and inexperienced, and as such it behoves us to feel our way slowly and warily. While teaching ourselves to walk boldly and upright before all mankind, we must still be careful ever to seek out the way where wisdom (not mere sentiment or desire) leadeth, treading softly, ploddingly, along the bright path illumined by righteousness and reason – the steep and thorny path, yet only one that will safely and surely lead us to our goal, the attainment of our rightful inheritance as sons of Africa and citizens of the South African Commonwealth.'
3. Odendaal, André, *The Beginnings of Black Protest in South Africa to 1912* (David Philip, South Africa, 1984) p. 191.
4. Blacks, or non-Europeans, were barred from service in the central legislature, and no non-white had so far gained entry to the Cape Legislature, but the importance of the black vote to a number of white parliamentarians in the Cape Legislature, and those contesting seats in the central legislature, theoretically ensured some native leverage.
5. Hancock, W. K., *Smuts, Volume 1: The Sanguine Years, 1870–1919* (Cambridge University Press, Cambridge, 1962) pp. 264-5.

Chapter 27 – The Mahatma
1. Olive Schreiner was also a close friend, correspondent and confidante of Jan Smuts, in whose purity of intent she maintained faith, and in whose spiritual and philosophical odysseys she followed and admired.
2. *The State*, September 1909, p. 257.

Chapter 28 – Labour Imperium

1. *Duragraha* can be defined as obstinacy, wilfulness and self-opinion.
2. Letters between Kallenbach and Gandhi reveal a depth of personal intimacy that under any circumstances would lead to speculation of a sexual interest between the two men. Gandhi, however, was celibate, and no records indicate any lapse from this, so actual intimacy between the two men was impossible, but a non-physical love affair of some sort was certainly not.
3. Edwina Mountbatten, wife of the last Viceroy of India, Lord Louis Mountbatten, was extremely close to both Gandhi and Jawaharlal Nehru, and almost certainly was party to a love affair, albeit a chaste one, with the latter.
4. A year earlier, in 1911, a vote had passed in the Union parliament finally halting the importation of Indian indentured labour into South Africa. Significant numbers of Indians remained under contract, however, and a large portion of the Natal Indian community remained subject to the tax.
5. 'Humbug, all humbug,' wrote V. S. in a lengthy open letter to the *Pretoria News* on 2 November 1912. 'Between ourselves, the Imperial Government, the Indian or Colonial Office, or the Department of the Dominions, I do not know exactly which, have made it very plain to the Government of this country that while in South Africa you should be "looked after", so you have had special railway coaches at your disposal, motor cars to convey you here and there, banquets have been organized at which "for the first time in the history of South Africa Indians and Europeans sat at food together".'
6. CIE: Companion of the Order of the Indian Empire, an order of chivalry founded by Queen Victoria in 1878.

Chapter 29 – Women and Children First

1. It was suggested in the judgment that the court should intimate that the woman might be allowed to land if the applicant agreed to legalize the marriage under Act 16 of 1860.
2. 'Transvaal Law Reports: Reports of Cases Decided in the Supreme Court By Transvaal (Colony). Supreme Court'.
3. According to Gandhi, an appeal was considered by the Satyagraha Committee, but was rejected on the ostensible grounds that such an appeal must enjoy the backing of the government, which the committee concluded that it did not.

Chapter 30 – Dénouement

1. Notwithstanding a union of the colonies, now represented as provinces,

provincial affairs in terms of immigration and various other aspects of administration were separately transacted.

2. Reading between the lines, it is clear from Gandhi's own account, and those of many others, that Gandhi was challenged considerably in maintain order on the march, and succeeded spectacularly when one considers the potential for difficulty in the unplanned movement overland of such a large body of relatively unsophisticated people.

Chapter 31 – An Omission of Inquiry
1. The existing polygamous marriages of resident Indians were also recognized.

Further Reading

Books

Aiyar, Sana, *Indians in Kenya: The Politics of Diaspora* (Harvard University Press, 2015)

Banerjee, Sukanya. *Becoming Imperial Citizens: Indians in the Late Victorian Empire* (Duke University, 2010)

Baxter, Peter, *Rhodesia, Last Outpost of the British Empire* (Galago, 2009)

Bhana, Surendra, & Vahed, Goolam H., *The Making of a Political Reformer: Gandhi in South Africa, 1983–1914.* (Manohar Publishers & Distributors, 2005)

Bulpin, T. V., *Natal and the Zulu Country.* (Books of Africa, 1969)

Campbell, Colin Turing. *British South Africa: A History of the Colony of the Cape of Good Hope from its Conquest 1795 to the Settlement of Albany by the British Emigration of 1819 [A.D. 1795—A.D. 1825]* (John Haddon & Co., 1897)

Desai, Ashwin & Vahed, Goolam, *Inside Indian Indenture: A South African Story, 1860–1914* (HSRC Press, 2010)

Gandhi, M. K., *Satyagraha in South Africa* (Navajivan Trust, 1968)

Gandhi, Mohandas K., *The Essential Gandhi* (Knopf Doubleday, 2002)

Gandhi, Mohandas & Duncan, Ronald (ed.), *Gandhi: Selected Writings* (Dover Publications, 2005)

Gandhi, Mohandas Karamchand, *The Story of My Experiments with Truth: An Autobiography* (The Floating Press, 2009)

Gandhi, Mahatma, *Hind Swaraj* (Sarva Seva Sangh, Rajghat, Varanasi, 2014)

Grant, Kevin, *A Civilized Savagery: Britain and the New Slaveries in Africa, 1884–1926* (Routledge, 2005)

Guha, Ramachandra, *Gandhi Before India* (Vintage, 2013)

Hancock, W. K. and Van der Poel, Jean (eds.), *Selections from the Smuts Papers: Volume 1, June 1886–May 1902* (Cambridge University Press, 1966)

Hancock, W. K., *Smuts, Volume 1: The Sanguine Years, 1870–1919* (Cambridge University Press, 1962)

Hancock, W. K., *Smuts, Volume 2: The Fields of Force, 1919–1950* (Cambridge University Press, 1962)

Hyam, Ronald and Henshaw, Peter, *The Lion and the Springbok. Britain and South Africa Since the Boer War* (Cambridge University Press, 2003)

Marsh, Peter T., *Joseph Chamberlain: Entrepreneur in Politics* (Yale University Press, 1994)

Millin, Sarah Gertrude, *Cecil Rhodes* (Grosset & Dunlap, 1933)

Millin, Sarah Gertrude, *General Smuts* (Little, Brown & Co., 1936)

Naoroji, Dadabhai *Poverty and Un-British Rule in India* (Nabu Press, 2010)

Neame, Lawrence Elwin, *The Asiatic Danger in the Colonies* (G. Routledge & Sons, 1907)

Odendaal, André, *The Beginnings of Black Protest in South Africa to 1912* (David Philip, 1984)

Palmer, Mabel Atkinson, *The History of the Indians in Natal* (Greenwood Press, 1977)

Ralph, Omar, *Naoroji, The First Asian MP: A Biography of Dadabhai Naoroji, India's Patriot and Britain's MP* (Hansib Publications, 1997)

Reynolds, David, S., *Walt Whitman's America: A Cultural Biography* (Vintage, 1996)

Rousseau, Jean-Jacques. *A Discourse Upon the Origin and Foundation of the Inequality among Mankind.* (R. & J. Dodsley, 1761)

Singh, G. B., *Gandhi: Behind the Mask of Divinity* (Prometheus Books, 2004)

Smuts, J. C., *Jan Christiaan Smuts* (Cassell & Co., 1952)

Smuts, Jan Christiaan, *Walt Whitman: A Study in the Evolution of Personality* (Wayne State University Press, 1973)

Smuts, Jan C., *Holism and Evolution* (Gestalt Journal Press, 2013)

Von Tunzelmann, Alex, *Indian Summer: The Secret History of the End of an Empire* (Henry Holt & Co., 2007)

Walker, Eric A., *William Philip Schreiner; A South African* (Oxford University Press, 1937)

Yap, Melanie & Leong, Man. *Colour, Confusion and Concessions: The History of Chinese in South Africa.* (Hong Kong University Press, 1996)

Pamphlets, articles & periodicals

Du Bois, Duncan, 'The Evolution of the Indian Question in Natal – 1860–1897' (University of KwaZulu-Natal Department of Historical Studies)

Dubow, Saul, 'Smuts, the United Nations and the Rhetoric of Race and Rights' in *Journal of Contemporary History* (SAGE Publications Vol 43(1), 43–72. ISSN 0022–0094)

FURTHER READING

Faulkner, Peter, 'Ruskin and the British Empire' in *The Journal of the William Morris Society* Volume XIV No. 1 (William Morris Society, 2000)

Gandhi, M. K. *et al*, *The Grievances of the British Indians in South Africa: An Appeal to the Indian Public* (1896)

Gauntlett, Jeremy, 'James Rose Innes: the making of a constitutionalist' in *Consultus* (General Council of the Bar of South Africa, 1988)

Glücksmann, Ralph, 'Apartheid Legislation in South Africa' (<http://www.smixx.de/ra>, 2010)

Hiralal, Kalpana, 'Indian Family Businesses in Natal, 1870–1950' in *Natalia* 38 (Natal Society Foundation, 2010)

Martiniello, Giuliano, 'Migrant Labour in Southern Africa: an Historical and Theoretical Perspective' (thesis, University of Leeds School of Politics and International Studies, undated)

Racism and Apartheid in Southern Africa, South Africa and Namibia: A Book of Data Based on Material Prepared by the Anti-Apartheid Movement (UNESCO Press, 1974)

Sarma, Christopher, 'Marx, the Mahatma, and Multiracialism: South African Indian Political Resistance, 1939–1955', (thesis, Wesleyan University, 2009)

The Review of reviews, *Index to the Periodicals of 1890–1902*, Volume 13 (Review of reviews office, Princeton University, 1903)

Vahed, Goolam, 'Natal's Indians, the Empire and the South African War, 1899–1902' in *New Contree*, 45 (North-West University, September 1999: 185-216)

Index

INDEX

INDEX